LIVES LIVED,
LIVES IMAGINED

LIVES LIVED, LIVES IMAGINED

Landscapes of Resilience in the Works of Miriam Toews

SABRINA REED

UNIVERSITY OF MANITOBA PRESS

Lives Lived, Lives Imagined: Landscapes of Resilience in the Works of
Miriam Toews
© Sabrina Reed 2022

26   25   24   23   22   1   2   3   4   5

University of Manitoba Press
Winnipeg, Manitoba, Canada
Treaty 1 Territory
uofmpress.ca

Cataloguing data available from Library and Archives Canada
ISBN 978-1-77284-009-4 (PAPER)
ISBN 978-1-77284-011-7 (PDF)
ISBN 978-1-77284-012-4 (EPUB)
ISBN 978-1-77284-010-0 (BOUND)

Cover art: *Day In, Day Out*, by Billie Rae Busby
Cover design by Alexa Love
Interior design by Jess Koroscil

Printed in Canada

The University of Manitoba Press acknowledges the financial support for
its publication program provided by the Government of Canada through
the Canada Book Fund, the Canada Council for the Arts, the Manitoba
Department of Sport, Culture, and Heritage, the Manitoba Arts Council,
and the Manitoba Book Publishing Tax Credit.

Funded by the Government of Canada   Canadä

To Cliff, Cynthia, and Alex

CONTENTS

A NOTE ON EDITIONS

When Vintage Press republished Miriam Toews's first three works, *Summer of My Amazing Luck* (1996), *A Boy of Good Breeding* (1998), and *Swing Low: A Life* (2000), Toews took the opportunity to revise her first two novels. Although the changes to *Summer* were not extensive, her edits to *A Boy of Good Breeding* were more substantial. Except where otherwise noted, all references within this book are to the revised Vintage Press editions of *Summer* (2006) and *Boy* (2005).

INTRODUCTION

Good fiction does not reinforce our complacent self-image; it makes us aware of identities outside our own. It brings to life complex characters who resemble real people, provides new points of reference, reclaims old territories and invents new ones, magnifies familiar moments into epiphanies. If anything, a good story will threaten the sanctity of the establishment and question the voice of privilege and tradition, and in doing so, evolve what it means to be a member of the community or the nation.
—MIRIAM TOEWS, "A NATIONAL LITERATURE"

Just because someone is eating the ashes of your protagonist doesn't mean you stop telling the story.
—MIRIAM TOEWS, *ALL MY PUNY SORROWS* (254)

Perceptive, controversial, topical, and achingly funny, the nine novels by Miriam Toews to date have earned her a place at the forefront of Canadian literature. Her work is studied in book clubs and in university classrooms (I myself have had the pleasure of teaching *All My Puny Sorrows*, *Irma Voth*, and *A Complicated Kindness* in my university classes) because it is highly readable and compassionate, with characters who resonate with readers because they exhibit resilience and humour in the face of loss, patriarchal bullying, poverty, and mental illness. The first epigraph to this Introduction comes from the keynote address Toews presented at the Edinburgh World Writers' Conference in 2021, where, in discussing what makes "good fiction," she also gave insights into what makes her own writing so powerful for so many people. Her writing is deeply personal, with complex characters who are often based upon her own lived experiences but who also stand on their own without reference to her biography. Toews often writes at the intersection between lives lived and lives imagined. As she explores her own psyche, she provides insights that inspire her readers to explore their own.

Toews has clearly taken her views on "what it means to be a member of the community or the nation" to heart. Whether she writes about life in Canada's smallest town, welfare housing, Toronto, or a tightly knit Mennonite settlement in South America, Toews explores how communities define their inhabitants by providing stability, support, and a shared identity, even while the constraints and expectations of these communities can restrict personal growth to the extent that individuals must leave them to begin anew. In her works, Toews challenges unexamined privilege in many ways, showing how monolithic systems—whether religious, settler colonial, or bureaucratic—undermine personal autonomy. Her most memorable characters encounter devastating traumatic events yet find ways not so much to overcome their experiences as to use them to help establish new lives and more nuanced attitudes both to themselves and to the worlds in which they live. Resilience, the ability to learn and grow from trauma rather than be destroyed by it, is an overarching theme in her writing.

Toews first gained sustained national attention when she won the Governor General's Literary Award for *A Complicated Kindness* in 2004. Her success inspired Vintage Press to obtain the rights to her three previously published works—*Summer of My Amazing Luck* (1996), *A Boy of Good Breeding* (1998), and *Swing Low: A Life* (2000)—so that they too could reach a wider audience than they had at first. Toews continues to publish books to increasing critical acclaim. In fact, the quality of her work and the topical nature of her subject matter, not to mention her ability to establish enduring connections with her readers through humour and compelling characterization, have made each of her recent novels a publishing "event" with widespread media coverage in Canada and abroad. Toews has also attracted interest from the world of cinema. An adaptation of *All My Puny Sorrows* (2014) came out in the fall of 2021, and an adaptation of her 2018 novel, *Women Talking*, is scheduled to be released in 2022. Toews is truly a novelist at the height of her career.

While I was writing this monograph, I considered several possible approaches to Toews's work. Her oeuvre could be studied, for example, in chronological order, beginning with her two comically oriented early novels and then moving to *Swing Low*, her account of her father's life and eventual death by suicide, and her subsequent turn to darker, yet still deeply comedic, works such as *A Complicated Kindness* and *The Flying Troutmans* (2008). I thought, however, that a chronological approach might do Toews a disservice by reducing her works to a discussion of correspondences with her own life. Although I discuss autofiction in Chapter 4, her work transcends her biography. Yes, Toews consistently refers to major events in her life in her work, from a description of what I call the "pink house" incident in the original version of *Summer of My Amazing Luck*, in *Swing Low*, and in *All My Puny Sorrows* to references to her father's heart attack and depression in *A Boy of Good Breeding*. However, Toews, like all great writers, builds upon the inspiration provided by her experiences, even as she selects memories and crafts details from which she can create independent fictional worlds. As Jeanette Winterson, a writer famous for her autofiction, says, "the photographer frames the shot; writers frame their world" (*Why Be Happy?* 8). For Toews, the guiding schema of the author tempers raw biography and makes it into art.

An additional avenue for entry into Toews's work is her Mennonite heritage. So far, six of Toews's books have been set in Mennonite communities or have characters who were raised as Mennonites, and naturally her work has been discussed by others with similar backgrounds. In fact, of the scholarly articles written on Toews, about half have appeared in journals or books that focus on Mennonite subjects, such as the *Journal of Mennonite Studies*, *Mennonite Quarterly Review*, and *Mennonite Life*. Although the number of articles on Toews in such journals suggests that many Mennonites engage with her work with curiosity and respect, others place her in the category of what Ervin Beck calls "Mennonite Transgressive Literature," writing that "often offends through character defamation, negative stereotyping of Mennonites, or distortion of Mennonite history or theology" (53). In an essay in which she discusses Miriam Toews's *Irma Voth* and Joanna Brooks's *The Book of Mormon Girl*, however, Rebecca Janzen counters such assumptions by saying that some readers evaluate the two authors' works "on the basis of whether, or how well, they represent a majority Mennonite or Mormon identity" (227) rather than looking at the works within their own contexts. Janzen makes a crucial distinction when she describes how Toews and Brooks focus on "experiences of religious practice rather than faithful adherence to religious doctrine" (227). Toews criticizes abuses within the church and, in Janzen's words, "encourages us to engage with structures of power" (227); however, as I discuss in the chapters on *Women Talking* and *A Complicated Kindness*, Toews also shows how the central tenets of her religion are still valuable when they are divorced from chauvinism. She says in an interview with Elizabeth Palmer that "what is harmful in the Mennonite tradition resembles what's harmful in any religion—when religious leaders use the authority of God to scold, shame, punish, silence, and shun people. . . . It's that abuse of authority—and witnessing first hand its destructive effects—that alienated me from the church" ("Novelist" 33). Toews is actually against fundamentalism, but because her background is Mennonite she situates her critique within her own faith community. Although there is no doubt that she is deeply critical of some aspects of the Mennonite Church, she considers herself a "secular Mennonite" and acknowledges that though she thought she "could somehow just move away from the community and escape and be fine . . . it gets under the skin and settles in there" ("'It Gets under the Skin'" 122, 121). In fact, rather than denigrating the spirit of her religion, most often Toews criticizes the self-serving excesses of religious elders who use their faith to enforce patriarchy, devalue women's voices, and shun those who do not adhere strictly to the status quo.

In answer to a question that some readers might ask, no, I am not Mennonite; in fact, one of my first tasks when I decided to write on Toews was to brush up on Mennonite history in general and on the history of Russian Mennonites in particular. Books that I found particularly useful include Marlene Epp's *Mennonite Women in Canada: A History*,

Arthur Kroeger's *Hard Passage: A Mennonite Family's Long Journey from Russia to Canada*, Harry Loewen and Steven M. Nolt's *Through Fire and Water: An Overview of Mennonite History*, James Urry's *Mennonites, Politics and Peoplehood: Europe—Russia—Canada 1525–1980*, and Robert Zacharias's *Rewriting the Break Event: Mennonites and Migration in Canadian Literature*. Assuming that not all readers of my book will know Mennonite history, I have included some of this research where it has relevance to my discussion of works by Toews, but I leave it to more informed sources to provide a detailed history of the Mennonite religion. In this book, I consider Toews as an author who draws extensively from her Mennonite background rather than as a "Mennonite" author per se.

Instead of a biographical or chronological approach to her writing, or a discussion of her Mennonite heritage, I have chosen a thematic approach that considers how the work of Toews reveals resilience in the face of trauma and hardship. Resilience, as Toews shows in her novels and her biographical work *Swing Low*, is not simply something that one is born with—an inherent trait such as height or hair colour—but a multivalent combination of biological inheritance, life experiences, and the availability (or the lack) of social and familial support systems. According to psychiatrist and expert on PTSD Steven M. Southwick and his colleagues, "most of us think of resilience as the ability to bend but not break, bounce back, and perhaps even grow in the face of adverse life experiences" (2). Certainly, many of her characters exhibit such abilities, but as Toews herself is aware, such a definition does not tell the whole story. In *All My Puny Sorrows*, for example, Elfrieda (Elf) and Yolandi (Yoli) Von Riesen are born into the same family, yet Elf, the more talented and successful of the two sisters, often expresses suicidal ideation, whereas Yoli, who admits that her life is a total mess, is able to survive and prosper. What, for Toews, makes one individual able to "fight" and another less able to take action? Why does a character such as Elf, who has a life that many would envy, lose her life to suicide, whereas Yoli, who grew up with the same family pressures as Elf, survives and endures even after the suicides of both her father and her sister? Toews would likely agree with Southwick and colleagues when they say that "determinants of resilience include a host of biological, psychological, social and cultural factors that interact with one another to determine how one responds to stressful experiences" (2). With the causes of resilience as complicated as life itself, it is doubtful that anyone can come up with a definitive recipe for resilience, yet it is important to discuss resilience in order to describe ways to move forward after trauma. Sometimes, as in the case of Toews's novels, models of resilience can inspire others to persevere.

Michael Ungar, a family therapist and the director of the Resilience Research Centre at Dalhousie University, summarizes how understandings of resilience have shifted over time. Early work on resilience in the late 1980s, he explains, focused on inherent traits possessed by individuals, but researchers later turned to what he calls a "social ecological" approach that focuses on a constellation of interventions and resources provided by outside support systems. "The problem has been partially the result of a dominant view of resilience as something individuals *have*," Ungar writes, "rather than as a *process* that families, schools, communities and govern-ments facilitate" ("Introduction" 1). He therefore argues for an approach to resilience that values individual strengths in the context of the ability to recognize and make use of the help available ("Social Ecologies" 15). The work by Toews resonates with such an approach, for she celebrates those of her characters who find the outer resources and inner strengths to surmount horrible obstacles such as having a murderous tyrant for a father (*Irma Voth*), the hospitalization of a beloved sister (*The Flying Troutmans* and *All My Puny Sorrows*), or the murder of a mother and a subsequent teenage pregnancy (*Summer of My Amazing Luck*) while showing compassion for and understanding of those who, for a variety of complex reasons, cannot.

In Toews's work, resilience tends to become manifest through four main thematic areas. First, Toews often highlights the ambiguous role of home or community in both fostering resilience and creating the situations and traumas that make resilience necessary. Second, she writes about how, when home or community fails, characters sometimes go on road trips to escape their situations and to find magical solutions to their problems, only to find that the strengths that they seek in others can be discovered within themselves. Third, Toews addresses her complicated relationship with the

Mennonite diaspora. Although she makes her distaste for fundamentalism amply clear, she also understands how the central tenets of the Mennonite Church can heal the very individuals who have been damaged by religious elders who use fundamentalism to control and to judge. Fourth, Toews uses autofiction, the translation of the author's life into thinly veiled fictional scenarios, to show how writing about trauma can be a means for reparation and resilience. Obviously, there is some overlap. Many of the novels by Toews have Mennonite main characters, so the theme of the Mennonite diaspora, its resilience in the face of hardship, and its relation to patriarchal oppression recurs in them. *Irma Voth* and *Women Talking*, however, most consistently address the Mennonite concept of "a people apart" and what happens when isolation allows patriarchy to flourish unchecked, so I concentrate on these two books in my chapter on the Mennonite diaspora. In the following section, I address these themes as they appear in the chapters of this book.

Home Is Where the Hope Is

In *All My Puny Sorrows*, Toews provides a quotation from D.H. Lawrence's *Lady Chatterley's Lover* (1928) that could sum up her characters' experiences of finding the strength and resilience to deal with devastating losses: "The cataclysm has happened, we are among the ruins, we start to build up new little habitats, to have new little hopes" (*All* 317–18). Sometimes, however, the very homes that we inhabit create the circumstances that call for resilience. In Chapter 1, "Home Is Where the Hope Is: *A Boy of Good Breeding* and *A Complicated Kindness*," I examine these two novels in terms of the complicated relationships of individuals with the notion of home. Toews often begins her novels with estrangement and broken homes, and the loss of one's home can be an ongoing trauma from which some characters never recover. Only these two novels, however, focus on making a home within the benign, or sometimes not-so-benign, world of small-town surveillance, with its ready judgements and pressures to conform. In some ways, the novels are reverse images of each other. *A Boy of Good Breeding* begins in disarray, but as it continues families come together, estrangements are healed, and a community becomes stronger. Meanwhile, *A Complicated Kindness* begins with Nomi Nickel mentioning on the first page that "half our family, the better-looking half, is missing" and that the furniture in her house "keeps disappearing" (1). Far from the situation improving, Nomi ends the novel alone in an empty house, shunned by her church, deserted by her father, and betrayed by her creepy boyfriend.

The contrast between the two novels stems, in part, from Toews's critique of religious fundamentalism, absent in *A Boy of Good Breeding* but front and centre in *A Complicated Kindness*. Although the Christian story, at its heart, is about resilience, foregrounding how lost souls can reclaim their lives through belief in Jesus Christ, Toews's controversial take on Mennonite religious fundamentalism suggests the opposite. Nomi's family is crushed by the weight of shunning, a practice that, for Toews, allows patriarchal tyrants to usurp the promise of forgiveness at the heart of the New Testament. Ironically, a fundamentalist focus on a heavenly home can destroy the earthly home, whereas resilience comes from resistance to overarching systems and a focus on forgiveness and understanding within the home place itself.

"On the Road" (with Children)

Whereas *A Complicated Kindness* concludes with a protagonist who might or might not escape her repressive community, in the second chapter, "'On the Road' (with Children): *The Flying Troutmans* and *Summer of My Amazing Luck*," I examine two novels that actually take their protagonists "on the road." Since the protagonists are accompanied by children, however, theirs is not the carefree experience popularized by Jack Kerouac. Whereas male-centred road narratives are often synonymous with freedom, the road trips in *Flying* and *Summer* include diapers, felt-tipped markers, and unglamorous Ford Aerostar vans. What Toews's road narratives have in common with the majority, however, is the theme of escape. The road trips in *Flying* and *Summer* ostensibly are quests in search of missing fathers who will somehow fix the untidy and difficult lives of the protagonists. In *Summer*, Lucy Van Alstyne, whose mother's death at the hands of a hitchhiker underscores the dangers to which women are prey when they take to the road, tries to cheer up her friend Lish by encouraging her to go on a journey to find the father of her two youngest children. In *Flying*, Hattie Troutman decides to take her niece and nephew, in limbo because their mother has been admitted to a mental health ward for depression and thoughts of suicide, on a journey to find the children's father.

Yet, though the two road trips are taken originally in search of fathers, they end with returns home and celebrations of the maternal self. In addition, as the evocation in *The Flying Troutmans* of Heisenberg's uncertainty principle implies, the characters in the two novels realize that there is no such thing as a perfect and predictable life. There are simply too many variables outside the protagonists' control, and changing one variable, as Heisenberg said, potentially changes everything else. Resilience means accepting that no person, place, or situation is foolproof. Instead, flexibility of thought and acceptance of uncertainty are signs of a resilient mind.

"All Trauma Presents a Choice"

In the third chapter, "'All Trauma Presents a Choice': *Irma Voth* and *Women Talking*," I describe how these two novels critique the Mennonite diasporic narrative (fleeing from persecution to start a new life) by showing characters who flee not *per*secution but *pro*secution. In both novels, it is not the Mennonite religion that is being oppressed, even though oppression is a historical part of the Mennonite narrative. Instead, those who live under abusive patriarchal authority must build resilience in the face of social and religious structures that unite to keep them in their place. In both *Irma Voth* and *Women Talking*, Toews—to use a word adopted by narrative research scholar Natasha G. Wiebe—*restories* the Mennonite migration narrative. Although the chronicle of what Mennonite author and critic Robert Zacharias calls "the break event," the violent persecution that Mennonites experienced in Russia after the First World War, focuses on Mennonites as a people who flee to escape oppression by hostile groups, in *Irma Voth* and *Women Talking* Toews divides this story in two. On the one hand, she describes how fleeing worldly life and external persecution can create a closed system that harbours its own cycles of abuse. On the other, she shows how the victims of that abuse must create their own exodus stories.

In *Journeys: Resilience and Growth for Survivors of Intimate Partner Abuse*, sociologist and expert in criminal justice Susan L. Miller describes the complexity of healing from abuse and attributes resilience to a combination of traits such as recognizing that "one is not to blame" for one's traumatic experiences, finding comfort and strength in religion and spirituality, "journaling or writing" as a means of self-expression, and being supported by friends, family members, or health professionals (178–83). *Women Talking* and *Irma Voth* address each of these elements, but Toews focuses on finding strength through re-envisioning central values that Mennonites hold dear: non-violence, love and support for family and community, and interpreting the word of God through personal insight. In doing so, Irma Voth and the eight women who meet in a hayloft in *Women Talking* also need to address the concept of blame. Fundamentalism condemns those who stray from a narrow path, but in each of these novels the blame heaped on the main characters is at least partially misplaced. The protagonists become more resilient when they are able to go beyond self-recrimination, reject the condemnation placed on them by patriarchal authority figures, and take responsibility for newly formed communities of care.

"Coming for to Carry Me Home"

In the fourth chapter, "'Coming for to Carry Me Home,'" I address another of Miller's categories of resilience: self-expression and self-discovery through writing. Here I discuss Toews's use of autofiction in *Swing Low: A Life* and *All My Puny Sorrows* and address the resilience of family members in the face of devastating personal tragedies: the suicides of her father and sister. Toews uses autofiction to address suicide survivorship. Her personal resilience is expressed through her ability to write out her pain, first by fictionalizing the thought processes of her father as he moved toward suicide and then by recounting how two fictional sisters in *All My Puny Sorrows*, Elf and Yoli, act at cross-purposes as Elf seeks death while Yoli frantically tries to keep her alive. In the end, Elf, like Toews's actual sister, loses her life to suicide, but the novel concludes with a statement on resilience as Yoli and her mother create a new life for themselves and look to the future rather than the past.

In a letter that Yoli writes to Elf after her death, Yoli says that "the pain of letting go of grief is just as painful or even more painful than the grief itself. It means goodbye" (314). As the theories of grief discussed in this chapter suggest, constructing a narrative about the deceased individual—and being allowed to speak of the deceased rather than having one's grief pathologized as excessive or self-indulgent—are effective ways to heal. As Toews poignantly says at the end of her prologue to *Swing Low*, "my father ... found a way to alleviate his pain, and so have I" (4).

The Fight against the Night

Toews's books often interconnect with one another as they address how families cope with deaths by suicide, and *Fight Night* continues this trend. Told from the perspective of nine-year-old Swiv, a child reeling from her father's desertion, her aunt's recent suicide, and her mother's anger and depression, the novel highlights resilience through the relationship between Swiv and her grandmother, Elvira. As the survivor of a repressive early life and the deaths by suicide of her husband and daughter, Elvira, with her many health problems, could be excused for giving up, yet she remains an inspiration for her granddaughter. Through Elvira, Swiv learns that tragedy can make us feel that life has stopped (or perhaps it makes us wish that it had), but the world continues nonetheless, and eventually we regain our enjoyment and perspective.

Lives Lived, Lives Imagined

Miriam Toews's protagonists do not lead easy lives. They face devastating sorrows: murdered loved ones, abuse, family members who die by suicide, and abandonment. Yet, even though they suffer more than their fair share of grief and trauma, something allows them to find the will to continue. *Swing Low*, Toews's fictionalized auto/biography of her father's experiences of bipolar disorder and depression, seems at first to be the exception to this pattern since it ends with Mel Toews's death by suicide. However, the paratextual elements of the text—Toews's Introduction and her statements about the power of writing to heal her own grief—indicate that resilience, in this case, shifts from the protagonist, Mel, to the actual writer of the text, Miriam.

In keeping with my overall discussion of resilience, the main title of my book, *Lives Lived, Lives Imagined*, reflects the futurity expressed even in Toews's bleakest narratives. The lives lived by her characters, and by Toews herself, are often saturated with psychic pain, to the point that it would be understandable for the characters to give up on life altogether. However, the subtitle, *Landscapes of Resilience in the Works of Miriam Toews*, reflects on how she creates characters who transcend their lives lived and move into a world of imagined possibilities for growth and even happiness. The humour prevalent in her writing wryly illuminates how some individuals can move beyond their own pain. Humour deflects sorrow and enables survival, and it creates the distance necessary to ensure resilience. One is in great pain but can still imagine life going on, even if grief fades but is never completely forgotten and exists alongside life.

This sentiment is expressed in *A Boy of Good Breeding* when Hosea Funk has a dream in which his best friend's wife, Dory, says "I like my stories happy, the sadness comes creeping out of the cracks in the story like blood, happy stories are the saddest" (234–35). Happy lives can lapse into sadness, and sorrow can be all the more intense when one mourns the joy that preceded it. But sorrow can also melt into contentment and finally even into happiness. One could thus turn Hosea's dream statement around and add that for Toews's many resilient characters—Lucy Van Alstyne, Knute

McCloud, Nomi Nickel, Hattie Troutman, Yoli Von Riesen, Irma Voth, the Friesen and Loewen "women talking," and Swiv and Elvira—extreme pain eventually "bleeds" into more positive emotions.

For these strong girls and women, being able to find the "joke" in impossibly sad situations can help them eventually to find ways to go beyond despair. Humour provides moments in which characters recognize the absurdity of their circumstances even as they feel the reality of being caught within them. Comedy, after all, can invoke different meanings: the slapstick comedy of the Marx Brothers or Dante's *Divine Comedy* with its promise of eternal life for the faithful.

"I don't intentionally set out to write comedy," says Toews in an interview with Avery Peters. "It's actually the way I see the world. It's dark and tragic. It's also ridiculously absurd and funny" ("Tragedy" 33). Toews might therefore agree with John Morreall, a theorist of humour who notes that comedy "is not about people doing well, but about people struggling in a world of conflict and confusion. Like tragedy, it deals with the disparity between the way things are and the way we think they should be" (126). Her humour expresses her tragicomic vision because her works often celebrate resilience and overcoming even though they describe traumatic events such as murder, rape, the death by suicide of a close family member, and familial abandonment.

To return to Dante, characters go through hell and purgatory before they can be admitted into a different world. Spanish philosopher and writer Miguel de Unamuno speaks of "the unbridgeable gap between desire and achievement, and . . . a conflict between the actual material order of the world and a preferred ideal order" that lies at the heart of tragedy (qtd. in Morreall 136; ellipsis in original), but as Morreall writes such disjunctions are also present in the comic vision. Toews's blend of tragedy and humour acknowledges the bleakness in modern life while presenting characters who, at least for those small moments in which humour breaks the tension, transcend the sadness of their situations, even if that humour is often bitter or rueful. Her dedications in *Women Talking* say it all. The first is to her sister Marj, who died by suicide in 2010: "For Marj, *ricordo le risate*" ("I remember the laughter"). The second, addressed to her partner, Erik Rutherford, says

"And for Erik, *e ancora ridiamo*" ("and still we laugh"). In spite of the tragedy of Marj's death, Toews remembers how she and her sister, whom she calls a "comic genius" in the Acknowledgements in *All My Puny Sorrows*, laughed together. In spite of everything that has happened in her life, Toews continues both to laugh and to write and to celebrate the spirit and perseverance of her family.

CHAPTER ONE

HOME IS WHERE THE HOPE IS?

A Complicated Kindness
and *A Boy of Good Breeding*

And my great wish is that young people who read this record of our lives and adventures should learn from it how admirably suited is the peaceful, industrious and pious life of a cheerful and united family to the formation of strong, pure, and manly character.
—JOHANN WYSS, *THE SWISS FAMILY ROBINSON* (237–38)

Don't let's be the kind of family discovered in freezers.
—MIRIAM TOEWS, *A COMPLICATED KINDNESS* (112)

The word *home* denotes a safe place, a centre for family and stability, yet—in spite of the security that the word generally evokes—individual experiences of home vary widely. For those fortunate enough to have grown up with loving parents and siblings in a house free from abuse and poverty, the idea of home creates feelings of nostalgia and belonging. However, for those who have experienced verbal or physical abuse, suffered from hunger, or lost a parent through death, illness, or a messy divorce, the idea of home signifies lack and failure. Because home resonates as a paradigm, not having the home of happy children's stories can leave individuals feeling bereft, reproached by an ideal that they long for but can never seem to attain. The fictional worlds that Toews creates often figure home as an absence or a lack. Parents, the bedrock of the traditional model of a happy home (though of course not the only model), are dead, missing, or unable to express the love that their children crave, leaving a gap that seems to be impossible to fill. In *A Boy of Good Breeding* (1998) and *A Complicated Kindness* (2004), the main characters—Hosea Funk, Knute McCloud, and Nomi Nickel—attempt to transcend the limitations of their homes and find new spaces where they can live on their own terms. In these two novels, resilience means finding ways to be "at home" in the world even when the pervasive models of what home should be have failed to materialize or are under threat.

Home in Canada: A Settler Colonial Context

Before turning to Toews's thoughts on how home both fosters resilience and creates traumatic situations from which individuals need resilience to recover, it is important to note how, in a Canadian context, the term "home" is problematized by settler colonial history. Like the Mennonite Heritage Village in which Nomi Nickel has a summer job, stories of pioneers tell of hard work, ingenuity, and home in an "empty" or, in the minds of many settlers, underutilized area. Critiques of Mennonite settlement patterns point to how Mennonites, like so many other settlers, moved into areas already inhabited by other peoples, notably in Russia/ Ukraine and then throughout the Americas.

Although he later qualifies his opening statement, Arthur Kroeger, a Canadian Mennonite born to parents who emigrated from Russia to Canada after the First World War, reflects the colonist's rationale for settlement when he writes about his ancestors' decision to move to what is now Ukraine. Kroeger describes how, in 1785, "an emissary from Empress Catherine the Great of Russia" approached Mennonites living in Prussia and "offer[ed] guarantees of religious freedom and exemption from military service if the Mennonites would colonize some of her largely empty lands" (10). Kroeger's use of the word *empty* highlights two common attitudes in colonial discourse. First, the word erases previous history. In this case, when Catherine the Great annexed the area now known as Ukraine, the land was not empty but newly conquered. As James Urry, a foremost authority on the history of the Mennonite people, writes, "new agricultural settlers were required for the territory" in order to secure the area under the tsarina's control (*Mennonites* 85). Second, colonial powers often justify expansion by saying that the land is not being utilized to the fullest. From Nova Scotian poet Oliver Goldsmith's description of the "bleak and desert lands" inhabited by Indigenous peoples and wild animals in "The Rising Village" (1825), to British immigrant Susanna Moodie's uncritical explanation in "The Wilderness, and Our Indian Friends," a chapter in *Roughing It in the Bush* (1852), that a "favourite spot" of the area's Indigenous people "had now passed into the hands of strangers" (298), the settler colonial mindset equates progress with altering or "taming" the landscape. The Dominion of Canada's stipulation that settlers "prove up"—that is, clear land and build a dwelling on it before gaining full title, clearly illustrates the link between "improving" the land and official possession of it.

Di Brandt, a Canadian poet and academic of Mennonite descent, writes in her essay "This land that I love, this wide, wide prairie" of "this stolen land, Métis land, Cree land, buffalo land. When did I first understand this, the dark underside of property, colonization, ownership, the shady dealings that brought us here, to this earthly paradise?" (*So This Is the World* 1). Toews similarly critiques opportunistic Mennonite land practices in *A Complicated Kindness* when Nomi completes a school assignment in which she criticizes the previous generation for buying land from the area's French inhabitants, many of whom were away fighting in the Second World War: "The Mennonites went and bought up a lot of their farmland really cheap from the women left behind who were desperate for money to feed their kids and just survive until their husbands and sons came home" (68). Given where this land is located, one can assume that at least some of the French-speaking individuals to whom Nomi refers are Métis or descended from Métis. Donovan Giesbrecht, author of "Metis, Mennonites and the 'Unsettled Prairie,' 1874–1896," explains how sections of the land that became the Mennonite East Reserve (where Toews's hometown of Steinbach is located) were originally claimed by Métis under the Manitoba Act of 1870, legislation that brought Manitoba into

Confederation and "promised the Metis title to the lands they currently farmed" (104). "Starting in 1874," Giesbrecht continues, "the Canadian government welcomed about 7,000 Mennonites to the Manitoba prairies, initially allotting them numerous townships on a land bloc that came to be known as the East Reserve. Unfortunately for the group of Metis mentioned earlier, the land promised to the Mennonites included the very land they had claimed four years earlier" (106). As has happened so often in Canadian history, promises made to Métis and Indigenous peoples were usurped by government policies on settlement. As Giesbrecht concludes, therefore, "historically speaking, Mennonites would be well advised to consider themselves not only as a voice for the oppressed but also in some cases as a cause of oppression" (109), a sentiment that Toews shares.

At Home in the Small Town: Isolation and Belonging

Although undoubtedly Toews is aware of how settlers, Mennonite and otherwise, have displaced Indigenous peoples within Canada, and though it is important to recognize how the concept of home is problematized by settler colonial history, when she discusses home she does so mostly within the context of second- and third-generation immigrant communities. All too often in her work, these communities actively undermine an individual's ability to feel at home by insisting on conformity and discouraging dissent. Thus, when Nomi tells her teacher about her research on unsavoury Mennonite land practices, she is "rudely rebuffed" and told that her insights are not "relevant" (*Complicated* 69) because they do not fit the community's vision of itself. She jokes earlier in the novel that, "when sin is used in the name of farming, Mennonites look the other way" (39), but this means that Nomi, who regularly challenges her town's deeply held beliefs, often is also discounted, rebuked, or ignored. Because she does not conform, the town closes ranks against her.

Deborah Keahey, author of *Making It Home: Place in Canadian Prairie Literature*, writes that "[home] can be a physical location or a psychological sensation. It can be individual, social, or communal. Similarly, 'place' can be a geographical location, but it can also be a symbolic, social, cultural, or psychic one. To know 'your place' can mean to know who you are, or how you are defined by others, and your relationship to the world around you" (11). In both *A Boy of Good Breeding* and *A Complicated Kindness*, the protagonists know their places very well, but they do not always feel at home in the spaces in which they live. The novels are different, however, in how they envision the connection between one's hometown and one's family. With its relatively small population and the closeness that comes when everybody knows who you are, the small town exists in correspondence with the life of the individual home. Robert Kroetsch goes so far as to say that "the rural or small-town setting remains the test place, the energy source" (46), for many Canadian writers, and indeed—from Stephen Leacock's Mariposa, to Sinclair Ross's Horizon, to Lucy Maud Montgomery's Avonlea, to Margaret Laurence's Manawaka, to Alice Munro's Jubilee—the small town has provided readers with many iconic and memorable places. Thus, in her aptly named article, "Beyond Horizon: Miriam Toews's *A Complicated Kindness* and the Prairie Novel Tradition," Claire Omhovère notes, "Although Toews's narrator introduces herself as 'Nomi from Nowhere,' the small town portrayed in *A Complicated Kindness* has been carefully mapped by her literary predecessors, who have conjoined the investigation of self with the investigation of place" (77). Referring to the opening of William Carlos Williams's *Paterson*, Robert Kroetsch writes, "A local pride leads us to a concern with myths of origin. Obviously, on the prairies, there has been an enormous interest in ethnic roots—that version of the myth of origin" (6). In *A Boy of Good Breeding*, the novel actually revolves around Hosea Funk's "local pride," which is very much tied to his search for his roots (meeting his father). As we will see, though, Nomi, while at first rejecting any pride in her home, will eventually grow to love aspects of the only place she has ever lived. At the moment when she is being forced to leave, she finds reasons to stay.

Set within the fictional small towns of Algren and East Village, Manitoba, respectively, *A Boy of Good Breeding* and *A Complicated Kindness* express the tension between group identity and individuation. With neighbours who know everybody's business, quaint Main Streets, and a general resistance to change, Algren and East Village resonate in the reader's mind and have a direct and lasting effect on the characters in the respective novels. Each town has a definite geography. The streets are choreographed, with houses and buildings named and placed in relation to each other. Reading these two novels, one can visualize Hosea Funk's office, the Wagon Wheel Café, and other landmarks. One can see Nomi as she prowls down Main Street or visits Mrs. Peters's house on Second Avenue.

As the mayor of a town of only 1,500 people, Hosea, one of the two protagonists in *A Boy of Good Breeding*, knows every inhabitant of the town, especially since he keeps tabs on who is born, who arrives, who leaves, and who dies. Hosea has never felt entirely at home in Algren, however, partly because of his unusual past. Fifty-two years before the novel opens, his mother, Euphemia Funk, lets herself be led into a field by a handsome cowboy stranger and conceives his child. Euphemia conceals her pregnancy from her family, delivers her son herself, and then tells her parents that a cowboy gave her the baby and asked her to take care of him. Euphemia decides to raise the child as "her own," and the town gives her credit for her self-sacrifice in adopting a child who is not even hers. Her family members eventually learn the truth, but they do not reveal it to the rest of the town for fear of tarnishing the family's reputation. When *A Boy of Good Breeding* begins fifty-two years later, Hosea is mayor of Algren, and he is a man with a mission. The prime minister of Canada, John Baert, has promised to visit Canada's smallest town, and Hosea is desperate that Algren receive this honour. In addition to being "Algren's Number One Booster" (15), he has an ulterior motive for wanting Baert to visit: on her deathbed, Euphemia told Hosea that his father is now the prime minister of Canada. The PM's visit will thus satisfy civic pride but also a deep need in Hosea to know and talk with his supposed father. The novel describes his obsession with keeping the town's population at exactly 1,500 people. Any fewer and Algren would no longer be considered a town. Any more and Algren might lose out to a town somewhere else in Canada. In spite of himself, Hosea secretly rejoices when ninety-five-year-old Leander Hamm dies and reduces the town's population by one person, but he despairs when Veronica Epp has the audacity to give birth to triplets.

Alone of all Toews's novels to date, *A Boy of Good Breeding* is written in the third person with more than one centre of consciousness. In the novel's parallel storyline, Knute McCloud has moved back to Algren to help her mother, Dory, after Knute's father, Tom, has a heart attack. Knute has a four-year-old daughter, Summer Feelin', conceived with her ex-boyfriend, Max, who took off for Europe as soon as he learned of the pregnancy.[1] He returns to Algren four years later to see his daughter, and Knute reconciles with him and forgives him for his earlier desertion. The stories of Knute and Hosea are linked through Tom, Knute's father and Hosea's best friend from childhood. Tom's health and mood decline throughout the novel, and after a second heart attack everyone expects that Tom will die. Hosea has confided his obsession to him, however, so Tom knows that his death will leave Algren one person short of the minimum of 1,500 people. In an uncanny effort of will, he keeps himself alive until after the population census has taken place, thus ensuring that Hosea gets his wish for Algren to be Canada's smallest town.

Through Hosea's efforts at population control, Tom's stubborn refusal to die, and pure luck, on the day of the population count Algren has exactly 1,500 people. In words that could describe the novel itself, the story of the town's "uncanny fifteen hundred exactly" becomes part of the nightly news broadcast, "the feel-good piece to put people to bed with, to leave them with the impression that not all was as bad as it seemed" (*Boy* 236). A quintessential politician, Prime Minister Baert breaks his promise to visit Algren, but Hosea no longer cares. Lorna has moved in with him, and he feels complete. Both Hosea and Knute have reconciled their physical homes with their emotional homes; they have found where they belong and where they can raise their families.

Unlike *A Boy of Good Breeding*, *A Complicated Kindness* is not a "feel-good" story, for it narrates the increasing mental distress of its protagonist. Sixteen-year-old Nomi is failing grade twelve English because she cannot write her final assignment—or, more accurately, because all of her attempts to write her assignment have been rejected as inappropriate by her teacher, Mr. Quiring. Readers discover in the final pages of the novel that Nomi wrote the book's first-person narrative as a way to fulfill her requirements for graduation. She lives with her father, Ray, in a state of almost constant confusion and grief. Three years before the novel begins, the Mennonite congregation that dominates town life shunned (excommunicated) Nomi's mother, Trudie, for her rebellious ways. The shunning took place just seven weeks after the Mennonite Church excommunicated Nomi's older sister, Natasha (Tash). Consequently, both mother and daughter depart from the community, devastating those whom they leave behind. Although incredibly articulate in her writing, Nomi has difficulty expressing her emotions in words, and she resorts to escalating inappropriate behaviour in an attempt to express her damaged inner life. By the end of the novel, she herself is shunned, and her father, in an attempt to lessen her feelings of obligation to him, has left her alone in an empty house.

The Secular versus the Sacred

The towns that Nomi, Hosea, and Knute inhabit are similar in many ways. Like Steinbach, Manitoba,[2] Algren is "only about forty miles away from Winnipeg" (*Boy* 6), and in *A Complicated Kindness* "the city," which, as literary critic Paul Tiessen points out ("Plotting" 29), is strangely unnamed, is "forty miles down the road" from East Village (*Complicated* 7). Nomi, in fact, can see "the lights come on in the faraway city. The magical kingdom" (74), made even more enticing because, Tiessen writes, it "represents a place used as a point of fear by petty Mennonite tyrants" ("Plotting" 29). If the city evokes suspicion among those who seem to despise her, Nomi reasons, then it must be the place where she belongs. In both *A Boy of Good Breeding* and *A Complicated Kindness*, the psychic rift between town and city makes the distance, a mere forty miles, seem to be much greater than it is. Characters either long to escape to the city or feel intimidated by it. In *Boy*, the main characters either stay in Algren or return to the town to live happy semi-rural lives, whereas in *Complicated* the motivation is very much to leave East Village and never go back.

The difference in attitude has much to do with religious fundamentalism or the lack of it. *A Boy of Good Breeding* is almost entirely secular in its orientation. Yes, Hosea is named when his grandmother sticks a pin in the Bible and it lands in the Book of Hosea, and his surname, Funk, sounds decidedly Mennonite.[3] When Euphemia was still alive, "the local churches brought her meals two or three times a week," and there is mention of "going to a Sunday school picnic" (97), but no priest or parson visits Tom as he is dying, people rarely pray, and the character most associated with the devil is Bill Quinn, a big black dog that sprawls in the middle of sidewalks as if to trip unwary citizens and that impregnates Mrs. Cherniski's dog, Pat. Mrs. Cherniski, the owner of the Wagon Wheel Café, tells Hosea that "that dog's got bad blood coursing through his veins. That dog's the devil's best friend, loyal to the end" (109); however, if this is the extent of the devil's inroad into Algren, then things do not seem to be very dire.

And then there is the town's other claim to fame: the so-called Algren cockroach. This fictional creature was apparently "brought to Algren on a plant or a sack of potatoes or something a hundred years ago from Europe and the rest was history." The insect has immortalized Algren in an encyclopedia, which describes Algren as "a small town in southern Manitoba. No mention of its being *the* smallest town in Canada, much to Hosea Funk's chagrin" (*Boy* 7). Although fictitious—Toews asserts that "there aren't cockroaches in Steinbach. The first time I saw cockroaches I was living in Montreal" (email to the author, 1 May 2020)—this pest makes its appearance throughout the novel, annoying the townsfolk with its persistent refusal to die.[4] Although Hosea finds the link disturbing, the fact that the town shares its name with a cockroach suggests its ability to bounce back no matter what happens, just as the town's inhabitants tend to do. Journalist Richard Schweid, author of *The Cockroach Papers: A Compendium of History and Lore*, writes that "the cockroach, regardless of species, is built for survival. This is the case for many insects, but cockroaches, as far as we know, are the oldest insect still abroad on the planet, a tremendously successful design in evolutionary terms" (6). No matter what Hosea does to prettify the town, the cockroaches remain, burrowing in Knute's newly planted flowers and generally annoying the people who come across them. Yet the many mentions of cockroaches in the novel situate Algren securely in the here and now. The Algren cockroach is "conceived in dirt. They love dirt" (*Boy* 150), and its presence in the town suggests a connection to the earth and to secular, rather than spiritual, concerns.

East Village in *A Complicated Kindness*, conversely, is a community dominated by fundamentalist Mennonite elders. The Main Street, with a sign depicting Jesus at one end and "another giant billboard that says SATAN IS REAL. CHOOSE NOW" at the other (47), suggests an either/ or world with little room for even small acts of rebellion. When Nomi was younger, she tells us, she believed what she heard in church and feared for her sister, Tash's, soul. "You'll burn in hell! . . . Forever!" thirteen-year-old Nomi screams (145), alarmed that Tash's behaviour jeopardizes the family's chance to "live forever, together, happily, in heaven with God" (17). Later, when Nomi "accept[s] boys and drugs into [her] heart" (158), at one point she finds herself floating with her boyfriend, Travis, on an artificial lake filled with little fires that they create when they light gasoline on the water, a fitting image of "that endless swim-a-thon in the Lake of Fire" to which the town's religious leaders believe she will be condemned if she continues her rebellious behaviour (200, 206). By the end of the novel, Nomi is excommunicated, which leaves her with little incentive to stay in a town that must, according to religious dictates, treat her as if she were a ghost. In her admittedly jaundiced view, life in the Mennonite community of East Village leaves little room for joy: "We are supposed to be cheerfully yearning for death," she says, "and in the meantime, until that blessed day, our lives are meant to be facsimiles of death or at least the dying process" (5). The promise of a heavenly home and the threat of eternal punishment exact obedience from the faithful, yet the former also provides a safe haven for believers. In Nomi's opinion, however, the town's emphasis on godliness and a future home in heaven has destroyed her home in the present. First her sister, then her mother, and then she herself are shunned by the community. They are no longer welcome or at home in East Village.

***The Critique of Fundamentalism in* A Complicated Kindness**
Nomi Nickel blames Mennonite authoritarianism for her family's problems, but as one would expect, actual accounts of Mennonites and their
namesake, Menno Simons, are more complicated than Nomi understands. In fact, in their earliest incarnation, Anabaptists were considered
iconoclasts for questioning the authority of church and state and insisting on their right to worship according to their own dictates. Central to
the Anabaptist faith is the idea of "adult baptism (hence, 'ana-baptism'
or 'baptizing again')" (Zacharias, *Rewriting the Break Event* 48). "Because
[early Mennonites] had already been baptized once in the Catholic
Church as infants, they had to undergo a second, 'believer's' baptism as
adults" (Peterson 18). The denial of infant baptism was political because
it undermined the authority of church and state. Infant baptism immediately made the child a member of a faith community, whereas adult
baptism made acceptance of faith a "personal decision," beyond the needs
of state and religious authorities (Loewen and Nolt 75–77). In addition,
with a few notable exceptions,[5] Anabaptists were pacifists who refused to
take up arms in service to the state or to participate in making or enforcing secular laws. Meanwhile, increasingly, Europe became a place "where
religious adherence would become inseparable from the social and political allegiances of different communities" (Urry, *Mennonites* 22), making
Anabaptists outsiders condemned for their beliefs.

   Born in the Netherlands and originally a Catholic priest, Menno Simons
(1496–1561) converted to Anabaptism in 1536. He preached non-resistance and helped to found "small, peaceful communities" of the faithful
(Urry, *Mennonites* 21). As the leader of a dissident community, Simons was
associated with tales of ingenuity in escaping from his persecutors (Loewen
and Nolt 98), and Magdalene Redekop speaks of "a Dutch Mennonite
trickster tradition" ("Escape" 10) in which the faithful managed to evade
arrest and make their pursuers look silly at the same time. As a people,
Mennonites, like their leader, showed considerable resilience in surviving
during periods of intense persecution, as elucidated in *The Bloody Theater or
Martyrs' Mirror of the Defenceless Christians Who Suffered and Were Put to Death
for the Testimony of Jesus, the Savior, from the Time of Christ until the Year A.D. 1660*

by Thieleman J. van Braght. Ironically, their faith in a heavenly home made Anabaptists unwelcome in many of their earthly homes, sparking waves of elective and forced migration to places where followers could practise their faith undisturbed.

As her life and works attest, Toews grew up in a Mennonite community founded as a result of one such migration, but it was not until *A Complicated Kindness* that she addressed her faith in a novel. Toews had already written two novels, *Summer of My Amazing Luck* in 1996 and *A Boy of Good Breeding* in 1998, neither of which mentioned Mennonites. Her third book, *Swing Low: A Life* (2000), was a fictionalized biography of her father, Mel, a man who deeply valued his Mennonite faith. Not only was *A Complicated Kindness* the first of her books to critique her religious heritage, but also—as a finalist for the Giller Prize and the winner of a Governor General's Literary Award—it reached a wider audience than had her previous works. Toews recounts how, when she went on tour in Germany with Rudy Wiebe in 2008, an audience member criticized her for having written a "filthy" book because the protagonist mocks Simons ("Peace" 20). This reaction to *A Complicated Kindness* was not uncommon. For instance, Al Reimer, a Mennonite writer and critic who also grew up in Steinbach, writes that the novel "raised the hackles of some Mennonite readers who know the Steinbach community and see the novel as a vicious attack against the town and, even more importantly, against the very principles of Mennonite faith and practice." Toews reports that when her mother, Elvira, finished reading the book she remarked, "well Miriam, it's a good thing we're Mennonites. At least you won't get shot" (qtd. in Schwartz).

Toews credits Wiebe as an inspirational figure who taught her by example to write of both positive and negative aspects of Mennonitism. In a 2016 article entitled "Peace Shall Destroy Many," she recounts her parents' and the Mennonite community's reactions to Wiebe's 1962 novel of the same name. In her words, the novel contended "that pacifism and non-conflict, core tenets of the Mennonite faith, may in fact be sources of violence and conflict, all the more damaging because unacknowledged or denied" (13). Her mother said that "Rudy Wiebe has aired our dirty laundry and it's about time" (14), but others were incensed to the point that, as Natasha G. Wiebe describes, he resigned as editor of the *Mennonite Brethren Herald* (35). Toews quotes Rudy Wiebe as saying that "'I guess it was a kind of bombshell . . . because it was the first realistic novel ever written about Mennonites in western Canada. A lot of people had no clue how to read it. They got angry. I was talking from the inside and exposing things that shouldn't be exposed'" ("Peace" 14). As Paul Tiessen writes, quoting an unpublished letter that Wiebe wrote to American Mennonite scholar Delbert Wiens in 1963, "the strong opinions about Wiebe's novel split the church into 'fairly equal groups of avidly for or avidly against, with not too many straddling the middle'" ("Re-framing" 78). One could argue that Toews created a similar "bombshell" when *A Complicated Kindness* was published in 2004.

Although generally positive about the novel, Magdalene Redekop wrote in a review that it is "chock-full of outrageous errors about Mennonite history. The notion, for example, that Mennonites are all fundamentalist and are in the habit of shunning each other for the slightest breaking of the rules is simply not true" ("Importance" 19). Reviewer James Neufeld similarly wrote that the novel "reduces the complexities of faith to the simplicities of its prohibitions" (101). Responding to criticisms that *A Complicated Kindness* exaggerates the prevalence of shunning within the Mennonite community, Toews commented, in an interview with Di Brandt, that shunning "still goes on all the time in Mennonite communities. People who say it doesn't are in absolute denial and are showing a complete disregard for the feelings of the people who have suffered from it. It might not be called shunning anymore, but it happens all the time, in different ways, and it's so destructive and sad and ridiculous and hateful" ("Complicated Kind" 23).

But Toews, of course, is not writing history in *A Complicated Kindness*, nor is she writing a full account of Mennonitism, which, as is the case with most denominations, houses people who range from exacting fundamentalists to permissive and secular adherents. In fact, she writes that the novel "is about a sixteen-year-old girl whose Mennonite family is torn apart by *fundamentalism*" ("Peace" 20; emphasis added). Toews echoes this sentiment in an interview with Natasha Wiebe, in which she says that her novel addresses "the destructiveness, the damage, that that kind of fundamentalism, with its adherence to ridiculous rules that have nothing to do with Christianity and love and goodness and beneficence, can cause human beings" ("'It Gets under the Skin'" 111). Moreover, in *Complicated*, readers encounter Mennonite life through the mind of Nomi, a deeply traumatized teenager with an eye for the ridiculous and ample reason to dislike the church that she believes has split her family apart. She has little interest in presenting an even-handed approach to a religion whose proponents she believes have wronged her.

To Nomi, Mennonites "are the most embarrassing sub-sect of people to belong to if you're a teenager" (*Complicated* 5), a group of joy-hating religious hypocrites whose favourite pastimes are judging others and finding new ways to be miserable. According to her, "the only reason we're not all snuffed at birth is because that would reduce our suffering by a lifetime," and she compares the church's founder, Menno Simons, to "the least well-adjusted kid in your school" (5) or "a delusional patient in an institute off some interstate in a pretty, wooded area. Shuffling off to Group, hoarding his meds" (6). By imagining him as a mental patient who lacks the inner resources to thrive outside a closed environment, Nomi does not see the historical Simons so much as she associates him with two central Mennonite men in her life: her father, Ray, and her uncle, Hans, her arch-nemesis in the novel.

Ray is a gentle man of faith who loves his religion with all his heart, but he is also ineffectual. He resorts to endless aimless driving, and—though Nomi's boyfriend shows his nastiness when he says it—there is some truth in Travis's description of Ray as a boy, "the one with his finger in the dike. Like standing there forever saving the town, like a hero, but kind of not, sort of goofy" (*Complicated* 76–77). Nomi acknowledges this opinion when she says that "Travis was right. I could imagine my dad standing forever with his finger in a dike saving a town that only mocked him in return. And not knowing it" (87). Ray, then, exhibits the less "well-adjusted" and vulnerable side of Nomi's description of Simons. Although Ray represents the Mennonite values of love and peaceful acceptance of others, he is unable to translate his faith into the ability to stand up for himself and his family.

In contrast, his brother-in-law, Hans Rosenfeldt, irreverently called "The Mouth of Darkness" by Nomi and her sister, Tash (*Complicated* 49), represents the unbending and exclusionary side of fundamentalist beliefs. Nomi mentions that her uncle used to be more easygoing, and she speculates that "he had tried to rebel against the thing he came back later to stand for and while living in the city doing God knows what he . . . I'm not sure . . . a girl ditched him" (50; ellipses in the original). Whatever the cause, The Mouth decides to return to East Village, as Nomi describes, "full of renunciations and ideas of purging every last bastion of so-called fun in this place" (50). She connects her repressive uncle to Simons himself, believing that both men became rigid because they could not cope with loss. Writing of Simons and his founding of the Mennonite faith, Nomi asks herself "what kind of childhood he must have had to want to lead people into a barren place to wait out the Rapture and block out the world and make them really believe that looking straight through a person like she wasn't there, a person they'd loved like crazy all their lives, was the right thing to do" (242). Her description of his supposed belief in shunning makes Simons sound much like Hans, and for both men Nomi equates religious rigidity with lack of resilience. To be resilient, after all, literally means to "bounce back," but in her jaded imagination both Simons and Hans reacted to personal hurt by imprisoning themselves in safe spaces that they could control. Like abusive relationships in which fear of rejection causes people to be hypervigilant about supposed slights, cutting off freedom for those whom they "love," Simons and Hans, in Nomi's mind, create homes defined by judgement and fear. Unwilling to risk loss, the men make it impossible for anyone to challenge their repressive and unhomely environments without experiencing harsh repercussions. Those who do not obey their rules, they fear, might spread such rebellion to others, and hence such individuals are cast out entirely.

As I will discuss further in Chapter 3, Toews consistently ties the Mennonite history of trauma and displacement to the reification of repressive religious values. Intolerance outside the community creates intolerance within the community itself. Natasha Wiebe comments insightfully on how *A Complicated Kindness* frames home in the context of "three interconnected stories of diaspora collapsed in the novel's pages" (35). The first narrative, as Nomi relates, is her account of her life as her response to an assignment from her English teacher, Mr. Quiring, who wants his students to write on the "Flight of Our People" (*Complicated* 132, 243) from oppression in Russia, the forced exodus after the First World War when Mennonites fled rape, murder, and disease in the wake of the Russian Revolution. The second narrative, as Wiebe says, "is that of the Mennonite or greater Christian diaspora, ... the good Christian's flight from this hard world for his or her heavenly home" (35). Quiring invites Nomi and her classmates to write the expected narrative of Mennonite migration in the face of persecution and intolerance, but Nomi challenges the status quo by writing instead what Wiebe calls a third narrative, "about the flight of her own family, not from the political upheaval surrounding the Russian Revolution, nor from the misery of this sinful world. Rather, Nomi's family flees the oppressive Christian fundamentalism of their contemporary Canadian Mennonite town" (35). Mennonite families fled Russia to preserve their way of life, but Nomi believes that keeping the Mennonite Church strong has wrenched her family apart. Toews repeatedly shows how, when fundamentalism is based upon exclusion, it imposes a rigid idea of home and actively discourages dissent. In structural terms, the word *resilience* implies being able to withstand stress without breaking, to bend rather than to shatter. Those living within a fundamentalist system, however, are forced down and broken rather than allowed to grow, heal, and expand.

Domination and Control: A Study in Contrasts

In considering the harms of fundamentalism as outlined by Toews, there is an interesting contrast between *A Boy of Good Breeding*, with its mostly secular focus, and *A Complicated Kindness* since each novel features a character who strives to make an ideal town, playing with others' lives in the process. Although totally committed to Algren, Hosea in *Boy* has a hidden agenda that causes him to ill-wish others and almost destroys his own happiness. Meanwhile, in *Complicated*, Hans seeks to control every aspect of life in East Village, even "purging" it of "the bar and the bus depot and the pool hall and swimming pool" (13), all amenities that might make living there more enjoyable but perhaps less godly. Claire Omhovère perceptively comments on Nomi's statement that in her town "there are no bars or visible exits" (53): "Punning on the double entendre of the plural 'bars,' the last sentence draws attention to the paradox of a topography which is simultaneously open and closed because it refuses the distractions of the present and, along with them, the very possibility of change" ("Pop Culture" 152). Nomi's dilemma highlights how difficult it is to live in place when one's society rejects the corporeal world.

Hosea, in contrast, fights to build a new ice rink and renovate an abandoned feed mill into a summer theatre. Hosea and The Mouth are similar in their avoidance of big cities and their experience of traumatic events when they were younger. Hosea was the victim of serious physical bullying as well as guilt for having revealed, at age four, his mother's secret about his origins. Although Euphemia's parents had suspected that he might be her biological child, they were willing to ignore that possibility as long as it was not said explicitly. But when Aunt Minty reveals the truth to Hosea, he repeats it at the dinner table, the family peace is shattered, and Euphemia and Hosea leave the farm and move to town. Perhaps his "nervous condition" (*Boy* 74), complete with panic attacks, can be attributed to his early childhood memories of bullying and "causing" his mother's rift with her family.

Once his mother informs him on her deathbed that his father is the prime minister of Canada (and neither Hosea nor the novel's readers can be sure that this revelation is true), he micromanages the town and its population. He becomes a nuisance to the town doctor with daily visits to check on those about to die and those about to give birth, and he even keeps a notebook with the helpful headings "Dying and Potentially Dead" and "Newly Born and Rumoured to Be Born" (*Boy* 37). His obsession is so strong that, when Mrs. Cherniski faints in the street, Hosea thinks "wouldn't that be a stroke of luck, after all, if Mrs. Cherniski was dead?" (109), followed by remorse for having had such a dreadful thought. Although greatly in love with Lorna Garden, Hosea resists having her move to Algren and live with him because she would increase the population of the town. It is only after she reveals her pregnancy that he realizes that his attempts to meet his supposed father might destroy his chance to *be* a father. He finally explains his reluctance to Lorna, and at the end of the novel the two are happily ensconced in Algren.

Unlike The Mouth, Hosea is finally a man of hope and forgiveness. In the biblical story, God tells Hosea to marry a woman who eventually betrays him with multiple partners. Yet, in spite of her betrayal, Hosea rescues his wife from slavery. According to various commentators, this story is an analogy for God's relationship with the people of Israel. Although God promised himself to Israel, the Israelites betrayed him by worshipping other gods. Hosea thus prophesies that Assyria will conquer Israel and that the people will suffer, but in the end God's love will transcend Israel's sinful nature, and God will send a redeemer to restore his covenant with his people. The name Hosea means "salvation" or "to be saved" ("Hosea Meaning"), so it is particularly apt for a character who is "saved" by others, notably Tom and Lorna, and who saves himself.

Hosea eventually recognizes how limiting his obsession has been. As *A Boy of Good Breeding* continues, he has many epiphanies that alert him to the needs of others. Johnny Dranger, for instance, wants nothing more than to fight fires, but he cannot be a volunteer firefighter unless he lives within Algren's town limits. In his attempt to reach a perfect 1,500 residents, Hosea keeps moving Johnny within and beyond the town's boundaries, a secular version of shunning, but when Hosea hears Johnny's story he realizes how unfair he has been. Johnny, it turns out, wants to put out fires because he secretly married a woman who died in a fire while she was pregnant with their child. Once Hosea understands Johnny's compulsion to fight fires, he realizes that "by moving Johnny out of the town limits he was destroying Johnny's chance at redemption. And for what? For his own personal gain" (115). Similarly, when Veronica Epp gives birth to triplets, Hosea is appalled by the increase in the town's population, but then—frustrated by the seeming indifference of her husband—she walks out on him and leaves the community. This is good news for Hosea and his statistics, but, as he realizes when he talks to the devastated husband, there is another side to the story. Hosea ruminates that "one Veronica, three babies, that makes four gone. Hurray, hurray, Hosea thought bitterly. And one broken man. Right here, right beside me" (202). He is learning to see people rather than numbers.

The same sort of thing happens in *A Boy of Good Breeding* when it appears that Summer Feelin's father, Max, has left town. Initially, Hosea hoped that "Max would leave town again, mysteriously disappear like before" (194), but when Max actually does go missing Hosea reflects on what that loss will mean for Knute and Summer Feelin'. He says to Knute "I hope you find him," and then Toews writes that "it was a pure thought, a simple wish, with no strings attached. He truly did not care about his fifteen hundred at this point. He hoped on every star and flying horse in the universe that S.F. would find her dad" (221–22). Hosea's story arc, in other words, shows how he grows from indulging in a self-absorbed and obsessive compulsion to meet his supposed father to a compassionate understanding of the needs of the community over which he is the secular leader. The book's final pages see him receive the bad news that John Baert has reneged, in fact, on his promise to visit Canada's smallest town and recount Hosea's message to the prime minister "not to worry, things come up, maybe next year. Please wish him a Happy Canada Day from the mayor of Algren" (237). Hosea now believes that the future is more important than the past. He has learned resilience by expanding his horizons to include others, and he has ceased to tie his identity to the myth of a famous father. "And I," Hosea realizes, "am not God" (116).

In contrast, in *A Complicated Kindness*, The Mouth exerts God-like control over East Village and especially, it seems, over the lives of his sister Trudie and his two nieces. Perhaps a more accurate way of putting it would be to say that Uncle Hans identifies so strongly with his role as the town's moral centre that he literally believes that he speaks for God and can shun anyone who does not obey him. Thus, whereas the biblical story of Hosea foreshadows God's forgiveness of his people, and his namesake in *A Boy of Good Breeding* embraces an inclusive community, Hans, in the words of Jeff Gundy, "is purely self-righteous and mean, a character so flat that he can be defined by a body part, which he apparently uses only to issue pronouncements and to binge on ice cream late at night." Of note, though The Mouth shows no compassion for Nomi, when she sees him eating ice cream in his darkened kitchen, she almost cries as she thinks of the "holes he could never fill with ice cream no matter how much he ate" (*Complicated* 51). She shows Christian compassion for Hans and an inclusive notion of what constitutes a family, thinking that "he's my uncle, I should love him" (52), instead of the judgemental scorn that he heaps on her.

Devoted to the Mennonite Church and its precepts, the gentle Ray provides the final word on The Mouth's Christianity when he writes in his parting letter to Nomi "and remember, when you are leaving, to brush the dust from your feet as a testimony against them" (240). In this passage, found with slightly different wording in several books of the New Testament, Jesus tells his disciples to lodge with people who accept their ministry; however, if a town will not accept the words of Jesus, then the disciples should "shake off the very dust from your feet as a testimony against them" (Luke 9:5, NKJV).[6] Although The Mouth would likely use this passage as a justification for rejecting others, Ray employs it to condemn The Mouth and his cronies. In direct contrast to his brother-in-law, for Ray intolerance is a bigger sin than any of Nomi's rebellious actions. Noon Park, author of "Rebirth through Derision: Satire and the Anabaptist Discourse of Martyrdom in Miriam Toews' *A Complicated Kindness*," has an interesting take on Ray's instruction to his daughter. Writing about the strong tradition of martyrdom within Christianity, a faith "founded upon the ideology and practice of voluntary sacrifice" (57), Park claims that Ray sacrifices his own happiness for the sake of his daughter and "subtly denounces the ecclesia before leaving East Village. Formally, Ray's letter reiterates the textual practices of early Anabaptist martyrs who wrote to their family and friends before imprisonment or death, urging steadfast faith" (61). Nomi believes that Ray sacrifices himself by leaving the town that he loves since he knows that she will never leave East Village as long as he remains there. If her interpretation is true, then he has performed a Christian act of self-abnegation.

Toews says in an interview with Di Brandt that

I wanted to use some verses in the Bible—for instance, the one from Luke that Ray leaves for Nomi: "And remember, when

you leave, to brush the dust from your feet as a testimony
against them"—to show a different interpretation of the
Bible—or the verse, which Ray also uses after being paid a visit
by The Mouth, which basically had to do with Nomi being
excommunicated: "And all our righteousnesses are as filthy rags,
and we all do fade as a leaf and our iniquities, like the wind,
have taken us away" [Isaiah 64:6, KJV]. Without being heavy-
handed about it, I wanted my wayward, messed-up, confused
and condemned characters to be able to hold up the Bible in
their defence, to be able to be comforted and supported and
vindicated by it. There should be a Take Back the Bible march,
I think, by all sorts of people who've had the "good book" used
against them as a means of punishment and condemnation.
("Complicated Kind" 44–45)

Toews implies that the Bible can be used as a force for good or as a stick
with which to beat others. Much depends on how readers translate what
they read into everyday life. The Mouth concentrates on the condemnatory parts of the Bible, those sections that discuss how the Israelites
failed God and deserved to be punished. Yet the New Testament provides
a message of forgiveness and hope. To return to the message of Hosea,
which to typologists prefigures the coming of Jesus Christ in its message
of redemption for the sinful, the question is whether or not one provides
another chance for the sinner to find redemption. Jesus actually references
Hosea 6:6—"for I desire mercy and not sacrifice, / And the knowledge of
God more than burnt offerings" (NKJV)—in Matthew 9:13, in which he
uses the verse "to defend his and his disciples' actions against the accusations of the Pharisees" (Viljoen 214). Like those Pharisees who follow
the letter of the law rather than its spirit, at first The Mouth keeps evil
influences out of the town by stopping its bus service (in *A Boy of Good
Breeding* the bus service is fully functional) and closing the town liquor
stores.[7] Then he further "purifies" the town by exiling those who do not
obey his rules. Ray, in contrast, rather than casting judgement on Nomi,
exiles himself.

Complicated Families in a Complicated World

Just as *A Boy of Good Breeding* and *A Complicated Kindness* describe different attitudes to being godlike, or at least being sure enough of one's righteousness to believe that one knows God's will, so too the novels have different trajectories when it comes to family life. "Part farce, part family saga" (Cook 51), *A Boy of Good Breeding* begins with families in crisis. Knute McCloud returns to Algren after her father, Tom, has a heart attack to find her parents coping badly with the situation. Medical complications have left Tom debilitated and with a faulty short-term memory; Tom's wife, Dory, has embarked on a mad scheme of renovations in an effort to relieve stress; and Knute, Dory intuits, needs a change from her life in Winnipeg. "Dory," Toews writes, "made it sound like she needed Knute desperately to help with Tom, to protect her sanity, and it's true she did. But Dory also had a sense that Knute was tired, really tired" (6). By reaching out to Knute, Dory shows that she understands her daughter and is willing to help her, just as Knute is willing to step in to help her parents.

Moving home, however, Knute encounters two people whom she neither respects nor trusts: Max, the father of her child, and Max's mother, Combine Jo. Knute has never forgiven Max for taking her at her word when she told him to leave after he responded unenthusiastically to her pregnancy. She also blames Jo for convincing Max to neglect his responsibilities as a future parent. Knute "really want[s] to hurt [Max] the same way he had hurt her" (118). She also refuses, at first, to talk to Jo and attempts to keep her away from her grandchild. When Max returns to Algren, Knute wants to deny him access to Summer Feelin' but soon relents, thinking "what was [she] supposed to do? She wasn't Isak Dinesen armed and living alone in the savannah or wherever. Blow his head off and nobody would ever know" (106). Instead, Knute lives in a town like that which Henry Tilney describes to Catherine Morland in *Northanger Abbey*, "where every man is surrounded by a neighbourhood of voluntary spies" (Austen 199). Eschewing dreams of harming Max, Knute learns to appreciate and trust him, underlining the theme of forgiveness and family unity that runs through the novel. When Dory worries that Max will not stay in town for long, Knute responds "I can't help it if he leaves again, but Summer Feelin' is better off knowing him, having seen him, and having had fun with him. She'll miss him but she'll be fine" (*Boy* 160). By the end of the novel, Max, Summer Feelin', and Knute are living together as a family. Perhaps it will not last, but they have come to understand each other well enough to try to make it work.

Knute realizes that revenge is futile not only with Max but also with his mother. Combine Jo has a sad history. After staying at her lover's house overnight, she returned home to find baby Max nearly frozen to death and her husband dead from a seizure. Her guilt drove her to alcoholism, and the town's disapprobation amounted to a kind of secular shunning. From her outsider's perspective, Knute's friend Marilyn says of Jo's drunkenness that "I would be too, if I was Max's mom and if I lived in this weird town and everybody was pissed off at me for something I did a hundred years ago" (123). As she gets to know Jo better, Knute realizes that Max made his decisions himself, not because of Jo, and she recognizes Jo's generosity of spirit. Max says of his mother "that she loved a lot of things, a lot of people, and that hers was a hard way to go, a potentially disastrous way of living" (175).

When Max tells Knute the story of how his mother once took him to a baseball museum, Knute has to reframe her image of Jo as a drunk too fat to take care of her son. Similarly, Hosea needs to reframe his image of his deceased mother when he finds "boxes and boxes of empty bottles" of rye whiskey in the basement of their shared home (129). Having believed most of his life that his mother was self-sufficient and unperturbed by life's vicissitudes, he suddenly finds out why his mother consumed such large quantities of Scotch mints. "Mother," he asks, "was your life unbearable?" (130). Hosea will never get an answer to this question since his mother has been dead for over three years, yet his new-found understanding that his mother was more than what he has assumed holds true for many of the book's characters. At crucial moments, they communicate their pain and are able to move on, finding resilience through the love and support of others. Not all characters in the novel are resilient; Knute's father, Tom, can conquer neither his initial illness nor his ensuing depression. Yet even Tom's death has a positive aspect, since he keeps himself alive long enough to fulfil Hosea's dream.

Like *A Boy of Good Breeding*, *A Complicated Kindness* begins with a family in crisis, but here a home is systematically destroyed by the pressures of fundamentalism rather than renewed by community and flexibility. Nomi's first words describe how "the furniture keeps disappearing" from the house and how "half of our family, the better-looking half, is missing" (1). Nomi, in her final year of high school, describes her probable future working in "Happy Family Farms," a chicken-processing plant. The smell from this "assembly line of death" (2) often wafts over the community, which seems, given the decided lack of happy families in this novel, to echo the miasma of oppression found within it. To make the point even clearer, Nomi also describes a memory of watching a young boy, Carson, try to slaughter a chicken. Obviously not ready for such a task, he whispers "instructions on how to escape. Fly away, idiot. Don't make me do this" (2–3) until his father steps in and finishes the job. Nomi's description of the chopping block as a "wooden altar thing" (3) hints at Old Testament animal sacrifice and a correspondence between religion and cruelty that continues throughout the novel.

Her mother, Trudie, however, comments on the Jackson Pollock–like beauty of the blood spray by saying "who knew it could be so easy?" Nomi, though, does not "know if she meant it's so easy to make art or it's so easy to kill a chicken or it's so easy to die. Every single one of those things strikes me as being difficult to do" (3). Situated at the beginning of the novel, the scene acts as an omen for Nomi's chances of escape at its end, where Nomi, who like her father "hates choosing" (3), tries to decide whether to stay in East Village as a shunned "ghost" or to leave town and start a new life. Carson desperately wants the chicken to escape, but, as Nomi later says, "every day at Happy Family Farms a few birds somehow manage to escape and fly away. Some of them end up dead in the ditches" (54). She juxtaposes this comment with her discovery of her mother's passport in her top drawer. Since Trudie always dreamed of travelling, her forgotten passport and failure to "pack *any* clothes for herself when she left" (54) suggest that she, as her brother Hans believes, "might have killed herself out of guilt and regret" (245). Nomi resists this interpretation, but it lurks in her mind until the final pages of the book. She remembers, for instance, how her friend Sheridan Klippenstein's mother lost her life to suicide after her husband was shunned. Mrs. Klippenstein, Nomi writes, "hadn't been aware of her options" (36; see also Soper 90), but shunning, by prohibiting family members from acknowledging each other, presents an incredibly hard choice: either one obeys the dictates of the church and ceases to talk to a loved one, or one risks losing the support of the church and the community.

Writing about *A Complicated Kindness* and Sandra Birdsell's *Children of the Day*, Paul Tiessen says that "both Toews's and Birdsell's novels are highly concerned with questions of home, but there is nothing straightforward about home for them. . . . In varying degrees, the two new novels by these authors emphasize a suppressed darkness that lurks within their respective Mennonite worlds in general and extends by implication to the domestic home" ("Revisiting Home" 128). Instead of fulfilling, as do the works by Mabel Dunham and Edna Staebler that Tiessen also cites, the stereotype of "an iconic Mennonite: hardworking and trustworthy, largely at one with his or her religion and community, and bearing the traits of a sustaining and invigorating home," he states that Toews "argues vividly and unequivocally that Mennonites have produced a society capable of nurturing and sustaining internal tyrannies" (129, 143). Yet the longing for home remains strong in *Complicated*, in which one can, in Tiessen's words, catch "glimmers of an ideal and elusive fantasy: a visit home" (146). Nomi fantasizes that her family will be reunited and once again live together in harmony. However, her desire includes a new dispensation in which her parents and sister can live without fear of retribution, accepted by their community instead of being torn apart by it.

One of the more positive images in *A Complicated Kindness* shows the potential for refiguring home in a way that includes freedom and movement. Nomi sees "two black dresses, the ugly Fortrel kind that many old women in our town wear on a daily basis, flying around like large crazy birds way up in the sky" (40). Strict Mennonites frown on dancing, so these dresses, "dancing all over the place, seriously shaking it in this crazy, free, beautiful way" (40), represent freedom to Nomi. Sarah Graham, however, notes that "neither dress escapes the village, one falling on a barn roof, the other landing at Nomi's feet as if the costume, and the feminine role it represents, is meant for her" (598). Yet, though the dresses eventually fall back to earth, Nomi writes in *Complicated* that "it was one of the best things that had ever happened to me, watching those dresses dancing wildly in the wind" (40), for as she watches them in the air, the dresses symbolize the potential for freedom and her ability to transcend the repressive world in which she lives.

The two dresses are unusual for being out of place, and as such they invite Nomi's gaze and approbation. With her heavy boots, short shorts, and eventually her shaved head, Nomi is also out of place, even on the modern side of town. Since she is eventually shunned for her anti-religious behaviour, she is also the object of the town's disapproving gaze, for she cannot seem to mimic compliance, unlike the other teens who congregate on Saturday nights for "drinking, dropping, smoking, swearing, screwing, fighting, swimming, home-made-tattooing," and other rule-breaking behaviours only to appear in church "the next morning when everyone would be back in the pew with Mom and Dad wearing nice (ugly) dresses and buttoned-up shirts flipping through Deuteronomy and harmonizing to 'The Old Rugged Cross'" (34). It is significant that Nomi chooses this book of the Bible and this hymn for her description, for they represent the dialectic found in fundamentalist discourse, at least as Nomi sees it. On the one hand, "The Old Rugged Cross" speaks of how Christ's sacrifice on the cross redeems believers from sin and promises forgiveness:

> On a hill far away, stood an old rugged Cross
> The emblem of suffering and shame
> And I love that old Cross where the dearest and best
> For a world of lost sinners was slain.[8]

On the other, in Deuteronomy Moses reiterates a strict set of laws, including prohibitions on eating certain foods, for the Israelites to follow. According to the New Testament, Peter has a vision of a vessel full of unclean foods and is told by God that "what God has cleansed you must not call common" (Acts 10:15, NKJV). Jesus, as the New Testament avers, comes to free humans from many of the injunctions against sin found in the Old Testament. Thus, Nomi's decision to highlight the biblical book most associated with Old Testament law, instead of the "good news" of Christ's teachings, suggests that, when it comes to the dichotomy between judgement and mercy, Deuteronomy prevails.

As Nomi explains, "but that's the thing about this town—there's no room for in between. You're in or you're out. You're good or you're bad. Actually, very good or very bad. Or very good at being very bad without being detected" (*Complicated* 10). The hypocrisy in East Village can be seen in how the community deals with substance abuse. Grace Kehler, a university professor and critic who has written extensively on Toews's work, mentions how Nomi's grandmother, like Toews's own paternal grandmother, "disguises her alcoholism through excessive but private consumption of vanilla, remaining a respected member of the community, whereas a man of the same generation (identified only as 'Bert's grandfather')" is shunned because his alcoholism is "overt" ("Heeding" 44). Actually, the townsfolk know that Nomi's grandmother is addicted to vanilla, but they put up with her behaviour because she maintains a superficial piety and stays out of the public gaze. Like Bert's grandfather, Nomi cannot hide her transgressive behaviour, and therefore she is cast aside by the community. In East Village, it seems, avoiding attention is more important than avoiding sin.

Christina's World *and the* Voyeur's Gaze

A visual representation of Nomi's predicament and the surveillance of her town, Andrew Wyeth's iconic painting *Christina's World* figures prominently in *A Complicated Kindness*, for its figure represents both the yearning for home and Nomi's difficulties in finding a secure place in a community that judges rather than helps its residents. According to art critic Zachary Small, early critics "harshly denounced the kitschy nostalgia of paintings like *Christina's World*, which ignored major historical and aesthetic events like World War II and Abstract Expressionism, respectively," yet the painting "is one of the most beloved works of American art," having been "viewed by hundreds of thousands of museum visitors, and generated countless reproductions" (Patterson et al. 647), one of which hangs

Andrew Wyeth, *Christina's World*, 1948. Courtesy of the estate of Andrew Wyeth / SOCAN (2022).

on Nomi's bedroom wall. In fact, Nomi explicitly references the painting four times. She stares at the poster while lying on her bed (*Complicated* 75), it falls on her head (99), and she makes "a word bubble coming out of Christina's mouth. FUCK YOUUUUUUUU! she said to that ugly old house off in the distance" (183). In the final reference, Nomi turns to *Christina's World* and blows her French horn as loudly as she can. "FUCK YOUUUUUUUU!" says Christina in reply (237). Nomi is no art critic, but she seems to intuit the unease that some art historians describe when commenting on the painting, the sense that there is something slightly "off" about how the painting portrays its subject. Nomi's "addition" to the painting might suggest her own, as well as Christina's, isolation in a world that pretends to be old-fashioned but actually is not, her feeling that she is being stared at by others, and her disdain for those who stare but do nothing to help.

Ella Soper connects Toews's allusion to the painting with the nostalgic past that the work celebrates, writing of how "the town itself is seen to grow ever more estranged from the agricultural past *Christina's World* invokes" (91). Soper discusses how Nomi's images of fields "in perpetual fallow" (*Complicated* 47), her fiery bonnet, and the chicken-slaughtering plant "are powerful signifiers of a connection to the land that has largely been lost," even as the town continues to portray itself as firmly connected to its idealized past (Soper 91–92). Meanwhile, Margaret Steffler, a literary critic who has written perceptively on many of Toews's novels, connects Nomi's poster to words on her sister "Tash's bedroom wall—'DON'T IMPOSE YOUR NOSTALGIA ON ME'—and the 'tiny, miniscule, pink embroidered letters that spelled EAT SHIT AND DIE' on Tash's jeans" (*Complicated* 103, 105; Steffler, "Fragments" 135). Although Steffler says that Wyeth's painting "suggests an entire narrative, which Nomi interrupts and reduces through the imposition of her two-word bubble" (135), an additional explanation suggests that Nomi understands the ambiguity of the painting. One of four paintings that Wyeth made of his neighbour, Christina Olsen, *Christina's World* has a disturbing subtext for some viewers. By the time that Wyeth painted her, she was severely crippled by "a degenerative muscle condition" and could no longer walk (Museum of Modern Art). Although initially people believed that her condition was "possibly polio" (Museum of Modern Art), Christina most likely suffered from "Charcot-Marie-Tooth disease, a hereditary peripheral neuropathy unfamiliar to most expert physicians at the time" (Radonjic 253).

As the painting conveys, Christina pulled herself around her property with her arms. Wyeth stated that "the challenge to me was to do justice to her extraordinary conquest of a life which most people would consider hopeless. *Christina's World* is outwardly limited—but in this painting I have tried to convey how unlimited it really is" (qtd. in Radonjic 253). Wyeth said that he was inspired to create the painting when he saw Christina from an upstairs window (Patterson et al. 647; Small), and thus "the painting's vantage point, looking down on the woman's youthful figure . . . constructs the viewer as a voyeur" (Griffin 36). Art critics Marc C. Patterson and colleagues also write of the painting's perspective: "The viewer looks over the woman's shoulder to share her perspective and identify with her predicament, whatever it might be. The diagonal orientation of the composition communicates uncertainty, isolation, and the challenge of a difficult task" (647). Although Christina Olsen was fifty-five when Wyeth painted her, her body looks much younger because he actually used his twenty-six-year-old wife, Betsy, as a model. Thus, there is an incongruity, as art critics mention (Griffin 31, 36; Small), between her "emaciated arms" (Griffin 42) and her youthful body. Randall C. Griffin goes on to explain how "Christina's idealized figure undercuts Wyeth's aim to expose the gap between the social category 'handicapped' and an actual person. Her body also reminds us that it is sometimes nearly impossible to untangle aesthetic from social ideals of the body" (46). Instead of portraying Christina's body as it was, Wyeth prettified it, thus implying that her world, in regard to prejudicial attitudes toward the disabled body, was not as "unlimited" as he suggested.

Soper connects Wyeth's painting to Nomi's friend Lydia, a young woman with an undiagnosed condition, presumed to be psychosomatic, that makes her hypersensitive to physical contact. At one point, Lydia makes a spectacle of herself by collapsing in the middle of the sidewalk and then refusing to let anyone touch her (*Complicated* 177; Soper 91). An even more apt correlative to the painting, however, is Nomi herself. After a fight with Travis, she returns home to find that Ray has sold their dining room table and their old freezer. He tells her that when he cleaned out the freezer he found Blakula, a pet cat that Tash placed there three years previously when it died and the ground was too hard for a proper burial. After they bury the cat, Ray leaves Nomi "lying in the grass next to Blakula." Nomi then writes that "I crawled slowly through the grass towards the back door. Its brown sections reminded me of a Jersey Milk bar" (168). Although she is incapacitated by depression and drugs rather than by long-term physical disability, her wording evokes Christina's position in Wyeth's painting as well as the painting's muted brown colour palette: both women are crawling laboriously toward home. In Nomi's case, the reassuring chocolate brown of her back door belies the increasingly stark environment behind it. As Ray sells off pieces of furniture, he makes the house less and less home-like.

Visible disability, though cloaked, makes Christina the subject of both the painter's and the viewer's stares, and her isolation in the painting's frame distances her from interaction, just as those with physical disabilities are often distanced by people's embarrassment, fascination, or aversion. Although Nomi is not physically disabled, her refusal to conform makes her disabled in the town's sight, and her increasingly unconventional appearance makes her what groundbreaking critical disability studies theorist Rosemarie Garland Thomson calls a "stareable" subject. As she brilliantly discusses in her book *Staring: How We Look*, all of us function as both "starers" and "starees." Thomson asserts that staring does not have to be an invasive act. "Staring here is more than just looking. The stare is distinct from the gaze, which has been extensively defined as an oppressive act of disciplinary looking that subordinates its victim" (9). Everyone stares. However, the stares that people direct at those with visible disabilities or, in Nomi's case, non-conforming appearances, have a particularly invasive quality as the able-bodied or conforming starers dehumanize the starees, reducing them to their disabilities/differences and limiting their right to be seen as people who exist as individuals. Thomson writes that "the visibly disabled body intrudes on our routine visual landscape and compels our attention, often obscuring the personhood of its bearer. Sometimes our startled eyes can stay with such a sight, and sometimes they flee in strained distress" (20). Individuals with disabilities/differences can be reduced through staring from individuals to anomalies, and thus, as Thomson writes, "how we look at one another can be a productive aspect of our interpersonal, even our political, lives. If all this is so, then the question for starers is not whether we *should* stare, but rather *how* we should stare. The question for starees is not whether we *will* be stared at, but rather *how* we will be stared at" (185). How we stare—whether we acknowledge a whole person rather than a stigma—becomes an ethical act.

A Complicated Kindness addresses the issue of staring through its discussion of shunning, figured as a kind of social disability that causes its victims not only to be marked as different but also to be ignored. Nomi, for example, describes a woman "who was shunned for adultery but didn't leave" (45). The woman has health problems and sometimes faints in public places, yet, "like the other town 'ghosts,' she receives no consolatory words or touch" (Kehler, "Heeding" 45). "People will leave sausages or cheese next to her sometimes but that's as much as they can do" (*Complicated* 45) because they are supposed to ignore her existence. In other words, the townsfolk clearly "see" this woman, but they cannot give her the kind of help that she really needs: acceptance and friendship. As Kehler writes, "no doubt this is a hyperbolic and historically inaccurate representation of Mennonite shunning, but Toews resorts to fiction in order to forge a narrative that reveals the worldly urgency of attending to persons who are not invisible but deliberately effaced" ("Heeding" 45). The Mouth suggests at one point "that when we look in the mirror there should be no reflection because who we are is something that we cannot see" (*Complicated* 115). In an odd paradox, Hans believes that the bodies of the devout are of little importance compared with their spiritual essence, yet when the same bodies are "seen" to have transgressed they are declared to be unworthy of notice. Ironically, the dictate that the shunned become invisible makes them impossible to ignore.

In the context of home, persons with physical differences or emotional disabilities ideally find belonging and some respite from the staring and judgement of others. Love, familiarity, and friendship replace embarrassment or distaste. Thus, in the Nickel household, Tash, Nomi, and Trudie are valued for who they are, whereas in the outside world they are surveilled and condemned because they challenge the status quo. Yet the home can also be a place in which both the "normate"[9] and the ill take out their frustrations on family members. In a pattern reminiscent of Toews's father, Mel, in *A Boy of Good Breeding* Tom gradually loses the will to live after a heart attack and a series of small strokes, until he ends up spending whole days in bed, unwilling or unable to engage with his family members or friends. His "depressive stupor" is difficult for his wife, Dory, who enters a support group for "women who love men who love beds" (165, 181). Toews accurately describes the conflicting reactions of those who love a disabled person: Dory is by turns exasperated, compassionate, angry, and despairing. "I don't know what to do. I don't know how to make him live. I don't know how to make him talk," she says. She goes on to tell Knute that

"I don't want him to die, sweetheart. . . . But sometimes I do" (158–59), presumably because his death would at least resolve the limbo in which Tom and his family exist. In spite of Dory's irritation, the family loves Tom and treats him well, but it is also true that homes can foster cruelty because a lack of outside scrutiny frees people to "be themselves," either for good or for ill. When Nomi says "don't let's be the kind of family discovered in freezers," she hints that the home can hide serious mistreatment and abuse.

"He Deserves Laura Ingalls Wilder": The Comforts of Nostalgia

In fact, traditional Mennonite beliefs in the primacy of home life—with clear roles for men, women, boys, and girls—are parodied in *A Complicated Kindness*. Nomi's mother, Trudie, is an indifferent housewife at best who goes reluctantly to the church basement, where she is expected to "cook for weddings and funerals, quilt, teach Sunday school and just generally get her ass in humble helping gear" (9). Her favourite activity is reading in her nightgown rather than partaking in the "endless domestic grind-a-thon" (8) that the townspeople expect women to embrace. Her talent for cooking with Klik, processed meat that comes in a tin, counters associations of Mennonite women with "down-home" cooking made from scratch. Indeed, once Trudie is forced to leave her home and Nomi has to take over the laundry and cooking duties—whether because Ray is grieving or simply untrained, he does not seem to be able to complete these tasks—she resorts to cooking food by alphabet, going sequentially through each letter. Her efforts at cooking, though, appear to be barely edible. This lack of domestic ability is very different from the philosophy expressed in *Homespun: Amish and Mennonite Women in Their Own Words*, in which women testify about their faith and how it manifests in serving (and feeding) others. One contributor to the volume, Rae Schrock, writes that "food, as we know, is the gem around which we gather to experience some of our most meaningful interactions" (15), and another, Vicki Kaufman, says that "home is the sharing of life with people you love, in both the mess and the beauty" (27). For the women writing in *Homespun*, the earthly home supports the family and might well be a microcosm for the far greater acceptance and joy that one will experience in heaven, yet it seems that for Nomi, Tash, and Trudie the fundamentalist expectations of women in the home can make life on Earth a hell.

The fantasy of home manifests itself in the other main industry in the novel: nostalgic tourism. Like Steinbach, East Village has a museum (Mennonite Heritage) village;[10] like Nomi, Toews worked there as a butter churner when she was young ("Complicated Kindness"). People often view a small-town past as a simpler time with fewer "modern" problems, and some researchers even "suggest that nostalgia helps people manage unpleasant or harmful psychological states. For example, nostalgia's role in regulating threats to well-being has been shown to counteract feelings of loneliness, meaninglessness, and boredom," and even physical pain (Kersten et al. 2). In spite of references to bullying and death, and though it is set in the present, *A Boy of Good Breeding* has this decidedly nostalgic feel. Knute, who has sought solace in Algren after being unhappy in the city, thinks that "nothing ever really changed in Algren" (35), and this nostalgia might account for how characters are drawn to the town and thrive within it. In contrast, the present, with all of its struggles and stresses, is in the fore-front of *A Complicated Kindness* even when characters attempt to remember simpler, happier times such as those described in *Boy*.

To Nomi, the museum village markets itself as an anachronistic utopia: "Americans come here to observe our simple ways. Here, life is so refresh-ingly uncomplicated" (*Complicated* 47). In fact, one critic writes about how "the museum's success . . . indicates a cultural longing for the traditional model of community and family seemingly embodied by the Mennonites" (Graham 597). But the nostalgia that the tourists seek exists side by side with a disappointing reality. The tourists who "wander the dirt lanes of the museum village" (*Complicated* 47) are disconcerted when they enter the modern town right next to it. "A tourist once came up to me," Nomi explains, "and took a picture and said to her husband, now here's a priceless juxtaposition of old and new" (53). Meanwhile, members of the younger generation, even while dressed up in old-fashioned garb, flout the rules whenever they can. A younger Nomi is immortalized in a picture taken after her bonnet caught fire while she was smoking a cigarette, and her boyfriend, Travis, who has been hired to pose as a father and dote over a Cabbage Patch doll with his young "wife," takes a break to smoke a joint with her behind a barn. In another example, while the American tourists listen to The Mouth deliver a sermon in the museum village, the majority of the town is watching the demolition derby. It is almost as if the fantasy of religious purity is demolished by the pull of the secular.

Nomi is quick to point out the hypocrisies of nostalgic tourism, but she herself longs for a simpler past within her own family, a past that she has lost and will never regain. The *Oxford English Dictionary* notes that the word *nostalgia* has its roots in the "ancient Greek νόστος [*nostos*] return home" plus "*algia*" or pain.[11] Nomi experiences this "pain of return" when she thinks of the family that she once had. Describing Trudie's tendency to say "*wheeeeee*" at "whatever little thing was turning her on," Nomi gives several examples: "We as a family in a little motorboat on big waves. We as a family coasting down a hill with the car in neutral. We as a family chopping down a Christmas tree. We as a family" (*Complicated* 8). Although she wistfully reverts to memories of better days, she also remembers how she feared for her family's future in heaven. Having bought into the rhetoric of heaven and hell preached by her church, as a child Nomi has nightmares about her rebellious sister, Tash, burning in hell. She narrates how she "spent a large part of [her] childhood praying for Tash's soul" because Tash seemed to be "intent on derailing [the family's] chances and sabotaging [their] plans to be together for goddamn ever" (16, 17). Nomi, as Margaret Boe Birns puts it, "has lost the protections of her childhood and is paradoxically longing for family and community at the time when both seem to let her down" (164). Her nostalgia, in a way, denotes the pain of *not* returning home.

In addition to the biblical stories and threats with which she has grown up, Nomi is exposed to a number of family dramas on television. She associates Trudie with two television shows, both of which represent a return to a simpler past. Set during the Korean War (1950–53), *M*A*S*H* (1972–83) at first might seem to be the opposite of nostalgic, yet its portrayal of caring doctors working in a war zone also privileges images of benign American intervention on foreign soil. "Trudie couldn't survive without

M*A*S*H," writes Nomi. "The melodic 'Suicide is Painless,' over the sound of helicopters, would tinkle out through the screen window around eight in the evening. . . . I'd always have this moment, this very brief moment, of thinking ah, now Trudie's happy" (*Complicated* 15). Ironically, suicide is rarely "painless" even though the melody that opens the show is upbeat rather than depressing. Nomi also narrates how Trudie "cried every single time she watched *The Waltons*" (19). *The Waltons* (1972–81), which gives viewers sentimental nostalgia centred on an agricultural family living through the Depression and the Second World War, also harks back to an idealized, simpler time when father and mother knew best, much like the Mennonite Heritage Village does.

Two other television shows evoke a world where happy families work together. When her father, for instance, asks Nomi if she minds "the way he was," Nomi responds by singing "the whole theme song to *The Partridge Family*," a sitcom that ran from 1970 to 1974 and features a family of five children and their widowed mother who form a band and travel together around the United States (*Complicated* 142). Certainly, Nomi and Ray could use some of the positivity that the theme song promises, with its exhortation to "Come On Get Happy" and love each other. Nomi also mentions another series, *Little House on the Prairie* (1974–83), when she says that "Ray deserves a better daughter than me. He deserves Laura Ingalls Wilder saluting him back exuberantly, clicking her heels even, and saying oh, Father, and gazing at him the way a daughter should" (73). "Everything was all right when Pa was there," says the young Laura in *Little House on the Prairie*, and Pa promises his daughter that "do as you're told . . . and no harm will come to you" (Wilder 225, 147). Whether in the book or in the television show, Pa Ingalls proves to be wise and capable, making furniture from scratch and protecting his children, a far cry, in other words, from Ray, who spends hours making a garbage hutch only to have the garbage men take it away because they believe that it was put out as trash (*Complicated* 29) and whose response to his daughter's predicament is to leave town.

Nomi's most extended reference, however, is to *The Swiss Family Robinson*, the only movie that Nomi (or, for that matter, Toews) was allowed to see as a child (Toews, "Miriam Toews Breaks Out"). Although Toews says that she has not yet read the work by Johann Wyss upon which the movie was based (email to the author, 19 March 2020), the book shows the same benevolently wielded paternal authority and family solidarity as *The Waltons* and *Little House on the Prairie*. After a shipwreck, a father, a mother, and their four sons are marooned on an island where they are the sole human inhabitants. Through great industriousness, not to mention a well-stocked ship stuck between the rocks that surround the island, the six castaways create a prosperous home complete with summer and winter residences, flourishing farms and plantations, and most of the comforts found in Europe. It helps that the father is a polymath who knows everything from how to make cassava flour, to how best to kill an iguana, to tame an ostrich, or to make porcelain. The mother is similarly brilliant when it comes to domestic life, sewing everything from dog collars to breeches and well able to make tasty meals from the various plants and animals that the menfolk bring to her. (The four boys' modus operandi is to shoot first and ask their father what they shot later.)

And, yes, this island contains an impossible variety of wildlife. Flocks of penguins and flamingos greet the stranded group, and they later encounter, among many other species, animals indigenous to four continents: kangaroos, tapirs, elephants, walruses, and turkeys. The book's narrator, the father of the four boys, imparts a series of helpful and edifying facts on the flora and fauna that they encounter. Nor does this father neglect the spiritual health of his family. He declares every seventh day a day of rest, complete with Bible readings and short sermons. The narrator tends to his sons' spiritual education by inculcating morals whenever the boys fail to live up to standards of generous manly behaviour. As he summarizes in the volume's penultimate paragraph, "it will make me happy to think that my simple narrative may lead some of these [children in other lands] to observe how blessed are the results of patient continuance in well-doing, what benefits arise from the thoughtful application of knowledge and science, and how good and pleasant a thing it is when brethren dwell together in unity under the eye of parental love" (278). Subjected to the malevolent surveillance of her uncle, Nomi longs for just such benevolent love, and, though she might have experienced such love in the past, in the present narration of the novel she sees it only in fiction.

Deprived of maternal love and sisterly companionship, Nomi looks back with nostalgia to moments when her family was together. Near the end of *A Complicated Kindness*, she recalls a particularly idyllic afternoon that her family spent together on an island in Falcon Lake. When their boat drifts away from the shore, the family is stranded, and Tash says "we [are] the Swiss Family Robinson now too" (*Complicated* 218). Unperturbed by their situation, they enjoy their day. Yes, Nomi still has a scar from where Tash accidentally lodged a fishhook in her head, but that pain is short-lived compared to the happiness that the family feels. Nomi and Tash explore the island while "talking about how we'd survive on the island for the rest of our lives and then have a movie made about us" (219). The Nickel family has such a good time that, when the boat reappears, they are "all quiet and disappointed," unwilling for their day to end (219). Remembering the beginning of the novel, where Nomi describes herself and her father as "little islands of grief" (28), marooned with Tash and Trudie gone, her nostalgia for the devoted family life of *The Swiss Family Robinson* makes sense. Nomi had to fight to see the film, and her argument to Trudie sums up, in a way, the theme of isolation and escape that runs through the novel: "A family, I thought. That lives on an island and is trying to get off. What's sinful about a family trying to survive and fight off things and get off an island, I asked her" (14). Perhaps, to a fundamentalist such as The Mouth, quite a lot. After all, he cancelled the town's bus service.

Nomi often acts in the adult role in her relationship with her father, a gentle and loving man with few practical parenting skills. Rather than cope with his domestic situation, Ray spends many leisure hours in the dump arranging the garbage into categories, an apt symbol of both the "garbage" that his life has become and the futility of his actions. In a particularly poignant insight, Nomi explains that "the dump was kind of like a department store for Ray, but even more like a holy cemetery where he could organize abandoned dreams and wrecked things into families, in a way, that stayed together" (159). Strangely, at the same time, Ray is emptying his own house of its furniture, divesting himself and his daughter of what makes their house a home.

In the end, Nomi is abandoned by both of her parents. Trudie decides to leave town (or perhaps to die by suicide) without saying goodbye to her younger daughter, and at the conclusion of the novel, when Nomi herself is shunned, Ray responds to the dilemma by also deserting his daughter. He leaves her the deed to the house and instructions on how to sell it, but surely this is too much responsibility for a sixteen-year-old girl who, only a little before, has confessed, "Dad, I'm so damn tired" (217). It is no wonder that Nomi fantasizes about *The Swiss Family Robinson* and *Little House on the Prairie*, for these works describe strong and benevolent parents who would never leave or shun their children. Although the Ingalls family moves several times during the course of Wilder's books, the parents work hard each time to create a home for their children. Likewise, though the Robinson family is marooned on a deserted island, the parents devote their energies to creating "New Switzerland," a home away from home. Both the Ingalls family and the Robinson family show resilience in the face of hardship. They do not give up, and hence their homes remain intact.

Alienation or Illness? Depression and Community Disruption

Neither the Robinson father nor the Ingalls father, of course, suffers from depression, an affliction that plagues Tom and, to a certain extent, Hosea in *A Boy of Good Breeding* and Ray and likely Nomi in *A Complicated Kindness*. Also found in *Summer of My Amazing Luck* and *All My Puny Sorrows*, the silent, withdrawn father is a staple in Toews's fiction. In fact, Tom's diagnosis in *Boy*—"he's had a series of small strokes, not big enough for anybody to really notice, except he knows it and he can't do things, you know, like he used to" (159)—sounds similar to Mel Toews's diagnosis in *Swing Low*: "dementia, due to small strokes, exacerbated by [an] underlying organic condition of manic depression, or vice versa, paranoia, I can't remember. Call it madness" (221). Tom's depression follows his initial heart attack and subsequent decline, whereas Mel was diagnosed with manic depression at age seventeen, but the similarity is there. Many of Toews's central male figures contain echoes of her father, who suffered debilitating depression for most of his life and died by suicide in 1998.

"Can the mind work when the heart is broken?" wonders Hosea after he discovers his mother's extensive stash of empty whiskey bottles. But the question could also be asked of his friend Tom, whom Hosea is visiting at the time (*Boy* 133). Knute's friend Marilyn compares Tom's depression to "a passive form of suicide, just letting go, checking out," but she philosophizes that "sometimes it's just the fucking sadness in the world, from the beginning of time, and no end to it in sight that begins to eat away at some people" (183). Tom's depression contributes to his decline and a second heart attack the day before the official population census that will determine the size of Algren. Far from being wasted, however, his life has been meaningful to many. Both Knute and Dory love Tom, he has been an upstanding citizen of Algren, and he is a true friend to Hosea not only in life but also in death. As children, Tom and Hosea were relentlessly bullied by older boys until Tom had enough and beat up one of the worst perpetrators. To the astonishment of Dr. François, who thinks that the second heart attack should have killed Tom, he remains alive in order to help Hosea. "What time is the count?" (232), he whispers, and then he keeps himself from dying through sheer will so that Hosea will get his wish to see his father.

For most of the novel, Hosea, as his surname indicates, is often "in a funk," prone to panic attacks and obsessive compulsions. His oft-repeated mantra is an old round:

> Man's life's a vapour, full of woes,
> He cuts a caper and down he goes,
> Down he, down he, down he, down he,
> Down he goes.[12]

Despite the many tragedies in the novel—the deaths of Tom, Combine Jo's husband, Johnny Dranger's wife, and others—its philosophy is mostly hopeful with a focus on those who persevere and show resilience rather than on those who suffer. Rather than staying in town and putting out fires to atone for surviving when his wife and unborn child did not, Johnny finally decides to leave Algren for new adventures (and possibly different fires). Jo finds acceptance and love as a grandmother to Summer Feelin', and the novel's two romantic couples—Max and Knute, Lorna and Hosea—have settled down to start new lives (and homes) together. There is, in fact, an air of hopefulness in Toews's first two novels that, with the exception of *Fight Night*, does not appear as strongly in her later works. As Toews has said, "things changed for me after my dad killed himself in 1998. And my writing changed, too. *A Boy of Good Breeding* had just been published a few days before he died in May" (email to the author, 1 May 2020). Add to this that she was reluctant to write anything critical about the Mennonite Church while her father was still alive, and one can see a reason for the differences in tone between her first two novels and *A Complicated Kindness*. Toews also mentioned that "I didn't want to hurt him. . . . Even though I think that the Mennonite community and the church and all of that stuff partially contributed to his illness, and death. But that was still the world that he knew and would have said that he loved and said he appreciated" (personal interview, 20 March 2020).

Attitudes toward depression and other forms of mental illness vary according to how they manifest in the individual and, to a certain extent, society at large. Certainly, *A Complicated Kindness* shows discrepancies in how health-care professionals and religious authorities identify mental illness and make allowances for it. Travis and Nomi have a conversation about his aunt, Abilene, for instance, in which Travis tells Nomi how "Aunt Abilene went nuts and after her funeral The Mouth said that like children and retarded people who were not capable of making an informed decision to ask Jesus into their hearts, Abilene, although she'd not attended church since she was sixteen, would automatically make it to heaven" (150). Later Nomi visits with her "simple cousin, Jakie," and tells him that he is "automatically saved" (153). Bert's grandfather, however, is not so lucky: "He'd been thrown out of the church a long time ago for being sick. Although the elders don't think alcoholism is a disease so it wasn't presented that way to the congregation" (79). Recent research on addiction shows that substance abuse often goes hand in hand with childhood trauma and loss,[13] but the elders obviously hold a still common belief that addiction is a personal choice and shows weakness of character.

A similar thing happens to Nomi, whose behaviours stem from a combination of grief, anger, defiance, and likely depression. No doubt she suffers from some form of mental illness. Toews comments on both Nomi and Ray: "As for the character Ray in the novel, Nomi never actually says he's mentally ill, but he's depressed, and so is Nomi in a way. They're grief-stricken, they're confused, they're bewildered, they're losing seemingly everything" ("Reader's Guide"). Reacting to the shunning of her mother and sister by the church elders in her strict Mennonite community, Nomi feels confusion and anger at the breakup of her family, and she becomes progressively more depressed, often weeping and trying to hide her tears. After another difficult encounter with her nasty boyfriend, for example, Nomi writes, "that night it rained softly. I could hear it through my screen. And then I felt it on my face, and it was warm, but it wasn't rain" (*Complicated* 127). Later she splashes Travis so that he will not notice she is crying (150), and a few pages after this incident, when she is rejected by two schoolmates, again she begins to cry (156).

When Nomi sees The Mouth's threatening sign, "YOU THINK IT'S HOT HERE ... GOD," she "started to cry and couldn't stop. Why couldn't the sign say: And you shall be like a spring whose waters fail not. Why not offer some goddamn encouragement?" (174–75; ellipsis in the original). But encouragement is in short supply for Nomi. Travis tends to insult her, even teaching her "how to walk" properly when her stride does not meet his requirements for sophistication (181). "You're beautiful, I told him, and . . . kind of mean," says Nomi, only to add "no, I didn't say that last part" (107; ellipsis in the original). She often censors herself because, she explains, "I almost never meant what I said . . . because I never knew what to say and yet felt the pressure to say things so I would try to but when I did they lacked all conviction and nothing made much sense" (106). For instance, when Nomi and Travis discuss "how it feels to be crazy," she knows that "he wanted me to say something almost as brilliant, but not quite" (149). She also lies in bed "remembering conversations and agonizing over things I'd said or hadn't said" (148). She is an intelligent young woman with keen insights, but she does not have the confidence to believe what she knows on another level to be true.

As indicated in her description of herself as "Nomi [no me] from Nowhere" (56), Nomi has little self-esteem. Although several critics have mentioned her penchant for lying and exaggeration (Neufeld 103; Redekop, "Importance" 19), she often bends the truth for fear of saying the wrong thing. Natasha Wiebe explains that, whereas Travis calls Nomi "a pathological liar" (*Complicated* 76), "Nomi tends to communicate indirectly and retract the direct statements she does make" (Wiebe 47). Wiebe explains insightfully that "Nomi's narrative style has been partly fostered by a culture that discourages and even punishes expression that runs contrary to the official religious framework" (48), but one could also say that her retractions are based upon her uncertainty. When Nomi tries to express her opinions aloud or in her schoolwork, she is shut down.

Nomi exhibits several other signs of depression. She spends many hours in bed or wandering aimlessly through the town, she has trouble sleeping at night but then falls asleep in school, she self-medicates with marijuana and Tash's expired Valium, and eventually she trades sex for drugs. Her "nightly face ache" (*Complicated* 136) started when Tash and Trudie still lived at home and Nomi was confused about what was happening around her, so this likely psychosomatic symptom has been recurring over a three-year period (146). Nomi also engages in an odd form of self-harm: she bites herself in her sleep. "I wondered what it meant to bite yourself in your sleep," she muses. "Would I soon begin to tear out clumps of hair? Would I be able to kill myself eventually without realizing it?" (127). She recognizes that her self-harm could escalate into even more damaging behaviour, but she does not have the inner resources to stop it.

Nomi's memoir implies, moreover, that she is alienated and depressed for good reason, for she recognizes and rejects the town's hypocritical fundamentalism and her supposed place in the community as a dutiful and obedient daughter of Christ. Nomi believes that women in the community have two options: to stay in the town and marry or "to travel to the remotest corners of Third World countries with barrels full of Gideon Bibles and hairnets" (7). Whereas she rebels actively against her designated future in the community, whether it be killing chickens or getting married, her friend Lydia Voth takes a passive route, becoming so sensitive to noise and touch that she is hospitalized. When the girls were younger, Ray Nickel nicknamed them Tom and Huck (31), indicating their closeness and inseparability, and indeed they are rather like friends adrift on a sinking raft. When Nomi comes to visit her, Lydia lies helpless in her bed, unable to perform even the simplest tasks because they hurt her so much. As with Nomi, at first the town does not recognize that Lydia might be suffering from mental illness. "How's the princess and the pea?" (33), one nurse asks Nomi, implying that Lydia in some way is faking her symptoms to get attention. Nomi, on the other hand, sees herself and Lydia as feeling "shared desperation" and recognition of "the familiar flickering embers of each other's dying souls" (33).

Erving Goffman, the famed sociologist and expert on stigma, speaks of how in some cases "the inability or reluctance of the mad person to play their designated social role, and thus fulfil the expectations of others, was the primary cause of their being labeled mad" (qtd. in Ussher 135). Indeed, the behaviours of both Nomi and Lydia make strange sense when one considers the lives laid out for them. Soper refers to a nurse's comment that both young women "needed to have [their] wings clipped" (*Complicated* 65), a particularly distressing metaphor given the nearby chicken-slaughtering plant. Soper writes that, "as the nurse's comment suggests, young girls are still considered chattel in the social economy of East Village; in the 'normal' course of affairs, the girls' apprenticeships in the slaughterhouse would be followed by marriage proposals from young men from the community. In her illness, Lydia passively defies this script, and her sensitivity, like Nomi's acute perception, is seen to threaten this status quo" (90). Yet their behaviours have an internal logic, for each young woman, in her own way, resists her future. Nomi makes herself difficult and unattractive; Lydia literally makes herself untouchable. Neither, then, is ideal marriage material.

Differences in how the people of East Village view mental illness mirror attitudes toward it in the world at large, especially when one considers that the book was published in 2004, at the height of the debate over treating depression with relatively new drugs such as Prozac. Prozac was first marketed in 1987 and enjoyed, according to Peter D. Kramer, the psychiatrist who famously published *Listening to Prozac* in 1993, "the fastest acceptance of any psychotherapeutic medicine ever—650,000 prescriptions per month by the time the *Newsweek* cover appeared, just over two years after Prozac was introduced" (xiv). Such wide adoption, along with Kramer's report that the drug made people feel "better than well" (*Listening* vii) created a backlash in which some worried that Prozac was the new Milltown or Valium, tranquilizers by then associated with medicating people, especially women, into accepting their dreary and unfulfilling lives. Moral philosopher Carl Elliott included a critique of the overuse of Prozac in *Better than Well: American Medicine Meets the American Dream* (2003), in which he said that antidepressants, though clearly necessary for some, could create artificial resilience in people who would be better off addressing the dissatisfactions prevalent in American life and changing their circumstances rather than being drugged into acquiescence to the status quo. Kramer responded with *Against Depression* (2005), in which he argued that depression is a disease and should be treated as such. In *A Complicated Kindness*, there is also controversy over prescribing antidepressants. Dr. Hunter, Nomi states, "liked to prescribe antidepressants. He'd written an article for the city paper that said our town has colossally huge numbers of depressed people" (134). The Mouth, of course, is adamant that the doctor is mistaken.

Divergence of opinion also exists on depression itself. Memoirs of those who have suffered through depression, for example, differ on whether the experience has intrinsic value. The "only saving grace" of depression, writes William Styron in his groundbreaking *Darkness Visible: A Memoir of Madness* is that "it is conquerable" (84). Although he shows how the depressed person, as the concluding statement from Dante's *Inferno* suggests, can "[come] forth, and once again [behold] the stars" (qtd. in Styron 84), he does not place an inherent value on the experience but focuses on the possibility of resilience. Others, however, have written personal accounts that insist on the value of depression. Andrew Solomon, for instance, writes in *The Noonday Demon: An Atlas of Depression* that "I do not love experiencing my depression, but I love the depression itself. I love who I am in the wake of it" (442–43). In a statement reminiscent of the Greek idea of *pathei mathos* (knowledge through suffering) or the Christian belief in *felix culpa* (the fortunate fall), Solomon continues that "I have discovered what I would have to call a soul, a part of myself I could never have imagined until one day, seven years ago, when hell came to pay me a surprise visit" (443).

Like many others, Solomon equates depression with a heightened sense of identity and ends up valuing his depression for the insight, depth of character, and sensitivity that it gives him. In *Against Depression*, Kramer writes of the many people who sent him their memoirs on depression: "But then more often than not, in these memoirs, hints of pride showed through, as if affliction with depression might after all be more enriching than, say, a painful and discouraging encounter with kidney failure. Expressions of value would emerge: *Depression gave me my soul*. . . . Despite their insistence on its ordinariness, the memoirs made depression seem ennobling" (5). Similarly, Nell Casey's collection of essays, *Unholy Ghost: Writers on Depression*, contains a mix of accounts, some of which value depression and others of which see mainly its negative aspects. Susanna Kaysen, for instance, writes in her essay, "One Cheer for Melancholy," that "melancholy is useful. In its aspect of pensive reflection or contemplation, it's the source of many books . . . and paintings, much scientific insight, the resolution of many fights between couples and friends, and the process known as becoming mature" (38–39). One characteristic of resilience, however, is the ability to move beyond a painful experience, valuing what has been learned while resolving to remain strong. Perhaps, then, these authors are celebrating their resilience rather than their depression itself.

Although Toews thoroughly describes the devastating effects of depression in *Swing Low*, *The Flying Troutmans*, and *All My Puny Sorrows*, her exploration of mental illness in *A Complicated Kindness* is made more complex by her use of the genre of the coming-of-age novel. For its first half at least, the novel can be said to be part of a tradition that includes Sheri Reynolds's *The Rapture of Canaan*, Barbara Kingsolver's *The Poisonwood Bible*, and even Charlotte Brontë's *Jane Eyre*, works that describe the plight of young women bound by fundamentalist authoritarian "father" figures and the subsequent struggles that these women undertake to clarify their own values and leave repressive communities. Other parallels include stories about young women who leave small towns to start life anew, such as Margaret Laurence's *The Diviners* and Alice Munro's *Lives of Girls and Women* (Steffler, "Fragments" 126).

In creating Nomi Nickel, Toews fashions a character whose obvious need for help is mitigated by her status as a fictional type. Soper writes of how *A Complicated Kindness* presents "an ironic commentary on the teleology of coming-of-age narratives" (87) and "likewise resists the conventional ending of the *Künstlerroman* and the emphasis it shares with the *Bildungsroman* on the teleology of *having become* (i.e., an artist, an adult)" (98). Unlike the traditional coming-of-age story, in which protagonists often surmount the obstacles that families and communities put in their way, Nomi does not leave her parents behind to start life on her own; rather, they and her sister leave her. As Steffler writes, "the shocking disappearances of all those who matter to Nomi are beyond her control: she is not the one initiating the break with her family, town, and past, but is instead the one being left behind by others" (Steffler, "Fragments" 126–27). If *Complicated* was true to the *Künstlerroman* or the *Bildungsroman*, then Nomi would reject her town's repressive environment and strike out on new adventures, yet at the end of the novel she is unsure of what she should do.

With the proviso that for many sufferers clinical depression causes extreme inertia, in coming-of-age stories, the suffering that comes with depression is often useful, for it allows those who experience it to see beyond the narrow focus of the community. Tash falls into this category as she rebels against community strictures. As Nomi writes of her sister, "and I had another thought: that Tash had stopped laughing for a good reason. And that she was the sanest person in our family. But that didn't make any sense at all" (*Complicated* 111). Tash becomes increasingly more desperate, saying to Trudie that "I think I'll go crazy. I can't stand it. It's all a fucking lie. It's not right and it's killing me" (146). Once she decides to leave, however, she smiles "a really tender genuine smile. . . . She'd freed herself. That's what the real smile meant. I knew it" (147). Her anger and sadness give Tash the strength to leave East Village and thus fulfill the "alienated-and-depressed-young-woman-escapes-entrapment" narrative that readers might expect.

Like her sister, Nomi has good reason to feel alienated, and thus her depression might have inherent value as a manifestation of her justifiable discontent with the world in which she lives. But that is more Tash's narrative than Nomi's, and Tash's situation actually differs from Nomi's in that Tash leaves town with her boyfriend, Ian, and Trudie is there to support her decision, provide her with money and food, and even help pack Ian's truck (146–48). Meanwhile, when Nomi contemplates leaving, her sister, mother, and father have all left town ahead of her. Although it seems that Tash had little community support, she did have the help of loved ones, something Nomi lacks.

In the second half of the novel, therefore, Toews questions the alienation narrative, focusing instead not only on how alienated individuals might be admired for their stance against the status quo but also on how they should be helped. Whereas Lydia receives an ambiguous sort of help, being sent to a mental institution where she will receive electroshock therapy so she can learn to "judge things better" (228), the punishment for Nomi's brand of rebellion is to receive no help at all from her community. Some readers—Jeff Gundy is a good example—get "so caught up in wanting to *help* her that [they can] hardly stand it that nobody else in the book seemed willing or able to throw her a lifeline." Similarly, German scholar Christoph Wiebe says that "Nomi is utterly deserted. No one helps her. Actually that is a declaration of bankruptcy of the Christian church as well as the community of people of the immediate location. Nomi needs help and support, but instead she is excluded and ostracized." Toews calls Nomi "a confused, grieving, misunderstood kid" ("Complicated Kind" 44); however, many in her community see her actions as wilful disobedience and fail to recognize that she has a problem. When her school principal invites her to the office for a chat, he begins by saying to Nomi that "clearly these are not the best years of your life." Feeling that she will finally be heard, she recounts how she "felt almost drunk with gratitude when he said that. . . . It was a type of understanding. I thought he was going to rescue me, but that's where it ended" (*Complicated* 170). The adults in her life are singularly incompetent when addressing the needs of this desperately struggling young woman; Ray tells Nomi at age thirteen that "he hoped [she] could thrive from benign neglect, like an African violet" (144), and Uncle Hans rejects her outright.

Others, like a hospital nurse whom Nomi approaches near the novel's conclusion, say that she is as "healthy as an ox" (228) and has no reason to be sad. When Nomi presses the point, describing her nightly face aches and her fear that she is going to die, she is "halfway there" already, the nurse patronizes her. "You're sixteen," she says, "that's a wonderful time in a girl's life. Go home and make yourself a cup of tea and try to relax" (229). Clearly, the nurse has forgotten how isolating one's teen years can be. The worst offender, however, is the person to whom Nomi ostensibly addresses her memoir, Mr. Quiring himself. He diagnoses her problem as "a general lack of self-esteem that feeds into an eroding sense of purpose" (118), in some ways an accurate description of depression, yet he continues to criticize Nomi instead of trying to help boost her confidence. He is also partly to blame for her losing her mother (he had an affair with Trudie and then threatened that he would lie about her promiscuity if she did not continue to have sex with him). Thus, Quiring should seek to make amends for helping to destroy the Nickel family, but instead, at one point, he throws a pencil case at Nomi so hard that she throws up (152–53).

As shown by the Protestant Reformation out of which Anabaptism emerged, Christianity is not a monolithic structure, and people worship with varying degrees of fundamentalism, secularism, and belief. The New Testament contains its fair share of condemnations for non-believers, but it also says "judge not, that you be not judged. For with what judgment you judge, you will be judged; and with the measure you use, it will be measured back to you. And why do you look at the speck in your brother's eye, but do not consider the plank in your own eye? . . . Hypocrite! First remove the plank from your own eye, and then you will see clearly to remove the speck from your brother's eye" (Matthew 7:1–3, 5, NKJV). In this sense, Nomi can be considered one of the most "Christian" individuals in her town. Although she is often flippant and disrespectful toward Menno Simons and The Mouth, Nomi also exhibits the compassion and care denied to her by others. She plays with the neighbour's child, she talks to a mentally disabled boy on the street, and she regularly visits Mrs. Peters, a woman whose son,

Clayton, drowned when he was four. "She loved to answer questions about Clayton," Nomi recounts, so she makes sure to ask some (*Complicated* 62). In other words, she contributes to the ability of Mrs. Peters to be resilient after her son's death.

Nomi also exhibits Christian charity when she construes the motives of the townsfolk in a positive light. In the novel's title passage, she qualifies her mother's "silent raging" against the town by writing "but there is kindness here, a complicated kindness. You can see it sometimes in the eyes of people when they look at you and don't know what to say. When they ask me how my dad is, for instance, and mean how am I managing without my mother" (46). She reiterates this concept when a woman comments on her lack of church attendance. Instead of thinking that the woman is a busybody who should stay out of her affairs, Nomi reflects that "when she looked at me she saw a child surrounded by flames, screaming. And that must have been hard for her" (186). Nomi also shows compassion for her best friend, Lydia, to whom she pays the respect of taking her complaints seriously. Perhaps most importantly, Nomi does not leave her father. Recognizing his vulnerability, she stays at his side and tries to take care of him.

After The Mouth and the other elders shun Nomi, Ray leaves town without saying goodbye, just as Trudie did earlier. In spite of her ongoing sadness, instead of constructing a negative story in which her parents sin against her, Nomi interprets their motives in a positive way. Ray's unsatisfactory answer to Nomi's poignant question "why didn't she take me with her?" is only "you were sleeping when she left" (192, 193), but Nomi fashions a better motive: Trudie knew that Ray needed Nomi more than she did. As Nomi elaborates, "I'm pretty sure she left town for his sake. It would have killed him to choose between her or the church" (194). Faced with evidence that her mother had an affair with Mr. Quiring, Nomi again interprets her actions in a compassionate way: "It was grief that drew my mom to you [Quiring] and love that pulled her back. Love for Ray. And for me and for Tash. And for the perfect idea, at least, of us being together again" (243). Trudie might have strayed from her marriage vows, but in the end Nomi wants to believe that she was loyal to her husband and children.

Nomi uses similar reasoning when her father leaves her alone in an unfurnished house. Ray leaves because he remembers her promise to him "that [she would] never leave him" (193). For Nomi to be able to leave East Village, therefore, Ray has to leave first. For Gundy, "that's a brave interpretation, but it's hard for me to buy. If he really loved her, I think, he would have said, Listen, Nomi, I've had enough of these people. Pack your stuff, we're moving to Winnipeg." Nomi, however, understands Ray's dilemma. As a true believer, Ray has to obey the edicts of his church, and his church has now shunned Nomi. Since it would be torture for him to ignore his daughter's existence, and torture for her to be ignored, he chooses to leave her behind. As was the case with her mother, there are problems with Nomi's interpretation. In a town with no bus service, and having left Nomi his car, how would Ray actually have left the town? The novel does not say, but Nomi, who has felt "stuck in the middle of a story with no good ending" (*Complicated* 194), finds a way to ignore the difficulties in her positive reading of events.

The brilliant double ending of *A Complicated Kindness* first gives readers the conclusion that they want and expect: a newly awakened heroine leaves her repressive home behind to start over in a new place. Toews has said that the original draft of the novel ended with "Nomi leaving town," but Toews "realized at the end of the writing process or just before [she] was about to submit the first draft, that that didn't make sense in terms of the story and Nomi's character. There are always surprises" ("Authentic" 11). "Truthfully," Nomi writes in *A Complicated Kindness*, "this story ends with me still sitting on the floor of my room wondering who I'll become if I leave this town and remembering when I was a little kid and how I loved to fall asleep in my bed breathing in the smell of freshly cut grass and listening to the voices of my sister and my mother talking and laughing in the kitchen and the sounds of my dad poking around in the yard, making things beautiful right outside my bedroom window" (246). Nomi has gained insight, and she might well leave East Village, but she is also paralyzed by her youth, her depression, and the fact that she has no real place to go.

"The Golden Dream of Home"

Nomi also hesitates to move because of her nostalgia for the home that she once knew and hopes will be established anew. After all, home is real, but it is also imagined. When Nomi recalls, for instance, her visits to an elderly neighbour, Mrs. Klippenstein, she describes how the older woman would recount "stories about her childhood in Russia, the golden dream of home" (*Complicated* 163). Yet her nostalgia for her Russian past is problematized by Trudie, who evokes the dark side of life in Russia when she tells Tash "that we could have stayed in Russia and had our barns set on fire and our stomachs torn out" (91). To live "the golden dream," Mrs. Klippenstein must efface hints of trouble that were undoubtedly brewing beneath the surface of the perfect rural life that she remembers. Perhaps she was too young to perceive the growing tensions between the Mennonite and Ukrainian communities, and perhaps, since she is an elderly woman, she remembers her distant past rather than her more recent past. However, her "golden dream" is based upon an ideal, and that ideal defines one aspect of small-town life in both *A Boy of Good Breeding* and *A Complicated Kindness*.

In Toews's writing, home is a place that we yearn to reach but is often elusive. When defined to include one's hometown or immediate community, it is also a place that can provide resilience but only if there is the will and expertise to do so. Michael Ungar speaks of how "social and physical ecologies potentiate resilience," and it is thus a combination of inherent personality traits and the availability and nature of community supports. "While individual agency is a component of one's ability to navigate to resources," Ungar continues, "it remains the role of families, communities, and governments to make those resources available in culturally meaningful ways that reflect the preferences of those who need them. Therefore, resilience is a shared quality of the individual and the individual's social ecology, with the social ecology likely more important than individual factors to recovery and sustainable well-being for populations under stress" ("Social Ecologies" 17). The differences in resilience at the end of *A Boy of Good Breeding* versus at the end of *A Complicated Kindness* have much to do with the reliability of community resources and supports. East Village itself is unresilient, for the community lives under fear of censure, has a high rate of depression, and does not recognize the problems of its members. In *Complicated*, fundamentalism pits family members against each other, paralyzes dissent, and cuts off resources that might promote healing. Nomi says of East Village that "somehow all the problems of the world manage to get into our town but not the strategies to deal with them" (52). "This town," she thinks, "is so severe. And silent. It makes me crazy, the silence. I wonder if a person can die from it. . . . The town office building has a giant filing cabinet full of death certificates that say choked to death on his own anger or suffocated from unexpressed feelings of unhappiness" (4). Toews emphasizes that the entire community, in fact, might be mentally ill, and Nomi, as one of the few people who recognize this fact, paradoxically, like her sister, might be saner than most. Like the children of an authoritative and abusive father, most people in the town have lost the courage to rebel and no longer question the arbitrary rules under which they live. As Toews says in an interview, "it keeps you childlike to live in an environment like that. You have to be childlike in order to follow, to conform to the extent that you're expected to—in that community and in the church" ("'Place'" 57).

In contrast, *A Boy of Good Breeding* describes a community with little to no religious affiliation that grows when it stops imposing boundaries (Hosea's exclusionary tactics to keep the town at 1,500 people, Knute's initial hostility toward Max and Jo) and moves toward forgiveness and understanding. The main characters in *Boy* are resilient. They carry on and form new lives. On the last page of the novel (237), all of Hosea's improvements to the town seem to be in place. The sun rises on "Canadian flags in the form of red and white petunias" and a town surrounded by "fields of yellow and blue." Up before her parents, Summer Feelin' plays with her newly adopted dog, Bill Quinn (the stray that Mrs. Cherniski earlier called the devil), and Hosea nestles beside his girlfriend, Lorna. No longer obsessed with seeing his supposed father, he takes the prime minister's cancellation of his promised visit to Canada's smallest town with aplomb. Clearly, Hosea knows who he is and where he belongs. Interestingly, though readers end *A Complicated Kindness* hoping that Nomi will leave East Village, those who finish reading *Boy* are unlikely to feel the same way about Knute, Hosea, Max, Jo, and Dory. One novel shows how a home place can provide stability, whereas the other shows how, when a town itself is made unresilient by fundamentalism, people have to leave it to preserve their own resilience and find new lives.

Perhaps Nomi, like her creator, Toews, rejects aspects of her town and the religion in which she was raised, but she is also loath to leave a place that contains both positive and negative memories. "While East Village is Nomi's place of exile," Natasha Wiebe writes, "it is also her home" (45). Clearly, Nomi is not Toews, yet Toews, who famously left town the day that she graduated from high school, and who has said in an interview that the Mennonite community is "a place you can't go home to" ("'Place'" 61), comes back to the small-town setting in *A Boy of Good Breeding*, and specifically to a Mennonite small-town setting in *A Complicated Kindness*, and in both *Swing Low* and *All My Puny Sorrows*. She said in 2005 that "I'm pretty sure I'm finished writing about Mennonites. . . . It's time to move on" ("Complicated Kind" 23); however, though Toews took a break from writing about Mennonites in *The Flying Troutmans*, in her next four books (*Irma Voth*, *All My Puny Sorrows*, *Women Talking*, and *Fight Night*) she returned to Mennonites, though not always to fictional versions of Steinbach. Home, whether the person's experience of it is positive or negative, has a habit of returning to be reimagined and rethought. *Boy* and *Complicated* are similar in their "return" to facsimiles of the small town in which Toews lived during her youth. However, because of her decision to write about the negative elements of her Mennonite past in the latter volume, they are different in terms of their takes on resilience and how communities can support or destroy the people who live within them.

A Boy of Good Breeding and *A Complicated Kindness* address how resilience comes not only from within an individual but also from community support and connection with others. In this sense, the novels are mirror images of each other: one shows characters who thrive within newly formed community relationships, and the other shows how both a family and a town essentially desert a troubled sixteen-year-old desperate for help. Her intelligence, sense of humour, and imagination will likely help Nomi to leave East Village, but this outcome is by no means certain at the novel's conclusion. *Boy* and *Complicated* essentially describe their towns as closed systems in which the outside world appears only tangentially, and thus their protagonists look largely within their immediate environments for support.

In the two novels that I discuss in the next chapter, *Summer of My Amazing Luck* and *The Flying Troutmans*, the protagonists, Lucy Van Alstyne and Hattie Troutman, try to find help by taking to the road. Both Lucy and Hattie feel overwhelmed by their responsibilities, and each envisions help from an elusive father figure whom she sets out to find. The road trips of the two women teach them two things: first, they learn that they have more inner resources than they thought possible; second, they find resilience within both themselves and the communities that they left behind.

CHAPTER TWO

"ON THE ROAD" (WITH CHILDREN)

The Flying Troutmans and Summer of My Amazing Luck

No squalling kids and mothers wielding strollers, no ten-cent hoods, no traffic jams on the freeway, no passenger with a ten-dollar bill when the fare is sixty cents and the sign's already told him I don't give change. I'm my own boss. I am free of the shrill and the halt purveyors of public transport. [Arachne Manteia on giving up her job as a city bus driver to become a travelling underwear salesperson.]
—ARITHA VAN HERK, *NO FIXED ADDRESS* (14)

We had been on the road for fifty minutes and not one out of the five—well, out of four, really; Dill had a diaper on—children had asked to stop to pee. There had not been one argument, not one shriek, not one bad word, not one painful accident (besides the car seat incident, but that was only painful for everyone watching it happen to Dill and not for Dill himself), not one spilled box of apple juice, not one object thrown from the window, and not one automotive breakdown.
—MIRIAM TOEWS, *SUMMER OF MY AMAZING LUCK* (163)

Miriam Toews admits that she "loves being on the road more than anything" and "enjoy[s] road stories, the reading and the pacing of them, in books and in film, the 'how are we going to survive?' kinds of challenges" ("Road Tripping"). Fittingly, Toews made these comments in connection with the debut of *The Flying Troutmans* (2008), her most sustained "road novel" to date. Only two of her works—interestingly, both non-Mennonite in focus—involve sustained road trips in which being on the road is as important to the story as the destination. (*Irma Voth* and *Fight Night* also contain significant travel, but in them the protagonists travel by air, and the focus is on what happens when the characters reach where they set out to go and less on the trip itself.) Yet, even when Toews focuses on extended car trips, her road novels feel different from the scenario popularized by Jack Kerouac in *On the Road* (1957). In his famous novel, the main characters, Sal Paradise and Dean Moriarty, escape their mundane lives by driving or hitchhiking across the United States, leaving their day-to-day responsibilities behind them. *Summer of My Amazing Luck* (1996) and *The Flying Troutmans* are similar in that their female protagonists, Lucy Van Alstyne and Hattie Troutman, seek to escape unsatisfactory home lives, but theirs are not footloose adventures into the unknown. They cannot make complete escapes because they take parts of "home" with them in the form of children and all the baggage, both physical and emotional, that comes with travelling with young people. Neither Lucy nor Hattie feels particularly resilient, and both are recovering from major traumas. They therefore set out on road trips to find others to help share their burdens, yet coping with adventures on the road allows them to see that they have resources within themselves.

Summer of My Amazing Luck begins in the "Have-a-Life" public housing facility in Winnipeg. Lucy, the narrator, is an eighteen-year-old mother with a nine-month-old son named Dillinger (Dill). Lucy was fifteen when her mother gave a ride to a hitchhiking bank robber who assaulted her and left her to die on the side of the road. After the death of her mother, Lucy dulled her pain with sex. In one of the many satires of reductive medical analysis in Toews's works, Lucy says of her mother's death that "they said I hadn't grieved properly over my mother's death. That was the reason I became promiscuous, they said. They said I snuck out of my bedroom window every night because I needed to forget. I needed to forget, they said, because I couldn't bear the sadness of remembering" (3). As readers find as they read her story, this diagnosis is essentially correct, but her reasoning and instincts are more complicated than the psychiatrists think, and her diagnosis makes Lucy more of a victim than her character suggests.

Lucy's first summer at the housing facility, nicknamed "Half-a-Life" by its denizens, is plagued by heavy rains, floods, and ravenous hordes of mosquitoes. There is a reason, after all, that novelty mugs proclaim the mosquito to be the provincial "bird" of Manitoba. Di Brandt underlines this point when she writes in her review of *Summer of My Amazing Luck* that "an incidental pleasure for Manitoba readers will be seeing our typical and legendary landscape tribulations documented here in loving detail. None of us will forget the summer of the rains a few years ago, which brought to life seven years' worth of drought-delayed mosquitoes all at once. The only consolation that year brought was its storymaking potential" (114). In *Summer*, the hordes of mosquitoes trap mothers and children indoors, and the overabundance of these pests prompts yearnings to escape to areas where children can play outside without fear of itchy bites.

On her first day at Have-a-Life, Lucy meets the flamboyant Alicia (Lish), a single mother of four daughters. Lish pines for the father of her two youngest girls, a street performer who left her after a one-night stand. As the rain and mosquitoes continue, Lish becomes listless and depressed, and Lucy, who relies on Lish's humour and strength of character, hatches a plan to make Lish happier. Lucy sends her a postcard, ostensibly from the departed busker, saying how much he misses Lish and wants to reconnect with her. Lish decides to drive to Denver to reunite with the busker, so she borrows a decrepit Ford Aerostar and embarks on a road trip with her two eldest daughters, her four-year-old twins, her surrogate daughter/friend Lucy, and Dill. Naturally, Lucy has to "kill off" the busker before they arrive in Denver. Lish handles the busker's "death" philosophically, and they drive back to Winnipeg. It turns out that Lish knew all along that the postcards were faked and that she turned the tables on Lucy by playing along. In an ending that one reviewer calls "somewhat contrived and less-than-subtle in its optimism" (Grekul 186), Lucy and Lish return home to find Lucy's estranged father, a boyfriend prospect, and most of the inhabitants of Have-a-Life anticipating the birth of a resident's baby. Lucy and her father reconcile, and things return to normal. Although the actual road trip is only three days long, it is the device that moves the plot as Lucy first tells how it came about, what happened on the road, and what transpires upon the women's return.

In *The Flying Troutmans*, the road trip takes up most of the novel. Narrator Hattie begins her account with "yeah, so things have fallen apart" (1). She has been living in Paris, where her boyfriend has just informed her that he is heading to "an ashram in India" and that she is not invited (2), when she gets a call from her eleven-year-old niece Theodora (Thebes). Hattie's sister and Thebes's mother, Min, has succumbed to another bout of the depression that has plagued her since childhood, leaving Thebes and her fifteen-year-old brother, Logan, to fend for themselves without maternal support. Hattie arrives to find Min incapacitated by depression and the house in disarray. After Min is admitted to the hospital, Hattie tries to take charge, but she feels inadequate for the task. When Min asks her to help her die, Hattie cannot tell the children what Min said; instead, she tells them that Min asked her to find their father, Doug Cherkis. He was a good father at first, but Min's resentment and depressive behaviour eventually drove him away. The children have not seen or heard from their father for about ten years.

Hattie decides to take the children on a road trip because she is desperate to avoid becoming their de facto parent and because she wants to protect them from Min's mental illness. Min has told Hattie many times "never to call her again" (53), but for "the first time" Min has now "refused to see her kids" (54). Hattie and the children are also afraid that social workers will discover that the family is in serious trouble and put Logan and Thebes in foster care. Hattie and the children therefore embark in Min's Ford Aerostar van in search of Cherkis, whom they eventually find in California. The adventures that Hattie and the children have along the way make her resolve to take responsibility for Min and the children in spite of the emotional toll that caring for Min has caused her in the past. In caring for her niece and nephew, Hattie discovers resilience that she did not know she had.

Summer of My Amazing Luck and *The Flying Troutmans* use the road trip as a central organizational device, but with a difference, for the freedom or release that the protagonists seek is tempered by the presence of children.

Traditionally, travel or quest stories, whether actual or fictional, are predominantly male and involve a departure from domestic life and the "refining influence" of women. In Homer's classic epic poem, Odysseus leaves his wife, Penelope, and son, Telemachus, on Ithaca when he goes off to war and further adventures; in Jonathan Swift's *Gulliver's Travels*, Lemuel Gulliver leaves his wife and returns to sea, where, like Odysseus, he encounters many strange people and places. Huck Finn decides to "light out for the Territory" to avoid being adopted and "civilized" by Aunt Polly. In contrast, as accounts by Catharine Parr Traill and Susanna Moodie illustrate, female tales of travel often centre on setting up a home place in "the backwoods of Canada" or describing "life in the clearings." It is the Alexander Mackenzies, Samuel Hearnes, or David Thompsons who record their ventures into putatively unexplored territories, often undermining the help that their Indigenous guides give them by describing them as servants of the cause of European exploration rather than the knowledgeable inhabitants of the landscape that they actually were.

As with narratives of exploration at sea, on foot, or by canoe, so with the car. Although, as women's and autobiography studies author Sidonie Smith has stated, some women, such as Edith Wharton, embraced road travel early (179), and "suffragists used automobility as a means to reach an increasingly widespread audience" (172), the car is more closely linked to the masculine than the feminine. In Smith's words, "mobile men have pursued self-discovery, expanded consciousness, profligate consumption, sexual release, and nostalgic return," with Kerouac's *roman à clef*, *On the Road* "as the quintessential tale (at least the quintessential North American tale) of man, auto, motion, and masculinity" (177). Bored with routine and dead-end jobs, men seek adventure and excitement through travel, leaving women behind to work their *own* dead-end jobs and take care of the children. Similarly, expert in mobility studies Alexandra Ganser notes that *On the Road* "is also the work that appears most often as an explicit or implicit intertext in contemporary road narratives" and "has arguably shaped the genre and its associative characteristics like no other text" (*Roads* 44). Kerouac's alter ego, Sal Paradise, and his friend Dean Moriarty (Neal Cassady) would prefer a world in which women "never [utter] a harsh word, never a complaint, or modified; her old man can come in any hour of the night with anybody and have talks in the kitchen and drink the beer and leave any old time. This is a man, and that's his castle" (Kerouac 192). Dean's statement reduces women to the role of unpaid help whose purpose is to take care of the household without complaint or criticism. At the end of *On the Road*, when Sal settles down with Laura, "the girl with the pure and innocent dear eyes that I had always searched for and for so long" (290), he still speaks of "all that road going, all the people dreaming in the immensity of it" (293), and feels regret that Dean, "the Idiot, the Imbecile, the Saint" (183), has also stopped his wandering. Tellingly, when Cassady's wife, Carolyn, published her memoir of the Beat movement, she called it *Off the Road* because she mostly held down a job and looked after the children while her husband travelled.[1]

Unlike Kerouac's travelling men, Toews's road-tripping women find their love lives challenged by the presence of their children. When Lucy meets a young man at a hotel, for instance, she admits that "I wanted to forget about Dill just for a while and feel those hard brown arms. I wanted to ride in the Dream Weaver with him and see those dirty hands of his holding onto the wheel. Driving fast. I wanted my life to go back about ten years so I could do it over and figure things out before I went ahead living it" (*Summer* 187). Hattie has a similar experience in *The Flying Troutmans* when she goes searching for Logan after he disappears. When she meets a group of young people who volunteer to help her find her nephew, she speculates that "it would have been a great time if I hadn't just lost my sister's kid" (203). Once she finds Logan, Hattie thinks "about the other options I'd had that evening, the roads less travelled. I could have been necking with a sweet, American hippie in the back of a truck under a full yellow moon" (210). Instead, she and Logan return to the hotel to find a distraught Thebes, who has called the hospital long distance only for Min to forget that she has a daughter. Feeling rejected by her mother and abandoned by her brother and her aunt, Thebes has been cutting herself. Hattie cannot escape her responsibilities for long.

Sinners, Saints, and Adventurers: A "Detour" on the Road Novel

Various critics have defined the term "road trip" both by what it is and what it is not. First and foremost, the twentieth-century road trip highlights the automobile. Unlike buses, trains, and airplanes, the automobile has no predetermined schedule and route. Travellers can start their journeys when they like rather than being tied, say, to the set times of airplane travel, with its instructions on when to arrive at the gate and long security lines. Except for the very rich, air, train, and bus travel are mass transportation without the privacy that the automobile can afford. Although cars can also be shared spaces, especially for the poor, the North American ideal of the automobile is private ownership and individual space. Thus, for every tale such as John Steinbeck's *The Grapes of Wrath* or Tomson Highway's *The Rez Sisters*, in which poverty and lack of access to transportation force extended family members to share cramped quarters in the same vehicle, readers encounter the freewheeling atmosphere of *On the Road*, in which the characters, albeit often too poor to have their own vehicles, exercise a great deal of choice as to when, how, and with whom they travel. In many ways a satire of the male-centric road novel, Aritha van Herk's *No Fixed Address* shares the trope of a solitary person who lives by her (his) own rules, rejects domestic life, travels freely, and indulges in sexual conquests.[2] As the only male traveller in either *The Flying Troutmans* or *Summer of My Amazing Luck* (aside from nine-month-old Dill), Logan desperately wants to live up to this stereotype of freedom. He knows that he looks "lame to be riding into a new town with his sister and his aunt. . . . Ideally he would have had us all duck down and make ourselves invisible while he drove around listening to his tunes, playing it cool, pretending he was something other than a fifteen-year-old Canadian boy in a leaking Ford Aerostar minivan" (*Flying* 197). His frustration with the vehicle and his embarrassing companions surfaces when Logan carves statements into the dashboard. But, as Hattie thinks, "who cares if it lowered resale value. It was a Ford Aerostar" (87)—and one in bad condition at that.

In many road novels, the car, far from being an anonymous means to a destination, becomes a character in its own right. The glamour of Arachne Manteia's 1959 Mercedes, the unreliability of the Joads' makeshift vehicle, not to mention the Aerostar vans in *Summer* and *Flying*, take centre stage, with characters developing, in many cases, symbiotic relationships with their vehicles. Moreover, even when there is a final destination, the emphasis in road novels is on the journey to get there and what happens while travelling. As Queen's University professor Heather Macfarlane puts it, "the major criterion is that the travelling itself is as important a part of the trip as the destination" (10). An early writer on the road novel genre, Ronald Primeau, writes of the "free-floating state beyond ordinary spatiotemporal bounds" (6), which gives road narratives their power. At home, one has a job or is perhaps castigated for not having one. With the proviso that cars themselves are a key indicator of wealth and status in North American society, being on a road trip, in the sense that Primeau means it, involves separation from day-to-day concerns and the possibility of adventure: "The lure of the road is simple adventure, escape, and the offer to break the routine. The appeal is in part the road's carnivalesque disruption of the ordinary. The freedom of the pilgrimage is a social alternative, a pure quest for something beyond the mundane" (15). Smith seems to agree when she says that "in their automobiles people sped away from the domestic constraints of home and the deadening routines of a rampant consumerism, and headed out across the land in search of new experiences" (169).

Likely because the road trip traditionally involves escaping domestic life and implies, in most cases, the freedom to move, Primeau writes that "the literature of the American highway has been dominated for most of its history by the values and attitudes of white males. When women and minority authors take to the road, they bring a different perspective and experience to their travels and writing" (x). Primeau acknowledges how "Native Americans, African Americans, women, and other minorities have moved around North America for centuries but not usually in the manner of the road quest conventions. We now have records of the tribal migrations of plains [*sic*] Indians, pioneer diaries by women, and stories of flight and migration in slave narratives and autobiographical prose by

African American writers" (107). What these groups lack, of course, is the privilege that comes with being male and white. Yes, poverty and joblessness lead to fines and encounters with the police in *The Grapes of Wrath* and *On the Road*, but for the most part white men can travel without being challenged for being "out of place." Meanwhile, people of colour often get stopped for police checks if they walk in affluent neighbourhoods, and they are more likely to be killed for simple acts such as reaching for a driver's licence. Racial segregation in the United States and the infamous pass system[3] in Canada restricted the movement of African American and Indigenous people. American and Canadian road narratives often celebrate the freedom of the open road; however, if one's history includes forced migration, racism, and laws that prevent movement, then road travel must be undertaken with caution.

Intersections of colour, class, and sexual orientation must be accounted for in any in-depth analysis, and likewise women know that they must take precautions when they travel. "This is certainly true," Macfarlane states, "for victims of the road—most notably Canada's missing and murdered Indigenous women, an estimated thirty of whom have gone missing on the 'Highway of Tears,' the part of Highway 16 in western Canada stretching between Prince George and Prince Rupert" (23). The dangers of travelling on the road are highlighted by the fate of Lucy's mother, "killed in a botched robbery attempt." Lucy recalls how "my dad and I told her over and over again she was crazy to pick up hitchhikers. Don't you read the papers?" (*Summer* 72). As a whole, women are raised to know the dangers of solo travel: they are warned not to hitchhike, to look in the back seat when getting into a vehicle at night, to park in well-lit places, and never, *ever*, to have a car break down on a deserted road. Should a woman have the misfortune to be assaulted while alone at night, she is often blamed for taking risks that put her safety in jeopardy. She can be blamed, in other words, for daring to be free from the rules that bind her to lighted places and travelling in groups.

Primeau comments that "women bring a calming influence to the American road" in the sense that, "with not as many highs to seek and maintain, the accompanying lows are modulated. The quest is not so manic, the goals are more realistic, and the state of mind more even" (116). However, that statement is contradicted by the fear that often accompanies women who travel alone or the irritation of women who travel with a car full of whining or screaming children. Ganser writes that "my own reading of women's road stories contradict[s] Primeau's generalizing statement, since most of the female characters in fact continue wrestling with their everyday lives, their bodily realities, and conventional domestic duties when on the road, thus experiencing both spatial and temporal limits" ("Asphalt" 157). We can recall here the second epigraph to this chapter, and anyone who has travelled with small children will recognize Toews's humour, for silence is the exception rather than the norm. And, of course, in *Summer of My Amazing Luck*, the calm does not last. By the time Lucy and Lish reach the American border, Dill's face and mouth are covered in fuchsia from chewing on an uncapped felt marker, one of Lish's twins is naked because she peed on her dress during a roadside stop, and Lucy is weeping because they have passed the site where her mother was murdered.

Smith writes that, in the early days of car travel, "a woman out for a drive was a woman out of place" (173). Short trips to the mall and grocery store were acceptable, but longer independent trips were associated with promiscuity and masculinization. Feminist geographers Mona Domosh and Joni Seager argue that "women on the loose are almost never valorized—in any culture. Indeed, geographical 'looseness' in women is assumed to be a universal marker for sexual wantonness—or at least cause for concern about their respectability. In contrast, 'footlooseness' is often held up as a signifier of 'real' manhood" (118). Similarly, speaking of "escape" novels, Heidi Slettedahl Macpherson writes that "a male character can step outside the domestic sphere with ease; he is constructed, in fact, in such a way as to make this escape natural, expected, accepted. Conversely, the female desire for escape must be explained, clarified, justified" (228).

Sidonie Smith, Deborah Clarke, and Alexandra Ganser, however, have all noted an increase in road novels by women and how these novels critique the commonly held quest or travel narrative in which a man goes off to find himself, with women playing the role of temptress, inspirational muse, or patient "Penelope" at home. These critics write of how, when a woman goes on the road, she takes the domestic sphere with her. As Macpherson suggests, "the idea that taking to the road (or the river, or the sea) is the ultimate expression of escape assumes a character free from family or social ties" (89–90). Not only are women more likely to have primary responsibility for child care, but also they are socialized to feel guilt when they leave their children behind. Therefore, when women take to the road, they are more likely to do so with dependants (Clarke 107; Ganser, "Asphalt" 157). Thus, in *Summer of My Amazing Luck*, an exasperated Lish asks "isn't travel relaxing? I told you we needed a holiday" (170). As single mothers on welfare, these women might most need a holiday, a break, from their children, but that is highly unlikely to happen. In both *Summer of My Amazing Luck* and *The Flying Troutmans*, the road to freedom is compromised by responsibilities for children, and the object of the search (on the surface at least) is a lost man invested with magical power to change each protagonist's life for the better. Each novel also contains cautionary stories of characters who go beyond boundaries and suffer the consequences. In *Summer*, Lucy's mother is murdered. In *Flying*, Hattie and Min swim "out farther than [they] should have" and their father dies trying to save them (9). Min is a rule breaker by nature, and she has achieved an ambiguous freedom from responsibility through her struggle with mental illness.

Road Trips with a Difference

Ironically, in spite of being road novels, in both *Summer of My Amazing Luck* and *The Flying Troutmans*, Toews spends a lot of time discussing immobility caused by poverty, depression, or closed bureaucratic systems. Not only are the women in the two novels driving unromantic family vans, but also the vans themselves are in lamentable condition. The Troutman family's van is "beat up" (*Flying* 4) even before the road trip starts, and hitting a deer does not help matters. Eventually, the ignition falls out, and Hattie can start the van only by using a screwdriver. The van develops an ominous sound that for a while turns the family's quest for a father into a quest for a reliable mechanic. But at least the van belongs to the family. In *Summer*, Lucy and Lish borrow an Aerostar from Lish's friend Rodger. The van works fairly well, except that its sliding door falls off around sharp curves, and they have to replace the windshield wipers within their first fifteen minutes of travel. Other delights include "a back bumper that we had to hang onto the van with wire" (152).

The women are also encumbered by the sheer weight of the "stuff" that they need when travelling with children. In a parody of war and adventure stories, for example, Lucy describes what she and Lish take on their trip. Tim O'Brien writes in his iconic Vietnam War novel, *The Things They Carried* (1990), that "the things they carried were largely determined by necessity," and then he provides a list of essentials, such as "P-38 can openers, pocket knives, heat tabs, wristwatches, dog tags, mosquito repellent, chewing gum, candy, cigarettes, [and] salt tablets" (2). Lish and Lucy also carry practical items such as toys, drawing supplies, diapers, and a stroller (*Summer* 152–53) even if they are not quite so evocative of manly adventures. Obviously, Lucy and Lish's adventure hardly fits the model of carefree spontaneity. The women also must wait until Lish's eldest girls are finished school for the summer, and Lucy has to make sure that her welfare officer does not pay her a surprise visit while she is out of town (welfare recipients are not supposed to travel out of province). It is therefore amazing that Lucy and Lish get on the road at all.

Although I classify *Summer of My Amazing Luck* as a road novel because it shows all of the preparations for a journey, the journey itself, and a return home, it takes over half of the novel for the women to be ready to leave. Toews spends much time describing the day-to-day challenges to mobility faced by poor women. As welfare mothers, Lish and Lucy have little money for food and lodging, much less for transportation. When Lucy thinks of visiting her father, for instance, she decides against it. She has never had a close relationship with him. Her father—like Tom McCloud in *A Boy of Good Breeding*, Jacob Von Riesen in *All My Puny Sorrows*, and Mel Toews in *Swing Low: A Life*—does not speak when he is at home. However, Lucy's main reason for not visiting him is her lack of mobility. Her father gave up driving after his wife's death, and Lucy figures that, "if he was too stubborn or terrified to keep a car of his own and use it to visit us, then damned if I was going to bus it to his place with Dill and bags and stroller and stuff" (*Summer* 159). Lucy also says that "none of us had cars or money for cabs. Even the bus was an extravagance. One bus fare can get you a box of Kraft Dinner or a litre of milk" (30). Even a trip to buy groceries is a major undertaking.

With vehicular transportation too expensive for every day, the women resort to walking with strollers. Originally, Lucy owns a broken-down stroller with a wheel that falls off every few feet. However, in a fit of pique in a mall, after one too many wheel emergencies and being stared at judgementally by fellow shoppers, she dumps her malfunctioning stroller and shoplifts the luxury stroller mentioned in the list above. Strollers, in fact, become a symbol of how public spaces restrict the movement of poor women. Activists have long described how the built environment creates and intensifies disability,[4] and for Toews it also creates obstacles for women who live in poverty. High curbs and flights of stairs, for instance, are hard for people in wheelchairs to navigate and prevent them from entering some spaces. Buses with large gaps between the vehicle step and the pavement make bus travel inaccessible for those with mobility issues, whereas a hydraulic step makes bus travel easier to access. Domosh and Seager make a similar point: "Most of the world's people live in built environments that are designed—unrealistically—for a physically unimpaired population." People with children, they continue, experience many of the same problems that the physically disabled encounter: "A parent maneuvering a baby carriage through the contemporary city will encounter many of the same limitations and built-in obstacles. . . . The design of public spaces, facilities, and transportation clearly favors the most physically fit, nonchildbearing, nonchild-caretaking segment of the population" (111). Women with young children might stay at home not only because of pressure to be good domestic labourers but also because the built world does not accommodate their needs.

What makes Lish really angry are "the people that make curbs at a ninety-degree angle so you have to break your back to lift the stroller over them or wreck your stroller or wake up your kid getting up them. There are no smooth curbs anywhere in this WHOLE GODDAMN CITY" (*Summer* 78). Not only are poor women restricted in their movements, but also they are restricted in where they are allowed to be. Lish articulates spoken and unspoken rules about children in public places as her children cause mayhem in a restaurant. Although readers will likely feel sympathy for the diners whose meals are interrupted by four-year-olds pretending to be drunk, Lish makes a good point when she says that restaurants that try to control children deny access to certain public spaces. Such businesses are like places that display signs "that say 'No Strollers.' Basically they're saying *No women and children*. Especially no poor women who have to cart their kids and everything else around in strollers" (78). Ever one to push boundaries in the name of equality and the livelihood of herself and her children, Lish decides that the best way to get money for the road trip is to exploit her father's embarrassment with her unconventional clothes and four children born out of wedlock. Lish takes her outrageously dressed self, Lucy, and their five children to the Four Seasons Hotel, where her father and mother are attending a conference on banking. Their first hurdle is getting the wagon carrying the children over the hotel's threshold since it gets stuck in the process—another indication that high-end hotels are not built for visiting children.

But the really sad point of all this is how easily Lish's father, John, coughs up $1,000 to spare himself the embarrassment of acknowledging his eccentric daughter and her rambunctious children. Just as the remittance men of old were sent to the colonies by families who did not want to deal with their behaviour, so too John bribes Lish to leave the privileged space of the hotel and return to public housing. Although she has achieved her goal, Lish cries all the way home. Also of note, her mother, Mary, wants to send her daughter home in a cab, but she "never really had money of her own" (113). Even women of high socio-economic status can be caught in the trap of having no discretionary income.

Along with her depiction of how the built environment, poverty, and children restrict access to certain spaces, Toews shows how the welfare system keeps the poor in their "place" in more ways than one. Literary scholar Alison Toron writes of the woman on welfare that "she must be kept in place so that she does not produce others like her. The welfare system not only deems women's bodies deviant, but it also suggests that women must remain physically, spatially, and imaginatively fixed" (69). In *Summer of My Amazing Luck*, for instance, Bunny Hutchison, "the minister in charge of welfare mothers," decides that they should not get the child tax credit. This decision is a huge blow for them because "fifteen hundred dollars is a lot of money when your annual income is only nine thousand six hundred" (98). Mothers not living on welfare continue to get the credit, so Hutchison's decision reeks of a belief that people on welfare should not be made too comfortable lest they become lazy and not try to find paying jobs. Hutchison, however, is capable of playing the system herself. Although she wants to prevent mothers from receiving additional public funds, she submits a false claim for flood damage, thus taking money away from those who actually have suffered during the flood (98).

As I discussed in Chapter 1, Toews believes that community supports are essential in contributing to resilience, but she has little good to say about support systems interested more in their own rules than in helping clients. Whether fundamentalist religion, the mental health system, or welfare, Toews critiques their tendency to insist on processes rather than on individuals. She says, for example, that she "always thought there are similarities" between the hospital and the church, and though she does not say so explicitly in the following quotation, one could add the welfare bureaucracy to her denunciation of how monolithic systems blame the vulnerable and in doing so often lessen rather than strengthen their resilience. In an interview with Alice O'Keeffe, Toews elaborates: "The language in the hospital reminded me of the church, for example the strange assumption of guilt on the part of the patient. 'Oh, you didn't stay out of trouble, you're back in the hospital.' 'You didn't take your medication or do what we told you to do and now you're here again.' Almost the assumption of some kind of weakness or guilt on the part of the patient for being in need, for being sick. And of course that's the backbone of the Mennonite church—guilt, sin, obedience, staying out of trouble" ("Miriam Toews: 'I Worried'"). Those who need social services are also subjected to guilt. Single mothers should have known better than to get pregnant, the judgemental might opine. Homeless people should stop being lazy and get jobs. Lucy, for instance, describes how the clients at the welfare office wait "to confess [their] sins of poverty and joblessness" (*Summer* 32), an apt analogy for how the language of blame creeps into the discourse on those who require public funds to survive.

The Flying Troutmans, which like the later novel *All My Puny Sorrows* fictionalizes aspects of Toews's sister Marjorie's mental illness, includes Toews's ongoing critique of the mental health system. Toews acknowledges the connection in an interview/essay in which O'Keeffe writes that, "when Marjorie read *The Flying Troutmans* (2009) in which a younger sister sets out on a road trip with her troubled older sibling's children, Toews recalls her saying, 'It's like a Valentine to me.' . . . And it really was" ("Miriam Toews: 'I Worried'"). When Min first arrives at the hospital, for example, the orderly asks Hattie, Logan, and Thebes if Min has "any sharps or fire or belts or shoelaces on her," to which Thebes replies "ask Min herself" (15). Already a veteran in dealing with the mental health system, Thebes recognizes how the question dehumanizes and infantilizes her mother. A few minutes later Hattie overhears "someone moaning and a nurse saying, That's enough, in a loud, too loud, voice. Like she was so sure of the limits, but the limits to what?" (15). Hattie also reports how Min's family doctor gave up on Min and decided that "there was nothing wrong with her that a little maturity wouldn't straighten out. She needed to grow up, basically, was his theory" (64). Whether religion, the hospital, or welfare, monolithic systems often blame the sinful, sick, and poor for bringing these things on themselves, but overemphasizing the culpability of the already weak ignores the complex web of factors that might have contributed to a person's so-called downfall. Popular culture similarly blames the weak, as evident when Hattie hears "Dr. Phil screaming at a woman for not loving herself more" (11). Often, when people seek help from the mental health system, social workers, or popular psychologists such as Dr. Phil, they do so because they have lost the resources to cope on their own. Perhaps, in other words, social systems should try to develop people's resilience rather than criticizing them for not being strong enough to face adversity and telling unhappy people to love themselves without giving them the resources to learn how to do so. In Toews's writings, characters often face devastating traumas, and they need help to recover from them, but it has to be the right kind of help, geared to individual needs rather than systemic rules and regulations.

Systems, Toews insists, tend to protect themselves, and the best way to do so is to impose rigid behavioural guidelines on their most vulnerable members. Her criticism of the welfare system in *Summer of My Amazing Luck* thus began a pattern that has continued throughout her career. When Lucy introduces herself to readers, she says that "I should tell you right now how I got to where I am: single mother on the dole, public housing, all that. It wasn't a goal of mine, certainly. As a child I never once dreamed, 'I will be a poor mother.' I had fully intended to be a forest ranger" (3). Right from the beginning, then, Toews rejects a common assumption about those on welfare—that they choose to embark on a life of sponging off the state because they are lazy, feckless, or just plain stupid. Lucy's circumstances are more complicated. Her life changed abruptly when her mother was murdered and her father lacked the emotional skills to help himself, much less his daughter. As mentioned above, he exhibits a common pattern in Toews's fiction, even when his wife was alive: "My dad was human when he was outside of our house. He talked a bit and smiled. . . . Inside the house he was dead, terrifying. He sat in his chair and silently shook his head at me when I made a lot of noise or ran around too much. On weekends when he wasn't working, he stayed in bed all day. We'd forget about him" (49). Having lost her mother and with a father who will not speak to her, Lucy turns to others for love and soon finds herself pregnant.

It is not choice, therefore, that brings her into the welfare system but a series of unfortunate circumstances or, to reflect Toews's title, some less than amazing luck. The same holds true for many of the other women in Lucy's housing complex, whose life stories Toews provides to show that going "on the dole" happens even to the most well-behaved and established women. Mennonite author and critic Daniel Shank Cruz writes of how "Lucy makes her neighbours visible" by explaining how they ended up at Have-a-Life, and he comments on how "their heartbreaking backgrounds show that in many cases women are forced to go on welfare as a result of systemic violence or as a result of men abdicating their parental responsibilities." Sarah, we discover, has a son by "either her brother or her father[, who] raped her and then denied the whole thing" (*Summer* 13). Naomi's first husband was a drunk who died choking on his own vomit. On the rebound, Naomi married a respectable fireman, only to "discover that his interest in [her daughter] Tina was sexual and his hatred for Naomi boundless" (*Summer* 22). She leaves her suburban home to protect herself and her daughter. Lucy also says that "a couple of the other women in Half-a-Life I got to know were more like me, not possessing any well-defined goals or on the run from nightmarish pasts. We were just there because we were poor and had kids" (*Summer* 24). Of all the women in the complex, Lish seems to be the most resigned to her life on welfare. She even thinks that once her four-year-old twins are in school she will have to get pregnant again, since the state makes welfare mothers find jobs once their children are in school.

Yet her desire to stay on welfare cannot be explained by saying that Lish is too lazy to work. Lucy comments on how "most of us in Half-a-Life were afraid of jobs." She explains that "we'd all had jobs at one time or another. Most didn't last long. We had a problem with authority. Maybe we were lazy. A lot of people figured we were stupid. But even being on the dole was better than working. We didn't want to leave our kids at a daycare or with a sitter" (116). Lish definitely seems to have a problem with authority, perhaps brought about by her mother's meekness and her father's bullying. But her rejection of working outside the home also has deeper roots. Lucy speculates that "a lot of us lacked confidence, too, in ourselves and in our ability to stick with a job and do it well. Having children was easy. There was no choice: we were stuck with them and this worked out for us, more or less. And besides, being on the dole and having children at the same time was a job. Who says we didn't earn our money?" (116). Ironically, social conservatives often say that women should stay home with their children, which the child tax credit makes a little easier, but a woman's decision to stay home and raise her children receives social sanction only if she has a husband who can bankroll her domestic labour. Single mothers who do not work outside the home are often deemed indolent, whereas married mothers who choose not to work outside the home are said to make the best choice for their children.

Once on welfare, people are trapped by rules created to prevent them from abusing the system but which have a side effect of abusing welfare recipients. For instance, those on welfare are not allowed to leave the province, so when Lucy needs a break she resorts to the subterfuge that she must attend her mother's funeral. Her welfare officer tells her that the regulations require a death certificate and a letter from the funeral officiant to prove the time of the funeral (115). The welfare system, then, restricts women's mobility by insisting that they remain in place, or it forces them to lie. In a parody of border crossings, the welfare office is a destination with entry points, wickets, and lines that tell clients where to go. Lucy has to "[get] past the receptionist" and follow the correctly coloured line toward her destination, her welfare officer (36), much as Lucy and Lish have to get by a suspicious customs officer when they reach the Canada-US border. The officer suspects that Lucy and Lish are not the "right" kind of travellers and asks them all sorts of questions about their "source of income" and the provenance of the children (176). Rather triumphantly, Lucy comments on the way home that "getting back into Canada was a breeze. They had to let us in even if they didn't want to" (199).

"Where Are the Fathers?"

In a great irony, "welfare equates men with financial support" (*Summer* 87) even when most of the children in Have-a-Life have fathers who are absent, too poor to pay child support, or refuse to do so. Some women, like Lucy, do not even know who the fathers of their children are. Or the women pretend not to know "to save themselves the grief of trying to extract cash from fathers long gone" (39) or whose violence they fear. Attending her "usual dole chat" with her welfare officer, Mr. Podborczintski, Lucy knows that she will be asked if she has "found out who Dill's father was," earned any money, or "received any gifts of money from [her] family" (120). In a previous meeting, Podborczintski patronizingly tells her to use a contraceptive next time, or to "obtain the identity of the male" in question (40), even if it means taking down the man's licence plate number.

But the image of the man driving away is rather the point. In *Summer of My Amazing Luck*, men often take to the road, and women stay behind, which is why Lucy and Lish's eventual road trip, short as it is, is so satisfying to readers. The father of Lish's twins has sex with Lish once and then leaves with her money, and as Lucy recounts, Lish "knew that it hadn't been her, it had been the road, and there was nothing she or anyone else could do about it. Some people were just like that. All the road had to do was look up at them and they were gone" (2). This anecdote, moreover, enforces how pregnancy and childbirth keep women in place. The itinerant lifestyle of the busker or musician does not easily support family life, even though Toews, who travelled widely for a time with her street performer boyfriend, who later became her husband, and their children, is an exception to her descriptions in *Summer*. More accurately, perhaps, she writes about the chaos of road trips with children because she knows what they are like first-hand.

In another example of how men in cars leave women behind, one of the tenants at Have-a-Life has three children, two from the same man: "The father of the oldest and the youngest was an Irish rock musician she had picked up in a bar. He had returned a second time to play in the same bar and had just about the same amount of time to kill before hitting the road" (27). Another tenant, Mercedes, was given her name because "the last thing [her mother] saw of Mercy's father after she told him she was pregnant" was his Mercedes pulling away from the house (53). Even though Lucy does not know who fathered Dill, she thinks of how the unknown father's life remains the same while hers has been irrevocably altered: "Somewhere out there in the suburbs, probably, some guy is living with his parents, fixing his car, studying for exams, drinking at socials with guys, trying to pick up girls, Dill's father. Doesn't even know it" (29). Tellingly, every Friday night "Deadbeat Dad's Row" forms in front of the housing unit, as the fathers who still want to see their children (or know they *have* them) "[line] up [in] their cars and half-tons" (28). The men swoop in for weekly visits and then drive away.

Fathers, in other words, come and go, are absent, or are elusive—and they have the vehicles to escape. One reviewer called *The Flying Troutmans* "a kind of reverse Odyssey—instead of the hero looking for his home and family, aunt and children go looking for [a] missing father" (Denham 196). Logan sums up the problem of absent fathers nicely when he tells Hattie that "there were three girls with babies in his Family Studies class." Answering her query about the babies' fathers, he parodies a social worker who has likely asked him the same thing: "He shook his head slowly, sighed like a burned-out social worker with an impossible caseload, and said in a fake earnest voice, Yup, where are the fathers?" (*Flying* 104). In fact, the paucity of fathers is generational. Hattie and Min's father drowned when Min was fifteen and Hattie nine, though in his case he died trying to save his daughters' lives. Lucy's father in *Summer of My Amazing Luck* is alive but absent, a cipher who cannot talk to his daughter.

It is no surprise, then, that Toews depicts the road trips in *Summer* and *Flying* as quests to find fathers who ostensibly will save the day. Even in the disillusioned world of welfare housing, where fathers often are absent, the women dream of "fathers coming home from work with treats and offers to do housework, to take the kids to the park, or read them a story. . . . Mom, Dad and the kids all playing on the same team" (*Summer* 9). The stories that Lucy tells, including one about how her father engaged in noisy passive-aggressive cleaning when his wife had visitors (73), belie the women's halcyon vision of the nuclear family, but as Lucy says, "a smoker dying of lung cancer always dreams of one more perfect cigarette" (9). In each novel, however, the quest to find a father turns out differently than expected. Lish knows all along that her juggling boyfriend did not ask her to go to Colorado; she embarks on the road trip so that she can have an adventure of her own. Indeed, though her depression before the trip is real, she provides Lucy and herself with a model of resilience in the face of a father-obsessed culture. When Lucy worries that Dill will be harmed psychologically by not knowing his father, Lish replies "'just as well.' The problem was knowing, she said, because as soon as you knew, you cared, soon as you cared, you lost." She reassures Lucy that Dill "could create his own dad in his mind and never be let down" (7). Coming from Lish, such a sentiment makes perfect sense, for her father has effectively cut her out of his life. For the most part, she models resilience in her stubborn independence and refusal to care about what people think of her, which is why Lucy is upset when

Lish's good humour turns to depression. Lucy initiates a fake search for a father figure because she wants to keep Lish resilient, for Lucy thinks that without the optimism of her friend she herself will not be able to cope.

In *Summer of My Amazing Luck*, Lish's father "ghosts" his daughter, and Lucy and Lish drive off to find another father who, they know, cannot be found. In *The Flying Troutmans*, the father whom Hattie, Logan, and Thebes search for is similarly unsatisfactory. Doug Cherkis, whose last name sounds much like "Jerkis," exhibits qualities that put him in the category of the elusive father. Cherkis, Hattie recounts, tried hard to stay with Min and make her better, but, as Hattie knows from experience, "he had no idea of the amount of shit that was about to fly. Eventually, though, he did come to understand, and he did what I did, and what so many others in her life have done. He left" (7). To be fair to Cherkis, he "wanted to be with his kids but Min had sent him packing" (61). She also spoke of potential suicide if he contacted their children and once called the police on him when he tried to visit them. "Cherkis," Hattie recalls, "wasn't the type of guy to hire a lawyer and fight for custody" (8). However, his abandonment of his children (he left when Logan was five and Thebes a baby) deprived them of a father who could have prevented their childhood from turning into what Hattie calls "one long march to the frozen Gulag" (149). Logan asks "but who would just do that? . . . Like, just leave. You know? Like, just disappear" (127). He and Thebes feel the loss of their father deeply.

The question of responsibility is a weighty one because, as *The Flying Troutmans* reminds us, sometimes one needs to save oneself at the expense of others. Hattie remembers her mother's final words: "Just before she slipped into unconsciousness she held my hand and told me that whatever happened, I was not responsible for saving Min" (63–64). Hattie later tries to tell Logan the same thing: "I wanted to tell Logan to set himself free, to live his life, not to worry about Min, he couldn't fix her, and he shouldn't feel guilty. But I didn't say any of that" (130). Hattie—who escapes to Paris, only to fill her apartment with psychology textbooks (*Flying* 130), and who tries to draw, only to find that every portrait she makes contains an element of Min's face (9)—knows that geographical escape is not the same as psychological escape. The former is relatively easy; the latter is almost impossible. In fact, caring for the mentally ill poses interesting problems when it comes to resilience: to get well, many people need outside support from family members, the medical profession, and friends, yet sometimes the weight of caring for the mentally ill leaves carers overwhelmed. In *A Boy of Good Breeding*, for instance, Toews writes that "Dory was worried about [Tom,] but at the same time she was restless and annoyed" (118). Frustrated by a husband who stays in bed all day and does not respond to her attempts to make him better, Dory embarks on a loud, and rather passive-aggressive, series of renovations, and she finds herself a part-time job. Neither action is necessarily what is best for Tom, but Dory needs time away from her husband to keep from sliding toward depression herself.

Caring for the mentally ill can be exhausting for family members, a mixture of hope for the future health of their loved one, grief when the loved one has a relapse, and constant vigilance. Even eleven-year-old Thebes watches over her mother, leaving notes around the kitchen with messages such as "*Cups! Glasses! Coffee off! I love you, Min! No more fires!*" (*Flying* 41). Her use of her mother's given name underlines how Thebes has been forced to "mother" her mother. As Hattie explains, "it's hard not to get a little hysterical when you're trying desperately to keep somebody you love alive, especially when the person you're trying to save is ambivalent about *being saved*." Thebes reminds Hattie of herself when she was younger, "rushing home from school ahead of Min so [that she] could create the right vibe" to keep her sister happy (6). After giving up university in order to take care of Min's children, Hattie finally "moved to Paris, fled Min's dark planet for the City of Lights" (8). She therefore identifies with Cherkis, who tried hard to make Min better but then couldn't handle her rejection.

Control versus Chance: Resilience as Acceptance of Uncertainty

Whether caring for mentally ill loved ones or having early pregnancies, the women in *Summer of My Amazing Luck* and *The Flying Troutmans* have responsibility thrust on them too early, and hence they desire not only freedom but also control. In *Summer*, Lucy inspires Lish to take a road trip both because she needs her friend to remain happy (control) and because she does not trust herself to take full responsibility for herself and her child. Lucy needs Lish to act as an emotional buffer and support. In *Flying*, Hattie wants to find Cherkis so that she can escape being a surrogate mother to Thebes and Logan. For both Hattie and Lucy, therefore, the road trip becomes a means to control the outcomes of their stories, rather ironic when one considers that the road is notoriously full of surprises and messy outcomes for both groups. Moreover, Toews connects the search for control in *Flying* to events in her own life. The uncertainty about Min's future, whether the family will find Cherkis, and how they will weather the storm of their lives come, Toews recounts, from her own feelings of uncertainty during this time. She was in the midst of a breakup with her first husband, her son was going away to university in New York City, her daughter was turning eighteen and would also soon be leaving the family home, her sister was succumbing increasingly to mental illness, and her mother was having heart trouble. As Toews commented in an interview with me in 2020,

> in that book specifically, . . . there was nothing in my life
> that I could control at that time, even though we understand
> that there is nothing we can ever control, other than our own
> reactions to things, but I just wasn't quite smart enough to know
> that, and it was that book, out of *all* of my books, where I felt
> everything's out of control, and all I can control is my writing,
> all I can control is that book. That was my lifeline, whereas all
> my other books, like *Swing Low* or *All My Puny Sorrows*, books which
> came after tragedies, I didn't have that same feeling because
> I'd already lost them. The chaos was over, the fight was over.
> We lost. But with the *Troutmans* there was still the possibility
> of maybe saving.

"At least in my writing," Toews joked, "I could keep my kids contained in a van" (interview with Reed). In *Flying*, though, the kids do not stay "contained" for long. Eccentric Thebes stages a personal rebellion against cleanliness, and Logan often escapes from the family for jaunts on his own.

Even the children's developmental stages are associated with upheaval. At fifteen, Logan is well into adolescence, and his natural desire for separation from his family members is in constant conflict with his heightened sense of responsibility for Thebes. Mostly cooped up in a van or a series of seedy motel rooms, he takes many brief flights away from his aunt and sister, causing Hattie considerable anxiety, but she gives him space to figure out who he is, if that is even possible. Still, she recognizes his restraint in not quashing his compulsively exuberant younger sister, even though her incessant talking and awkward questions must be hard to take. Like Logan, Thebes is also in developmental transition. Margaret Steffler calls her a travelling "tween" who inhabits the "now familiar qualities allocated to tweenhood, including the power and advantages that come with the occupation of liminal space between girl and teen, innocence and experience, naiveté and disillusionment, hope and cynicism" ("Thebes" 127). Toews herself writes of Thebes: "For me the name Thebes was significant because in my mind it was a place where a lot of wars were fought. And I thought that was appropriate for my character, a little girl with a lot going on inside, conflict, fear, bravery, fighting, etc. I also had this notion that it became kind of a lost city, or a secret city . . . and that also seemed to fit" (email to the author, 1 May 2020; ellipsis in the original). When the reader first meets Thebes, she is caught between being a child, running sobbing into her aunt's arms, covered in candy necklace dust, and being an adult as she takes on a "maternal" role with her mother, coaxing Min to eat, lining up her pill bottles, and interpreting her needs to the newly arrived Hattie. Thebes, who spends a lot of her time in the van making gift certificates and novelty cheques out of paper and popsicle sticks, makes an apt coupon for herself: "*This Certificate entitles Theodora Troutman to become an actress at any time she chooses*" (*Flying* 173). Yet surely Thebes has had little choice in her life, and she acts out various roles more for self-protection than for profit. Perhaps this is why, at a time when most tween girls are learning how to conform their inner selves to outside expectations on cleanliness, polite behaviour, and fashionable dress, Thebes insists on non-conformity to the point, as Steffler says, of parody ("Thebes" 128). Strongly encouraged by Hattie to change out of her encrusted and stinking blue terrycloth ensemble, Thebes chooses a new outfit, a "white double-breasted suit jacket and trousers, shirt, vest and tie" (*Flying* 167). Aside from being "not a good choice" (165) for someone who hates washing as much as Thebes, the white suit, especially once she pairs it with a plastic gun and holster, mocks various "rules" on how to dress appropriately for the occasion. Steffler compares Thebes's self-presentation to the minivan, "a kind of protective shell holding together the bodies within it," yet it "leaks oil in an alarming fashion just as Thebes's colourful eleven-year-old female body releases its excessive bodily fluids, contributing to the blurring and erasure of conventional bodies and borders" ("Thebes" 134). Her body and clothes become rigid with dirt, glitter, blood, tears, and food, forming a kind of "crust" that both protects Thebes and makes her an object of ridicule (Steffler 136). In some ways, self-parody is a protection since it suggests that the subject is beyond the criticism of the docile masses and is performing difference on purpose. However, since hegemonic structures are deeply invested in maintaining their sway and self-perpetuate by seeming to be natural and beyond challenge, the parodist also places herself in danger of rejection.

From Thebes's dirt, to Logan's cast, to the papier-mâché mannequin head that the children change into a social statement, *The Flying Troutmans* is full of protective coverings and camouflage. Logan provides a parodic statement about the head, which is covered in "blood" and "depict[s] a fictional young victim of typical street violence, attaching a certain level of humanity to a conventional urban casualty." He further explains how "the images on the lower neck represent two contrasting influences on the dying kid, one material, violent and destructive, and the other loving, peaceful and uplifting." Logan sees "the presence of these two divergent influences as a fundamental conflict within everyone" (179). As he signals here, the novel uneasily straddles the gap between hope and despair, health and illness. When, for instance, automotive artist Logan carves "*the f—ing Troutmans*" into the van's dashboard, Thebes employs her ever-ready glitter pen and changes the message to "*the flying Troutmans*" (265, 266). She transforms Logan's disparaging message into one of hope, yet the word *flying* implies both the freedom of flight and flying/fleeing from harm.

From the untidiness that comes with travelling with children, to a dead battery and a van door falling off in the street in *Summer of My Amazing Luck*, to setbacks that include hitting a deer on the highway, Logan breaking his wrist, and Thebes engaging in self-harm in *The Flying Troutmans*, the novels' road trips reflect how easy it is for things to fall apart. Although the road trips begin from a desire to keep certain circumstances the same, Lucy and Hattie soon realize that road trips are inimical to certainty. They introduce, to use Heisenberg's term, an "uncertainty principle" into the mix—particularly when such trips include decrepit vehicles and children. Toews refers directly to that principle in *Flying* when Hattie's new-found friend Adam asks Hattie if she has ever "heard of the Heisenberg Uncertainty Principle." Formulated by Werner Heisenberg in 1927, it states that the more certain one is of the position of a subatomic particle, the less sure one can be of its velocity, or, as Adam explains, "the momentum and location of a certain particle cannot be determined at the same time" (204). Hattie meets Adam and enlists his help driving in circles through Flagstaff, Arizona, trying to find Logan, and the uncertainty principle highlights conflicting trajectories. The family travels through the United States, more or less following the famed Route 66, in search of the elusive Cherkis, yet within that journey, ironically immortalized, as Hattie is all too aware (234), in the lyric "Get Your Kicks on Route 66," those in the van move erratically, focused on yet unsure of their psychic destination.[5] Certainly, the "kicks" promised by the song's title fail to materialize.

Two other popular cultural references highlight the conflict between determinism and indeterminacy in the novel. After yet another discouraging telephone chat with Min's nurses, Hattie begins to feel faint. She recounts how "I closed my eyes and tried to pray but all I could do was channel Bowie" (155–56). David Bowie's description in "Space Oddity" of an astronaut untethered in space and powerless to save himself accurately echoes her feeling of dislocation as Hattie drives across America in an Aerostar to find a man whom she is not sure wants to be found.

Around the same time, Thebes watches *Run Lola Run* on a motel television and becomes obsessed with running alongside Lola. As Hattie explains, "she was going to go all the way with Lola and save that guy's life" (131).

Tom Tykwer's 1998 movie famously repeats the same scenario three times, for Lola has just twenty minutes to find $100,000 and save her boyfriend from death. In the first scenario, she dies; in the next, her boyfriend, Manni, dies; in the third, she miraculously times everything just right. Lola wins enough money at the casino to pay the debt owed by Manni, though ironically he no longer needs the money because he gets it back from the man who took it in the first place. Film critic Tom Whalen writes about how "Tykwer begins his film's philosophical project of disrupting determinism, and for the next 81 minutes, like Lola, we, too, if we work at it, can become the player rather than the played" (40). In a film that illustrates the "butterfly effect" by showing how small actions change lives, determinism seems to be the norm, but Lola will not accept her and Manni's fates. "In her third and triumphant version" of the story, therefore,

> she brooks no opposition. She wills the casino cashier to give
> her the chips even though she is short of the required funds and
> improperly dressed. She wills the bouncer to allow her one last
> play. Lola refuses the tragic or comic pattern that is summarized
> by the woman's description of the casino (read: Life): "You buy
> chips and you gamble them away." Like the new young Germany,
> Lola won't take loss for an answer. Undaunted by the weight of
> the past, the corruption around her, and a discouraging future,
> she strives and then re-strives until she gets what she wants. But
> then Tom Tykwer's Lola is lucky. Unlike most of us, she's living
> in a brilliant post-modernist fiction. (Yacowar 564)

Running to save her *mother's* life, Thebes indulges in some magical thinking, for—as Tykwer explains while commenting on how, in the movie, a series of dominoes creates a chain reaction, and one after the other falls— "the world is a stack of domino stones, and we are one of them. . . . On the other hand, the most important statement is the end: Not everything is predetermined" (qtd. in Whalen 39; ellipsis in the original). Although Min's fate seems to be fixed by her pattern of recoveries and relapses, Thebes, in spite of the odds, might be able to assist her mother back to health. Resilience stems from making one's own luck. However, Toews also complicates the narrative by showing that making one's own luck—if that is even possible—does not always work, and we must be able to accept failure and then keep going forward in order to create opportunities to find happiness in the future.

There is certainly luck involved, for instance, in finding Cherkis, one man in a vast continent, after receiving only some vague clues to his whereabouts from others. However, he is not the man whom Hattie desperately wants him to be. Evidenced by his status as an unofficial watcher at the US-Mexico border, Cherkis himself is a transitional figure, without a steady home or job and with one family in Winnipeg and another in California. Logan quickly realizes that Cherkis will not return to his Canadian family, and he tries to give Hattie an "out" of sorts when he tells her "I'm not stupid. . . . You can go back to Paris, or wherever, you don't have to take care of us. I've got it" (*Flying* 230). But at fifteen Logan is not doing a good job of caring for himself, much less his younger sister. His bravado in facing up to the fact that his aunt does not want him or his sister makes Hattie begin to see that she is not a child who can run away but an adult who must stay and fight. As she tells Logan when she offers to let him spend the summer with Cherkis, "however Min deals with it isn't your problem. It'll be my problem, ok? You should hang out with your dad for a while if that's what you want to do" (270). Now that Hattie has succeeded in her quest to find Cherkis, she gains the strength to let Logan have a life of his own, if only for a while. Just as her mother told Hattie that she was not responsible for keeping Min happy, so too Hattie gives Logan the gift of self-care. She has no illusion that Min will make a complete recovery and never again relapse, for she has lived with her sister's depression her entire life. But Hattie also knows that the children need time and space to grow into adulthood rather than having premature adulthood thrust onto them. Logan's "beautiful, heart-stopping smile, all badly disguised tenderness and tentative joy" (270), is a reward in itself. Hattie might bolster his resilience at the expense of her own, but she remembers both the times that Min inspired her and the times that Min hurt her. She also sees that she is not, as she thought, "the world's worst guardian of children . . . like the neighbourhood cat lady, but with kids" (226), but someone capable of courage, invention, and strength. As her dream of dumping Logan and Thebes into the capable arms of their father fades, she finds that she has resilience and ability that she did not know she had.

Hattie optimistically remembers how Min once celebrated an eclipse not for the loss of light but for its return. As Hattie resolves to "become a cartographer of the uncharted world of Min" (259), she undertakes not only a physical road trip back to Canada but also a spiritual road trip to find her sister. She speculates that "Min was in the universe. She was a dim and falling star, but she was alive. She hadn't loved watching the sun's eclipse as much as she'd loved watching it reappear. If she had really, truly wanted to die she'd have succeeded a long time ago. She loved the brink, going to it and returning from it" (258). Min is an explorer who goes to the edge of psychic pain but returns to live another day. She travels to uncharted territory, but she does not, as some early mapmakers believed, fall over the edge of the world into oblivion. Although Min cannot chart her own experiences so that others can understand them, perhaps Hattie can learn to read her sister better and help her to live in a world that her insights make both more vivid and more unendurable. Maps are useful mainly if you know your destination, but perhaps Hattie—like Logan when he explains his philosophy of basketball, "I'm always sure the next one will go in" (242), or Thebes when she perks up as she crosses the state line in Arizona—can find ways to continue in spite of disappointment. Steffler celebrates the optimism inherent in Thebes as "she [sits] up in her seat" and "look[s] around with fresh eyes, like things might be radically different now that we had crossed an invisible state line" (*Flying* 187). According to Steffler, "Thebes insists on possibilities instead of drawbacks," and thus it is "Thebes's 'fresh eyes' and her tween comfort with permeable borders and liminality that push the Troutmans and the family into flexibility" ("Thebes" 138). Thebes is a troubled young girl, but she also has imagination and resilience.

Luck is also a major theme in *Summer of My Amazing Luck*, in which Lucy, who has suffered a great deal of (un)amazing luck in her life, remembers how her mother "was always telling [her] Good Luck Lucy, Good Luck" (45). Now that her "life seem[s] like one big mistake from start to finish,"

Lucy thinks of her mother and "wonder[s] if it hurt her to see me this way, that is, if she could" (45). Lucy even names her son after John Dillinger, a figure whom she believes to be lucky. Dillinger, the Depression-era "public enemy number one" who travelled across the United States robbing banks and was admired by many as a handsome rebel, was shot dead by the FBI in 1934, but to this day there are those who believe, as does Lucy for a time, that he did not actually die and that another body was buried in his place.[6] As she says, "I wanted Dill to be a lucky boy, as lucky as his namesake, John Dillinger. Some people believe he's still alive. I do. His girlfriend only pretended to be setting him up." In addition, Dillinger, according to Lucy, "never killed anybody; he just said, 'Lie down and nobody gets hurt.' He was a lucky man" (100). Given that her mother was killed when she picked up a hitchhiker who had just robbed a bank, Lucy's name for her son represents her irrational desire—half a belief—that her mother's supposed death was actually "an elaborate plot on her part to get away from" her husband. After all, her mother had been so "beat up" that Lucy was not allowed to see the body before the funeral (100). In Lucy's mind, unlike the man who murdered her mother, Dillinger was not a killer. In fact, though, he likely killed one person, a police officer who tried to stop a robbery ("John Dillinger").

By the end of *Summer of My Amazing Luck*, however, Lucy has revised her optimistic dream. She and Lish arrive back at Have-a-Life to find that one of the inhabitants, Mercy, is in labour after having successfully concealed her pregnancy from everyone in the building. Even more surprisingly, the two people locked in the bathroom helping her are (rather improbably) Lucy's father, who has been living in her apartment after being forced out of his home by a flood, and Harley, a man whom Lucy last saw jumping out of her window to avoid being discovered by the welfare officer. Always the predictable member of the Have-a-Life community, Mercy holds down a job, goes to bed at exactly the same time every night, and keeps herself, her child, and her apartment compulsively clean. The one erratic element in her life, "the only unpredictable thing she could handle" (54), is the father of her only child, a married man who shows up at his convenience and treats her badly. For Mercy, whom Lucy has typecast as always being in control, to be in labour makes Lucy realize that her attempts to control her environment, whether through altering Lish's moods or magical thinking about her mother's continued existence in another country, have little bearing on what actually happens. Lucy begins to cry: "If this much could happen, find a beginning and an end, and lead to more and more events transpiring, over a short period of three days, then how much had happened over the three years since my mother had died? And how would I be able to remember her when so much was happening?" (206–07). Mercy symbolically leads the way for Lucy when she embraces "a new life philosophy: to name what you fear, to look it in the eye and embrace it" (212). Mercy even names her new daughter Mayhem so that she will never forget this revelation.

The birth of Mayhem also helps Lucy to see her father in a different light and, in a way, find the father whom she was seeking on the road. She has believed that her son's big hands are a genetic inheritance from his unknown father but suddenly realizes that this trait was inherited from *her* father. After years of resenting her father for his awkward aloofness, Lucy begins to appreciate him through their joint love for Dill. Lucy explains that "I hadn't, up until then, really had anybody else to enjoy Dill with. And it was a wonderful feeling. I mean I had Lish and the other women in Half-a-Life, but my dad was far more thrilled with the little things Dill did. He saw them as incredible achievements. I think he was even proud" (214). The love of a grandfather for his only grandchild trumps the affection of mothers with children of their own.

Lucy realizes how, in addition to fabricating a story for Lish, she has fabricated a story about her mother and thinks "I couldn't bear to lose her all over again, the woman I had created in my mind. Speeding down the highway with her elbow resting on the door and her hand tapping on the roof of the car. At that moment, all I wanted was to have my mother back" (207). In effect, Lucy has manufactured an actual road trip to support her mother's imagined escape. Giving Lish hope has meant giving herself hope, but now Lucy realizes that she must accept the reality of life without her mother. "Things were happening," she says, "without me making them happen. What wasn't happening was my mom wasn't catching a flight home to Winnipeg from somewhere in South America and John Dillinger wasn't alive and well. . . . [The father of Lish's twins], dead or alive, was never going to show up and neither was Dill's father, the way Podborczintski kept hoping he would" (207). Somehow her epiphany on arriving home to so much chaos has made Lucy realize that she cannot "make things happen" or completely control her life, only live it. Identities, whether of those alive or those dead, are changeable and surprising. Toews would likely agree with Del Jordan in Alice Munro's *Lives of Girls and Women* that "people's lives, in Jubilee as elsewhere, were dull, simple, amazing and unfathomable—deep caves paved with kitchen linoleum" (210).[7] No matter how mundane lives look from the outside, people have their secrets. We can no more predict what makes other people do what they do than we can completely predict what will happen in our own lives. Resilience means finding ways to keep going even when life deals out devastating challenges.

Alexandra Ganser notes that "transiency, from the Latin *transire*—to go across, to pass—highlights the simultaneity of the spatial and the temporal dimension in narrative subject formations. On the temporal level, it emphasizes the fact that identity is always already in transition, a constant process, and historically contingent; as a consequence, this relativity dismantles essentialisms and 'being-s' by pointing to the performative aspects of identity and embodiment—as constant *becoming*" (*Roads* 25; emphasis in original). Toews's emphasis on fluctuating identity formations brings to mind Ganser's adoption of the term "transdifference" to describe what happens in many road narratives written by women. Unlike binary formulations such as home and away, chaos and stability, sanity and insanity, childhood and adulthood, imprisonment and freedom, or ignorance and knowledge, the concept of transdifference, according to Ganser (who echoes John Keats's famous letter to his brothers on "negative capability"),[8] "requires the acceptance of uncertainty, incommensurability, doubt, and indecisiveness" (26). Thus, though a traditional quest narrative might see the protagonist redeemed by the successful quest, and a traditional travel narrative might show an explorer finding and settling on "untamed lands," transdifference allows for uncertainty and non-completion. Speaking, for instance, of Chelsea Cain's *Dharma Girl: A Road Trip across the American Generations* (1996), Ganser describes how the author "makes use of the road trip in order to recover a broken connection *without erasing difference*, regressively idealizing the maternal, or privileging the daughterly over the mother's perspective" (143–44). Ganser then concludes that the story "fundamentally rewrites the quest narrative by creating the road as a dynamic space not of territorial discovery but of spiritual recovery" (144).

Toews emphasizes "spiritual recovery" in both works discussed in this chapter. She uses the road trip to show how people strive desperately to control their fates and those of others. But, as Ganser has shown, the quest motif often morphs from a journey toward accomplishment and fulfillment into a messy journey with no real ending. The best that you can do, like Thebes, is to look at the world with "fresh eyes" or, like Logan, to have faith that at least one aspect of your life (in his case basketball) will work out in your favour. Perhaps Min is the best example of how *Summer of My Amazing Luck* and *The Flying Troutmans* unsettle the road and quest narratives. In the first few pages of *Flying*, Hattie describes Min as "travelling in two opposite directions at once, towards infancy and death" (7), or "living permanently in an airport terminal, moving from one departure lounge to another but never getting on a plane" (8). The metaphor of the airport terminal reappears at the conclusion of the novel as Hattie recalls an incident that occurred when Logan was young. Returning home after a visit with friends, Min gets stopped in the "Arrivals" area because she cannot pay the airport tax. Spontaneous and beautiful, Min puts her hat on the floor and dances until her fellow travellers donate money to her so that she can pay the fee. In this instance, she is successful. Not only does she flout convention (airports are notoriously humourless places), but also she impresses four-year-old Logan and those watching from the other side of the glass. So much so that the man next to Logan tells him that "she was great, Logan was lucky" (274). Given Min's subsequent hospitalizations for depression, her children's "luck" is debatable, but in Min Toews shows the changeable face of the mentally ill. When she is in remission, Min is inspiring and original, full of life, and an excellent mother. When she is depressed, she cannot care for herself, much less her children. Although Hattie and Thebes are about to return to a newly recovered Min, they do not know what they will find. In order to be released from the hospital, she has told its authorities that Hattie is at home to take care of her, but Hattie is many days away. Hattie hopes, but is not sure, that Min will be there when she gets back.

The final paragraph of *The Flying Troutmans* underlines the difficulties of maintaining closed systems: Thebes and Logan play Ping-Pong while Hattie and Cherkis watch "the white Ping-Pong ball bounce back and forth across the net for a while, it was kind of mesmerizing, and then Thebes spiked it hard and it hit Logan right between the eyes, and he laughed and the ball went spinning off into the darkness like a tiny plastic universe out of control" (274). If life is like a Ping-Pong ball, then sometimes it does hit one right between the eyes. Sometimes it goes in the right direction, and life goes on as planned, and sometimes it flies off into the darkness, and one must search for it. Sometimes our lives take trajectories that we do not expect. We are both the casualties and the beneficiaries of uncertainty.

Toews's characters might try to escape responsibility for a while. They might try to control the outcomes of their lives in attempts to find safety. In the end, though, they find the resilience to accept the duties that life has given them with love and with grace. Hattie realizes that her home is not in Paris but in Winnipeg with her sister and her sister's children. Lucy realizes that she is resilient enough to be a mother for Dill, even without Lish, or more importantly without her own mother to give her advice and support. Lucy returns to a community of people who will likely both irritate and support her. She says at the end of *Summer of My Amazing Luck* "Winnipeg, Manitoba, city with the most hours of sunshine, the centre of the universe. I was home" (220). Hattie's life is likely to be difficult, and, though readers hope for Min's recovery, that might not be the case, as indeed it was not the case for Toews's own sister Marjorie. In a way, though, being on the road has given the protagonists time to appreciate what they have. Things are not ideal at the conclusion of either novel. However, being on the road and returning home have taught both Lucy and Hattie that they have inner resources to deal with whatever the future holds. They are stronger and more resilient than they believed at first.

Naturally, not all life circumstances allow for a return home, and, though Lucy and Hattie grow into the homes that they have recognized as their own, sometimes resilience requires that characters leave home altogether. In the next chapter, I examine two novels in which Toews frames resilience as the ability to leave repressive environments and start life anew. In *Irma Voth* and *Women Talking*, she returns to her Mennonite heritage, framing the Mennonite religion not only as a source of spiritual solace but also as the root of repression and violence in the two communities in which the novels are set. According to Mel Toews in *Swing Low*, "the Mennonites have a long history of moving from place to place in search of religious freedom" (13), but for the women in *Irma Voth* and *Women Talking* persecution comes not from outside the community but from within it. Faced with crippling violence within their communities, these women must leave behind homes that have damaged them and undermined their resilience. In choosing to leave their homes, they find resilience anew.

CHAPTER THREE

"ALL TRAUMA PRESENTS A CHOICE"

Irma Voth and *Women Talking*

And do not be conformed to this world, but be transformed by the renewing of your mind, that you may prove what is that good and acceptable and perfect will of God.
—ROMANS 12:2 (NKJV)

And hope for the unknown is good, better than hatred of the familiar.
—MIRIAM TOEWS, *WOMEN TALKING* (106)

"Motivated by religious persecution, a desire for community isolation, and in search of economic opportunities" (Epp xi), Mennonites have migrated a number of times, and their migrations tell of righteous suffering in the face of oppression. Over their nearly 500-year history, Mennonites often have chosen to leave their physical homes rather than desert their "home" in faith. Those who have chosen to migrate, the story goes, have done so to preserve their way of life in the face of persecution or temptation by a secular society. From the first Christian martyr, Saint Stephen, to a host of Catholic saints, to the Mennonite believers commemorated in the *Martyrs' Mirror*, Christians of various denominations tell stories of the virtuous few who stand up for what they believe, even in the face of severe trauma and sometimes death. Such stories of sacrifice reinforce the value of particular belief systems, for they suggest that the martyr's faith was precious enough to die for. We rarely celebrate those who converted to save themselves from death or who led uncontroversial lives following the status quo. It is those such as Maeyken Wens, an Anabaptist woman "burned at Antwerp with a tongue screw in her mouth," to which we return, just as her sons did when they searched through her ashes to "find the screw to keep in memory of their mother's Christian witness" (qtd. in Redekop, "Escape" 16). For many North and South American Mennonites, such stories culminate in the horrors of Russia at the end of the First World War, and in this sense Mennonites, by themselves, can be said to be a "resilient" people who have, as one definition of the term puts it, "survived or surmounted daunting and seemingly overwhelming dangers, obstacles and problems" (Leshner 2). In the novels of Miriam Toews, however, the survival of a people is sometimes predicated on enforcing values to the point of abuse. Resilience implies surviving trauma while maintaining equilibrium and the ability to move forward, whereas non-resilience implies a wound that will not heal and instead forms a debilitating sore that constricts and limits movement. The truly resilient person can adapt and grow, whereas others reify boundaries and distinctions at the expense of the vulnerable within their own faith groups.

The story of "four centuries of mass flight away from intolerance," writes Natasha Wiebe, "helps us to understand what it means to be Mennonite" (34). Having named themselves *die Stillen im Lande*, the Quiet in the Land" (Brandt, *So This* 110), some Mennonite groups have tried to this day to isolate themselves from secular influence in order to live godly lives, forming new homes in Mexico, Paraguay, and Bolivia. These groups "[shun] the world to maintain a community" (Redekop, *Making Believe* 40). Thus, Di Brandt writes of a "sober profile of humble serious hardworking folk" who want to be left in peace but "bow to no one, except God. If you force us to work in your factories or fight in your armies, we will pick up our things and move somewhere else to start over again" (*So This* 109). Better to give up land and home than to compromise deeply held principles. *Irma Voth* and *Women Talking*, however, contradict narratives of righteous migration by including male characters who flee not *persecution* but *prosecution*, for Toews examines how extreme patriarchal communities discount violence against women in the name of religious autonomy and the larger (male) good.

Set in a Mennonite community in the Mexican Chihuahuan Desert, *Irma Voth* tells the story of its titular character, a young woman born in Canada but transplanted to Mexico seven years before the story opens. When the novel begins, Irma has been shunned because she has married outside her faith. As in *A Complicated Kindness*, ostracism, or shunning, represents a form of violence since it cuts individuals off from family and community and designates them as unworthy of human contact. With her husband away, little means to support herself, and desperate for communication with others, Irma accepts work as a translator and factotum for Diego Nolasco, a famous director making a movie with Mennonites as the main characters. As many readers will know, the inspiration for this scenario came from Toews's experience starring in a film by Carlos Reygadas, *Stellet Licht* (*Silent Light*), about a Mennonite man torn between his wife and the woman whom he truly loves. Reygadas approached Toews to play the role of the scorned wife when he saw her picture on a book cover and thought she looked perfect for the part. The movie that Irma works on, *Campo Siete* (Campo Seven) has a similar plot, is also shot in Plautdietsch (Low German), and also uses amateur actors.

Eventually, readers learn the reason for the Voth family's relocation from Manitoba to Mexico. While seeking to prevent his rebellious daughter Katie from leaving for Vancouver, Irma's father, Julius Voth, hit Katie with his truck and killed her. This act was likely intentional since, as the police say, the day that she died was "exceptionally clear and sunny and anybody driving down the road would have been able to have seen a running girl on the shoulder," even though Julius says that it was snowing (*Irma Voth* 228). Near the end of the novel, Irma explains to another character that "my father doesn't like us, I said, he doesn't like girls. He doesn't like it when we get older and ... there's something about his daughters that makes him crazy and ... that's all" (204–205; ellipses in the original). Julius, it seems, goes "crazy" when his daughters become young women and try to assert some autonomy over their lives and bodies. Although he might think that he is saving his daughters' souls by beating their bodies into submission, his physical violence prompts Irma to fear that her younger sister Aggie will suffer the same fate as Katie. And it is not just Aggie and Irma who are afraid. When Irma tells her mother that she is taking herself and Aggie away from the violence, her mother entreats her also to take her newborn daughter, Ximena, presumably to save her from future abuse when she, like her three older sisters, challenges the strict rules of their father.

Like *Irma Voth*, *Women Talking* addresses egregious violence against women. Given its subject matter, one wishes that the novel was not based upon a true story; however, as Toews says in the note that precedes the novel, she wrote it in response to a series of horrific attacks that occurred in the Manitoba Mennonite colony in Bolivia between 2005 and 2008. Women "would wake up in the morning feeling drowsy and in pain, their bodies bruised and bleeding" (*Women Talking*), with no recollection of what had happened to them. It eventually became clear that a group of men were using veterinary anaesthetic to sedate whole households so that the perpetrators could sexually assault the women. In interviews, Toews describes *Women Talking* as an attempt to allow the victims of this atrocity, largely silenced by the patriarchal structure of their strict fundamentalist sect (at the trial, five *men* acted as plaintiffs on behalf of the women) to speak. Depending on the source, as many as 100 to 130 women were documented as victims of the attacks, though the total number of women was likely under-reported. Eight men were eventually convicted for these crimes; however, follow-up interviews with women in the affected communities suggest that not all of the rapists were caught or convicted, and some witnesses state that the attacks have continued.[1] Toews recounts how members of the Manitoba colony were reluctant at first to believe the women who reported physical injuries from sexual assaults that they did not remember occurring, coining the term "ghost rapes" to imply that no real perpetrators existed. The colony's elders attributed the women's pain and bleeding to visits from the devil, lies "to cover up adultery," "wild female imagination,"[2] or *Narfa*, a word that Toews translates from Plautdietsch as "nerves" ("How Miriam Toews Gave a Voice") or "nervousness" (*Women*

Talking 3). She believes that the term "ghost rapes" "reinforces the lies that were told to deal with these attacks" and asserts that the term "diminishes the reality that these were real men that [the women] knew who perpetrated these crimes against them" ("How Miriam Toews Gave a Voice").

In *Women Talking*, Toews illustrates how language can be manipulated to undermine the truth of women's testimony and to undercut the trauma of patriarchal abuse. As the novel begins, readers learn that the group's male members have opted not to banish the perpetrators and have gone to the city to pay bail so that the rapists can return to their homes and be forgiven by their victims. Worse, at first the elders of the colony chose to do nothing, turning the rapists over to the authorities only when one victim, Salome, attacked the perpetrators for sexually assaulting her three-year-old daughter and some members of the community took justice into their own hands and hanged one of the accused rapists. In effect, the colony's leaders protected the rapists from violence yet did little or nothing to protect the victims.

Faced with the imminent return of the offenders, the colony's women must decide whether to

Do Nothing.
Stay and Fight.
Leave. (6)

Although some of the women decide to stay and do nothing (the mandatory forgiveness option), others are torn between staying and fighting or leaving the colony. With the men away, the women designate eight of their "sisters," representing three generations, to debate the last two options on behalf of the others. Greta Loewen and Agata Friesen are the grandmothers in the group. Mariche and Mejal are the daughters of Greta, and Ona and Salome are the daughters of Agata. Autje is Mejal's daughter, and Neitje is Ona and Salome's niece and the daughter of Mina, a woman who died by suicide after a particularly horrific attack on Neitje (57). Each of the eight women has been the victim of multiple rapes. Ona is pregnant with a rapist's child, Greta had her teeth knocked out for crying out during an attack, and Salome is the mother of Miep, a three-year-old girl who now has venereal disease. As the conversation unfolds, Toews shows how the intersection of rigid gender roles, the lack of outside medical and psychological care, and the tendency to discount female complaints as a sign of mental illness have created a climate of abuse that made the rapes possible. As the eight "women talking" claim their right to testimony, they assert that their minds and bodies deserve care and respect. As they put it, "we want our children to be safe. We want to keep our faith. And we want to think" (120). Through their conversation and their eventual decision to leave their homes, these women prove their resilience in the face of systemic and sustained abuse.

The Trauma of Russia

Toews's indictment of violence against Mennonite women is set against a narrative of violence against the Mennonite population as a whole, especially the history of persecution in Russia after the First World War. Although Toews is descended from Mennonites who did not personally experience the violence that occurred after the Russian Revolution, in each of her Mennonite novels she makes explicit mention of the trauma that Mennonites experienced during that time. To understand why she returns again and again to a history not directly her own, it is important to know the background of the Russian Mennonites in Canada. From the 1530s onward, Mennonites began to move from the Netherlands to avoid persecution. Many settled in Poland, where they flourished until, as a result of the partition of Poland, Frederick II of Prussia took over the territory that the Mennonites inhabited and imposed high taxes in lieu of military service, placing the pacifist faithful in the uncomfortable position of supporting the military (Loewen and Nolt 139). Meanwhile, Catherine the Great of Russia was extending the borders of her empire. First in 1763 and then in the 1780s, she issued an invitation to prospective settlers to make their homes in her newly expanded territory. In 1789, after they reached an agreement that gave Mennonites large tracts of land, "freedom of religion and exemption from military service" (Urry, *Mennonites* 87), many Mennonites emigrated to Russia, and more followed in the early 1800s.

The move initiated a period of peace and prosperity "often referred to as the Golden Age of Mennonite society in Russia" (Kroeger 13). Largely undisturbed by the Russian government, the Mennonites established several prosperous colonies (eventually referred to as the Mennonite Commonwealth) in which they could practise their religion in peace, build their own schools and hospitals, and establish their own systems of community governance. The first major threat to Mennonite autonomy came in the 1850s when Tsar Alexander II began a series of reforms. Although he did not withdraw the military exemption entirely, Mennonites were mandated to finance and take part in alternative forms of service, such as working in forestry or in hospitals. In addition, Russian was made the language in all schools, so the Mennonites were no longer able to instruct their children in High German. The colonies were also beginning to run out of land for new members. As a result, "nearly a third of Russia's Mennonites emigrated to North America in the 1870s, including some 8,000 to the Canadian prairies" (Zacharias, *Rewriting* 51). The Mennonites who settled on the prairies at this time became known as the Kanadiers. The term "'Kanadier' appears to have been an invention of the 1920s immigrants" who came to Canada after the Russian Revolution and wanted to differentiate themselves from the original Mennonite immigrants of 1874. To the later group, "the 1870s groups, through their emigration, obviously had abandoned the right to be connected with the 'Russia' to which so many Russländer still felt attached" (Urry, "Of Borders" 519). The Russländer were forced to leave Russia to escape ongoing violence against them, whereas the Kanadiers had chosen to leave of their own accord. Toews's parents, Mel and Elvira Toews, are descended from Kanadier immigrants.

After the exodus in the 1870s to North America, the population of Mennonites who stayed in Russia grew to "nearly 100,000, owning more than 3 million acres of land by 1917" (Zacharias, *Rewriting* 50). The abdication of Tsar Nicholas II on 15 March 1917 brought new and unimaginable hardships as Ukraine became a battleground in the Russian Civil War. "Large numbers of soldiers deserted, many with their weapons, and armed bands roamed the steppe, attacking villages and estates more or less at will"

(Kroeger 45). Between 1918 and 1921, the pro-aristocracy White Army battled with the Bolshevik Red Army, but the most feared group of all were the anarchists under Nestor Makhno (Loewen and Nolt 234–35). Fuelled by long-term anger at the Mennonite occupation of their ancestral homelands, many Ukrainian peasants supported Makhno. A period of great violence ensued, and the Mennonite population was further weakened by famine brought on by drought, hyperinflation, and widespread looting (Kroeger 66–71; Loewen and Nolt 234–39).

When the fighting ended and Vladimir Lenin's Bolsheviks came to power, the Russian Mennonites were faced with a completely unsympathetic government. They therefore sent out emissaries to other countries to seek places where they could preserve their religion, practise non-resistance, and establish their own schools. A mass emigration of Mennonites from Russia to the Canadian prairies followed, with about 20,000 people coming to Canada from 1923 to 1930, when hard economic times in Canada caused the government to restrict access to the country (Kroeger 83, 167). Those fortunate enough to come to Canada left behind about 80,000 of their compatriots to what Kroeger calls "tragic fates in the USSR" (83) and brought with them memories of extreme violence.

In *Rewriting the Break Event*, Robert Zacharias sums up the importance of the collapse of the Russian Commonwealth for Mennonites in Canada: "Given that it is arguably the most dramatic moment in Mennonite history since the martyrdoms of the sixteenth-century Anabaptists, it is hardly surprising that, as E.F. Dyck wrote in 1988, 'the Mennonite imagination is ... fixated on the traumatic Russian experience'" (56; ellipsis in original). Using a term from Robin Cohen's *Global Diasporas: An Introduction*, Zacharias names the 1920s flight from Russia a "break event": that is, an event of such cultural significance that it becomes a marker of group identity and a common trope to designate a people's character.

Toews does not set any of her works in Russia, but the experience of exile from Russia is nevertheless a recurring reference. Characters in *A Complicated Kindness*, *Swing Low*, *Irma Voth*, and *All My Puny Sorrows* tell of "murderous anarchists" (*All* 215), "thousands of Mennonites who stayed behind, in Russia, [who] were eventually killed by the army" (*Swing Low*

13), or family members "slaughtered by soldiers on a road somewhere in Russia" (*Irma Voth* 13), and they hint at how collective trauma can become manifest in inherited despair and reactionary attempts to preserve a threatened culture. In *A Complicated Kindness*, Nomi Nickel remembers her mother "telling us about the Mennonites in Russia fleeing in the middle of the night, scrambling madly to find a place, any place, where they'd be free" (148), and in *Fight Night* Grandma laughs at her daughter's love of Russian spa treatments by saying that "it was funny that a hundred years ago we—which doesn't mean *we*—had narrowly escaped getting whipped and murdered by Russians and now Mom was voluntarily paying big bucks to get whipped and murdered by Russians" (29). August Epp expresses the combination of nostalgia and trauma experienced by the Russländer when he says in *Women Talking* that "our members had for centuries inhabited the shores of the Black Sea, near Odessa, and had experienced, until we began to be slaughtered, much peace and happiness" (34). Although the assaults upon which Toews based *Women Talking* took place in the Manitoba colony, the novel also signals the Russian experience by naming the fictional Bolivian colonies in which it is set Molotschna and Chortiza, the two most prominent colonies that the Mennonites founded in Ukraine.

Toews uses Russländer trauma to explain, at least partially, recurring generational depression, the despicable behaviours of some patriarchs, and her characters' expulsion from various home places. In *All My Puny Sorrows*, for instance, Yoli asks her best friend, Julie "do you think you're still suffering from your grandparents being massacred in Russia?" It is small consolation when Julie replies that only her grandmother died: "She couldn't run because she was nine months pregnant" (103). Yoli and her sister Elf also know a sure way to make their parents "start clawing the air": that is, to mention anything to do with "the land of blood," especially in a positive way (18). Even though the events in Russia are two to three generations removed, they still have resonance because the break event lives on in the collective memory, even for Mennonites without direct ties to it. Toews herself recounted how "there were always waves of Mennonites coming to our town. You know, growing up, and certainly when my parents were young, it was just 100 percent Mennonite. . . . But there were always stories, always stories, and so relatives of ours, not my parents, and friends, they would have stories of how they escaped in the '20s and even in the '40s" (interview with Reed).

Why Mexico? Why Bolivia?

Toews's many references to the trauma of 1920s Russia bring to mind what Magdalene Redekop calls "archetypal patterns. The Reformation martyr-doms are relived in the experience of suffering in Russia and the escape to Canada re-enacts the exodus" ("Charms" 210–11). Yet the Mennonite history of migration and settlement is also subject to competing narra-tives. On the one hand, from their inception, Anabaptists have been persecuted in their home countries, forcing them to migrate in search of religious freedom. On the other, Mennonite settlement has often been connected to the host government's desire to control territory, as was the case after Catherine the Great conquered what is now Ukraine and when the Canadian government offered Mennonite immigrants "reserves" in Manitoba on lands already settled by Métis and Anishinaabe peoples. Mennonites of European origin have often moved to contested areas where they are valued because of their whiteness and ability to reclaim lands that rulers believe to be "underutilized" by their current occupants.

The extent of the Mennonite diaspora in North and South America can be gauged by Toews's references to Paraguay in *Swing Low* and *A Complicated Kindness* as well as an offhand comment from Nomi about Mrs. Peters, whose children live in "Bolivia and Akron, Pennsylvania" (*Complicated* 61). Nomi also describes how some Mennonites "ran away to a giant dust bowl called the Chaco, in Paraguay, the hottest place in the world" (5), and others "left town for Paraguay for even more hardship and isolation than this place could provide" and were returning to East Village (129). In setting *Irma Voth* and *Women Talking* in Mexico and Bolivia, respectively, Toews chose two Mennonite communities known for their strict values and traditional ways, including traditional dress for both men and women and separation from the outside world. Geographer Dawn S. Bowen affirms how, "historically, two major forces have stimulated Mennonite migration.

One has been the loss of exemption from military service. . . . The second reason has been state interference in their education system" (463). Just as they had in Russia in the 1870s, so too the more fundamentalist members of the Mennonite community in Canada were disturbed by the government's establishment of public schools with common curricular goals: "Conservative parents rejected the official curriculum, and provincial courts responded by handing down thousands of fines, upheld by the Canadian Supreme Court" (Loewen and Nolt 170–71). In 1921, therefore, a group of Canadian Mennonites visited Mexico to find an alternative homeland.

Martina E. Will, a historian of Mexico and Latin America, notes that the leaders of the Mexican Revolution (1910–20) "had promised *tierra* to the nation's peasants" (353), but these promises did not always lead to action. After the revolution, the Mexican government was eager to stabilize the region, restore agricultural prosperity, and encourage settlement by those "of European descent" (375). A group of Mennonites legally purchased land from a family of wealthy landowners, but Will argues that, "by encouraging the sale of a large tract of land to a group of foreign farmers, the [Mexican] federal and state governments in effect appropriated the very lands that otherwise could have been parceled out to the peasantry" (354). After receiving guarantees of government non-interference, the first group of Mennonites migrated to Mexico from Canada in 1922, and "it is estimated that there were about 80,000 Old Colony Mennonites in Mexico in 2003" (Bridgemon 72).[3]

Irma's comment in *Irma Voth* that her people "started to move all around the world in colonies looking for freedom and isolation and peace and opportunities to sell cheese" (12) tells only part of the story. As in Ukraine, Mennonites displaced others who had lived on the lands. Toews explicitly mentions Mexico's history of colonization in two ways. First, Irma is fascinated by a Tarahumara Indian family that she passes on the road who are "just there." As precolonial inhabitants of Mexico, they "didn't seem to be walking anywhere" (47). Yet the Tarahumara, who claimed this land as their original home, are doubly dispossessed, first by the Spanish colonizers and then by Mennonite settlers. Irma subsequently dreams of the family (53), and when she envisions leaving the area with Aggie she thinks "we'll have no place to live. We'll have to stand silently by the road like that Tarahumara family. Forever" (108). Although Irma is the daughter of interlopers in the area, she identifies with the displacement of the Tarahumara. She has been moved from her original home in Canada, shunned by her family in Mexico, and now must leave again in order to protect herself and her sisters from her father's violence.

Toews also refers to the Mexican history of colonial conquest when Irma references Diego Rivera's famous mural, *México a través de los siglos* (Mexico through the Centuries):

> If I had known more about anything I might have pointed out
> how Diego Rivera was asking all Mexicans to look squarely
> at the history of their lives, at the beauty and the misery and
> the pain and the struggle and the wreckage created by that
> profligate Cortés. I could have added too that Diego Rivera was
> completing his mural around the time the seven Mennonite
> men came to the palace to ask for the land in Chihuahua, now
> the scabby homeland of Aggie, Ximena and Pancho Villa, and
> how Mennonites always choose to live in places nobody else
> wants to. (173)

Irma overestimates the undesirability of the land, for one assumes that the Tarahumara, like the Ukrainians and the Anishinaabe, want to live in the area that they inhabited before others came to use it for their own purposes. Irma might assume that Mennonites settle lands that no one else wants, but her description of Rivera's mural introduces a competing narrative. Through her description, Toews conflates the Mexican history of colonial conquest with the arrival of Mennonites in Mexico—a peaceful appropriation but also a "conquest" of sorts.

Consisting primarily of a conversation among women who have never gone beyond the borders of their colony, *Women Talking*, set in Bolivia, has little to say about Indigenous peoples and their displacement, yet it is important to remember that the Molotschna colony in which the women live also has a history of displacement, in this case of Indigenous groups in the semi-arid Gran Chaco region of Paraguay and the Chiquitano dry forest of Bolivia. According to Ben Nobbs-Thiessen, "Mennonites benefitted from a racialized ideology of immigration as 'whitening' even as their settlement was conditional upon a legally sanctioned refusal to assimilate into national society" (585). Miriam Rudolph writes that "in 2014 Paraguay had the highest deforestation rate in the world" (28), a result of land owners, including Mennonites, clearing native vegetation for cropland and grazing. "Unfortunately for the flora and fauna of the Chaco," says Sarah M. Hanners, "the Anabaptists are a hard-working people, who have a history of overcoming environmental obstacles to become exceptionally skilled farmers" (204). As she goes on to say, the Chaco and Chiquitano regions' famed biodiversity has suffered because of soy farming and cattle ranching. Although international conglomerates are now the main culprits, Mennonite settlers paved the way by showing that lands previously believed to be inhospitable to farming could support agriculture. Mennonites "are among the wealthiest landowners in each country and enjoy a high per capita income and share of the land" (203). The displaced, in other words, are also displacers.

Reimagining Mennonite Precepts

Historically, Mennonites migrated to shield the faithful from corrupting outside influences and to protect core values, but, Toews asks, what happens when insular faith-based communities are corrupted from within? If, as happens in *Irma Voth*, a Mennonite family moves to Mexico because the Canadian police are about to arrest its patriarch for murder, does the fundamentalist community ethos protect the faithful or allow some of them to prey on others? If, as in *Women Talking*, a community leader prevents victims of assault from getting medical help on the ground that outside doctors will be privy to the colony's shame, does that not question the idea that insularity protects the faithful from evil influence? Quoting Irma's sarcastic comment on how Mennonites "pack our stuff up in the middle of the night and move to another country where we can live purely but somewhat out of context" (*Irma Voth* 12), Rebecca Janzen asks "but what does this purity mean if murder can go unpunished?" (233), as it does in *Irma Voth*, or, for that matter, if serial rape goes unpunished, as it does in *Women Talking*? Toews seems to echo historian Marlene Epp that "many of the myths and images that characterize Mennonites should be read in newly gendered ways. Such an endeavour is potentially subversive because it attempts to deconstruct themes and ideals that are viewed as 'fundamental,' 'natural,' 'universal,' and 'core' to Mennonite thinking and praxis." Epp mentions how "favourite terms and phrases such as 'the Anabaptist vision,' 'the quiet in the land,' '*Gelassenheit*,' 'discipleship,' [and] 'separation from the world'" must be reimagined in the light of female experience (11). Toews does just that in *Irma Voth* and *Women Talking*, but in addition to tearing down patriarchal interpretations of what these terms mean she postulates a feminist vision of what being a Mennonite should (and can) be.

Epp writes that "the quiet in the land" relates "to Mennonites' perceived historic withdrawal from interaction with culture and politics outside their communities, to their agriculture-based economy, and also to their overall obedience to the structures from which they nevertheless withdrew" (12). As Irma irreverently puts it, "different countries give us shelter if we agree to stay out of trouble and help with the economy by farming in obscurity. We live like ghosts" (*Irma Voth* 12). Both *Irma Voth* and *Women Talking* critique the notion of the quiet in the land in a number of ways. There is the obvious point that Canadian, Mexican, and Bolivian laws do not condone murder, assault, and rape, though in practice much violence against women is discounted, excused, or hushed up. Truly to be quiet in the land, Mennonites should obey the laws of the land and accept punishment when those laws are broken, yet Julius Voth does neither. Similarly, Molotschna colony's Bishop Peters tries to subvert the rule of law by discounting the stories of the women and then trying to get the rapists back home on bail, even though they might reoffend. But more than this, the quiet in the land can be a tool to cover up abuses in order to maintain the illusion of righteous living.

Speaking of the assaults in Bolivia, Toews comments that many in the faith community condemned what happened, whereas others were less critical: "I think there was and continues to be a concerted effort to keep quiet about it, to sweep it under the carpet, to deny the fact that it happened and that it was serious, or that it was exceptional. There were people saying, "These types of things happen in every kind of society" without looking at the culture of the remote colonies—the male entitlement and the submissive roles of women" (qtd. in Kreizman). Thus, in *Women Talking*, Bishop Peters forbids "outside helpers from entering the colony" because they "would gossip about the colony and . . . people would become aware of the attacks and the whole incident would be blown out of proportion" (30, 43). How, a reader might wonder, can a crime as heinous as the systematic rapes of multiple women and children be "blown out of proportion"?

We also learn in *Women Talking* that August Epp's parents were excommunicated, ostensibly because his father brought a prohibited art book into the community, thereby exposing vulnerable minds to the filth of the Old Masters. As the story unfolds, however, we learn that August and Peters look much alike. A second explanation of the banishment, then, is that Peters slept with August's mother and fathered her child. August writes that "we were sent away because by the age of twelve, as I approached the brink of adulthood, I bore a remarkable resemblance to Peters and I had become a symbol, in the colony, or at least to Peters, of shame and violence and unacknowledged sin and of the failure of the Mennonite experiment" (213). This idea takes on an even more problematic cast when August wonders "did my mother once love Peters?" (167) and especially when we learn that the veterinary anaesthetic used to sedate the colony's women is kept in the garage owned by Peters. As August speculates, "is it for good or for evil that Peters is the caretaker of the belladonna spray?" (207). Did August's mother, in other words, have a sexual relationship with Peters because she loved him or because she, like so many other women in the colony, was sexually assaulted?

Admittedly, the rapes committed by the jailed men occurred more recently than August's birth, and Peters could be keeping the anaesthetic in his garage to prevent other men from using it. Yet Peters acts hypocritically on more than one occasion. He confiscates a member's clock because time is "irrelevant," but he mounts the clock on his study wall (48). Alone of all the members of the colony, he owns a cellphone, which he uses to play games "while the other men are working in the field" (190). Needless to say, this is a strange occupation for a man who recommends that a fellow colonist be banished for eight weeks for succumbing to the "worldly influence" of "organic farming manuals" (83). Old Colony Mennonites often follow closely traditional techniques because they want to live according to the old ways; if that is so, however, then playing games on a cellphone is a worse transgression than researching alternative farming methods. Given that some of the real-life perpetrators of the rapes in the Manitoba colony retracted their confessions, saying that they had been given "only under threat of lynching" (Luis Loza, qtd. in Friedman-Rudovsky, "Verdict"), and that some believe that the convicted men were forced to confess "in order to cover up widespread sexual abuse and incest" (Braun, "Modern Ghosts," Part 1), Peters might be even more sinister than his patriarchal prejudices imply.

But the most egregious "quiet" in the novel is that of the women themselves. In patriarchal societies, women are often accused of being unrelenting talkers and gossipers who rarely let their menfolk get a word in edgewise. Yet work by linguists Jennifer Coates and Deborah Tannen shows that women talk less than men when they are in each other's company. "By and large, sociolinguistic research into mixed talk exposes the fact that women and men do not have equal rights to the conversational floor" (Coates 124) and that, when men and women are in mixed company, men tend to interrupt more often than women (Coates 115–24; Tannen 188–92). Yet in *Women Talking* August explains how his surname, Epp, was derived from "Aspen, the Trembling Aspen, the tree with leaves that tremble, the tree that is sometimes called Women's Tongue because its leaves are in constant motion" (3). Readers quickly intuit that the novel's title represents an anomaly rather than the status quo. Although most of the men are away during the two days that the novel covers, Klaas Loewen, who returns to get more funds to post bail for his jailed brethren, twice tells the women, in just a few minutes, to "be quiet" (137). Even though Klaas considers August "a half-man, and deemed, barely, able to receive this type of business news," it is August whom he addresses when he explains the reason for his return, not the eight women also present, including his own wife, Mariche

(134). Although Mariche speaks in the presence of the women in the loft, repeated beatings by Klaas have effectively discouraged her from talking back to her husband. According to her mother, Greta, Mariche "will say nothing to him" when once again he beats her and the children (61). In addition, the women of Molotschna have been told over and over that their experiences did not happen, and they have been denounced for making up or exaggerating their traumatic assaults. Truly, as Ona says, "[they] are women without a voice" (56). The power of the title reflects how "women talking" can give voice to their grievances and plan for the future, how the support of a community of sisters, mothers, and cousins can provide the strength necessary to leave violence behind. For these women, even forming their own opinions constitutes a form of resilience, for they have been beaten for smaller infractions.

Speech or Silence? August Epp as Narrator

August Epp is an interesting case when it comes to Toews's critique of enforced female silence, for he exists in a liminal space within the community and has suffered his own traumas from which he is still recovering. He, too, in other words, is searching for ways to become resilient and overcome his past, and he often resorts to nervous talking to try to put himself at ease. Held in contempt even by some of the women, he is considered a "*schinda*" or "tanner of hides," the "king of insults" in a community that values farming above all else (*Women Talking* 61). The men leave August behind, along with the mentally incapacitated and boys under fourteen, when they go to the city, presumably because, as the community's teacher rather than a farmer, he is not considered fully male. Yet, even though August is diffident, with a history of being bullied, he still makes his presence felt when the women meet. Toews says that "I like the idea of August representing all men. . . . He can record, but the women will do the talking and the planning and the acting. He can sit and he can listen and he can learn" (qtd. in Kreizman). Toews also speaks of how, "if there is a hierarchy" in the novel, "it's an inversion. With the women being the planners, the philosophers, and August being the secretary" ("Miriam

Toews on What Forgiveness Means"). Theologian Martin W. Mittelstadt even counts the number of pages that August devotes to the women's discussion rather than his own ruminations in order to "establish Toews's goal that Epp gives voice primarily to women talking" (41). August cares deeply about the women's plight and does his best for them, even stealing the community's safe so that the women can have money for their journey. However, his role as supportive male, amanuensis, and minute taker tells only half of the story.

Traditionally, the minute taker is silent because a secretary records what is said by others and does not usually intervene in the meeting. Rarely does the minute taker interject more than a quick clarification. This is not the case with August. Ona asks him to take notes at the women's meeting because none of the women can read or write, and she apparently wants a record of what is said. As we learn at the conclusion of *Women Talking*, August believes that Ona has an ulterior motive. Encountering him when he is about to take his own life, she asks him to take the minutes to give him a sense of purpose, not because the women really need their words recorded. Whatever the case, the novel is told from his point of view. To return to the metaphor of the trembling aspen, then, it is sometimes *his* tongue that "waves," not those of the women. From the beginning, August inserts himself into the text, giving readers an account of his history: his family's shunning, his education in England, his arrest for stealing a horse, his eventual return to Molotschna, and his love for Ona. The first lines of the novel, "my name is August Epp—irrelevant for all purposes, other than that I've been appointed the minute-taker for the women's meetings because the women are illiterate and unable to do it themselves" (1), suggest his self-deprecation and willingness to remain in the background, yet almost immediately August tells readers why he is able to speak and write English and why he has chosen to record the women's words in a language that they do not understand. (Plautdietsch is an oral language.)

Margaret Steffler writes about the importance of August in the novel: "He provides an outside, male perspective that results in the hayloft becoming a relational, interactive, and dialogical space, thus putting into play an exchange of words and ideas that initiates movement, change, and the future" ("Breaking Patriarchy" 61). Unlike the majority of men in the colony, August listens to what the women have to say. As Steffler points out, he is similar to the women in that his opinions are discounted and ignored by the majority of the colony's men, yet "the perpetual condition of not mattering at all belongs, without question, not to August Epp but to the women of the colony" (61), something that he does not always remember.

August's verbal and written utterances are of two types. First, he provides a silent commentary, writing interjections on the page while he listens to the women. Often this commentary provides necessary background, telling readers what happened to Melvin (formerly Nettie) Gerbrandt to make him stop speaking to adults and identify as male, that Ona's father lost his life to suicide, what happened when Salome tried to get antibiotics for her daughter Miep, and so on. Such comments enrich the novel because the women talking in the loft would not naturally stop to explain what occurred in the past. They *know* what happened, but the reader needs August's exposition to understand the colony's extreme dysfunction.

Second, August utters more problematic statements. When, for example, he describes Neitje Friesen's illustrations of the women's three options—printed on the inside covers of *Women Talking*—he writes that "'Do Nothing' was accompanied by an empty horizon. (Although I think, but did not say, that this could be used to illustrate the option of leaving as well)" (6), he expresses a personal opinion and suggests that he has deeper understanding than the women. When Ona laughingly calls the sun a "coward" for leaving August and her in darkness, he writes that "I grappled with the idea of explaining hemispheres to her, how we are required to share the sun with other parts of the world. . . . But instead I nodded" (2). Steffler argues that August shows restraint by not correcting Ona ("Breaking Patriarchy" 72); however, he would show even more restraint by keeping his aside out of the text altogether.

In another example, when Salome talks about not being a member of the colony but a servant, August reports her speech as follows:

We're not *members*! she repeats. We are the *women* of Molotschna.
The entire colony of Molotschna is built on the foundation

of patriarchy (translator's note: Salome didn't use the word
"patriarchy"—I inserted it in the place of Salome's curse,
of mysterious origin, loosely translated as "talking through
the flowers"), where the women live out their days as mute,
submissive and obedient servants. Animals. Fourteen-year-
old boys are expected to give us orders, to determine our fates,
to vote on our excommunications, to speak at the burials of
our own babies while we remain silent, to interpret the Bible
for us, to lead us in worship, to punish us! We are not *members*,
Mariche, we are commodities. (Again, a translator's note about
the word "commodities": similar situation to above.) (*Women
Talking* 120–21)

Partially, August wants to be accurate; however, taken with his attempts
to educate the women about various facts that they might not know, the
tone of his silent interventions is somewhat condescending, even though
he censors himself by not vocalizing his thoughts to the women themselves.
Steffler points out how August wants to get the gist of what the women
say into "the concrete logic and reason of print," but in doing so he flattens
their exuberant and imaginative verbal expressions ("Breaking Patriarchy"
71). Since Peters and the men of the Manitoba colony have used the phrase
"wild female imagination" to undermine the women's accounts of sexual
assault, August's reduction of the women's figurative language to terms
such as "patriarchy" and "commodity" highlights both the impossibility
of reducing their complex experiences to a couple of words and his belief
that it might, in fact, be possible to do so.

Perhaps in an attempt to impress Ona, August often interjects arcane
facts into the conversation. He writes at one point that, "since we concluded
our first part of the meeting with a hymn, I say to the women, Would it be
acceptable if I were to begin our next part with a fact that could act as a
metaphor and inspiration?" (*Women Talking* 34). Given permission to do so,
he mentions that the Black Sea has a calm surface, "Yet underwater there is
a river, a mysterious river that scientists believe can sustain life" (34). Most
of the women are perplexed, but Mariche, who has turned away at the start
of his speech, accuses August of implying that the "lower layers" represent

"the women who would somehow, mysteriously, thrive in spite of being beneath the severe and lifeless pressure of the men" (35). The women are then drawn into a discussion of the meaning of his metaphor, effectively distracting them from their main topic.

August interrupts them again when he asks if he "may share with them a fact related to the hymn that Greta has suggested: 'Nearer, My God, to Thee.'" His relation that the band played this hymn as the *Titanic* sank is not, he quickly realizes, the ideal story to tell women about to embark on an unprecedented voyage of their own (167–68). To be fair to August, his sometimes misjudged commentary adds humor to the novel, and most of his interjections come when someone asks him for his opinion. Thus, when Agata asks him "what do you make of all this? Do you have an opinion too?" he speaks of "the Korean poet Ko Un." When the women do not comment on his story, he becomes defensive, explaining that he "had meant only to articulate [his] feelings about the meaning of meaning" (42–43). Mariche seems to be particularly annoyed by his interesting facts, telling him that he was invited to the meeting "to translate and to write, and [he] should not feel obliged to offer inspirational counselling" (35). August also seeks occasionally to control the meeting, suggesting adjournment (29), asking "for a quick breather" (46), and requesting that the women "move on to the Cons of Leaving" (61). After this last intervention, Mariche "reminds [him] that they, the women, will determine what happens in these meetings" (61). She, at least, thinks that August has overstepped his role.

Toews defends August by saying that "he's not talking as much as he's having thoughts about different things that are being expressed, obviously, but . . . I just really like that play between them. And for the rhythm of it, I needed somebody to move back from the intensity of the conversation. A kind of give and take. Plus I really feel that with everything we are attempting to do—you know, feminists—we absolutely need men involved" (interview with Reed). In a society as gender segregated as Molotschna, August is "demasculinized" by his tenderness, his love for Ona, and his erudition. One should remember as well that he has been victimized by other men both inside and outside the colony. His previous traumas manifest in nervous habits such as compulsively scratching his head, at one point literally tearing his hair out (*Women Talking* 191). August and his parents were shunned by Peters, and upon his return to the colony many years later both men and women treat him with considerable contempt. As well, August has been scarred by having spent time in prison for allegedly stealing a horse, though in his account he was trying to save it from panicking during a "protest in Hyde Park" (143). In prison, August is beaten for being too sensitive. For instance, when he tells his cell mate that he likes ducks, he receives a "severe beating" (142, 32), and the "part of [his] scalp" that he "scratch[es] at wildly" "was removed, brutally," when he quoted Flaubert to his fellow inmates (214). August tells Ona that he was beaten "daily" while in prison (144), and since sexual assault is common in carceral institutions readers might speculate about an additional reason that he empathizes with the women of Molotschna (Hensley and Tewksbury 236–41).

As Toews is aware, male-on-male sexual violence occurred in the real-life Manitoba colony (Friedman-Rudovsky, "Ghost Rapes"), and the women in the fictional Molotschna colony are therefore nervous about what will happen if the girls and women leave the colony and the boys thirteen and fourteen years old are left behind (*Women Talking* 75). Thus, August functions as a bridge between the world of men and the world of women, life beyond the colony and life within it. Toews says in an interview with Christine Fischer Guy that he occupies a "liminal space": "In my mind, it was important that it was a male narrator, because I was thinking, it's time for the men to listen and to record and to stay quiet. It's time they learn and understand what the women's lives are, and how they need to change. In the end, the women will write their own stories" ("Women Will Write"). Like the women, August is often silenced and despised by the men, so his past experiences make him more able to understand the women's oppression, even if he sometimes interrupts them or attempts to guide the meeting.

Insight into August can be gained through a comment by trauma theorist Kalí Tal, who criticizes two respected writers on trauma, Shoshana Felman and Dori Laub, for "appropriative" behaviours (55). Tal writes that those who listen to trauma sometimes commit "hubris" by placing their experience of listening at the same level as the experiences of the actual victims. Speaking of and quoting Laub, she writes that "he makes no distinction between the primary trauma suffered by the Holocaust survivor and the sort of secondary stress suffered by the testimonial audience, claiming that the listener 'can no longer ignore the question of facing death; of the limits of one's own omnipotence.' ... The survivor herself has disappeared from the picture, reappearing only as a device for pushing the listener to self-examination" (56–57). Although this analysis is harsh when applied to August, his continued self-reflexive comments and his tendency to use much of the account as an analysis of his relationship with Ona suggest that Tal's point might have some validity. As he reports the women's testimony, for instance, August often believes that Ona sends him hidden messages. When she sings a song about ducks to Miep, August wonders "does Ona remember the happiness and consolation I feel when I hear the sounds ducks make?" (*Women Talking* 95). In another example, he writes that "I embrace Ona, in my mind, and she embraces me" (54); in another, he states that "Ona speaks, rescuing me yet again" (113).

Since readers are not privy to Ona's thoughts, there is no way of knowing whether August is accurate in his wistful desire for her attention. Just before the women leave, however, her mother, Agata, asks August "wouldn't you marry my Ona?" He replies that, though he has asked Ona many times, she has consistently declined. According to Agata, Ona "loves everyone," but August wants an exclusive love that she seems to be unwilling to give him (197). Stylistically, his "romance" with her brings some lightness to a story of horrific cruelty and trauma, but it also shows that August, for all his sensitivity to the women, places himself in a central role in the story. Perhaps, however, that is part of Toews's ingenious creation of this character. Romantic novels often centre on women who pine for men and wonder whether the men will notice them, only to discover ecstatically, after many pages of doubt, that the men whom they desire return their love. Toews not only inverts the trope of the unfulfilled woman who will be made whole through love but also subverts the stereotypical romantic ending. August and Ona do not marry, and it is August who remains behind when the women eventually decide to leave the colony. By the end of the novel, he has learned an important lesson. Rather than joining the women as their wise guide to the outside world and the supportive husband of Ona, he tells Salome "don't come back. . . . Don't ever come back, any of you" (208). Rather than educating the women, as he has tried to do for much of the novel, August has received his own education.

Tellingly, he decides to impart his knowledge to the boys in the colony, realizing that he is "of more use being alive and teaching basic reading, writing and math, and organizing games of Flying Dutchmen, than lying dead in a field with a bullet in my brain" (215). More importantly, August can teach these young men how to view women as equal participants in the colony rather than as chattel. In addition to teaching them the basics, likely he will impart his respect for women so that these young men might create, in the future, an environment—a new kind of home—that women will not have to leave.

The Quiet in the Land in Irma Voth

Like *Women Talking*, *Irma Voth* addresses unacknowledged violence and the silencing of women's voices, revealing that the notion of the quiet in the land might sometimes project an image of pacifist tranquility while hiding criminal activity such as sexual and physical assault and even murder. Once again the image of the happy home—with its stern but benevolent father, its devoted wife and mother, and its obedient children—does not hold up to scrutiny. In *Women Talking*, the women have been sexually and physically assaulted in their own homes, and they must leave their community if they are to avoid further abuse. In *Irma Voth*, the quiet in the land is best represented by Irma's absent sister Katie, murdered for wanting to leave her family. The reason for her death goes unacknowledged till the end of the novel, when Irma admits that she betrayed Katie's trust by telling their father, Julius, of Katie's plan to move to Vancouver. He responds by driving after Katie and running her over with his truck. At the time of the murder, Irma tells us, her parents lied to the police, saying that Katie's (non-existent) boyfriend accidentally ran her over with his car and then fled. When the police become suspicious of this story, since they can find no boyfriend and Katie probably died two days before Julius says she did, they take Irma aside and ask her what really happened.

But she has learned her lesson about speaking the truth. Only thirteen and trained to be dutiful, Irma lies to support her father's story and much regrets doing so later. She writes in her diary that "I lied to the police about everything because I didn't want my dad to go to jail and because of that we had to move to Mexico where the life gradually drained out of my mother" (246).

Irma reveals the truth to her younger sister Aggie only seven years after the fact in order to stop her from fantasizing about returning to Canada to be with Katie. When Aggie indignantly wants to turn Julius over to the authorities, Irma replies with a sobering understanding of patriarchy both within and outside the Mennonite community. If Aggie calls the police, Irma says, then the police will believe his version of events, partly because Julius will bribe them and partly because male testimony matters the most. "They'd call you a mischief-making runaway," Irma tells Aggie, "and they'd take you and Ximena back home and that would be the end of it except for Dad beating the shit out of you and probably out of Mom for lying to him about Ximena being dead and I would never see you again and it wouldn't bring Katie back to life and you'd be dead inside forever!" (236). As Irma says here, physical violence is a potent silencer. Just as how in *Women Talking* Mariche will not speak of Klaas's abuse, though she is blind in one eye from having a hoof pick thrown at her (80) and shows up on the second day of the conversation with a bruised face and her arm in a sling, so too Aggie might lose her spirit, as her mother did.

Because *Irma Voth* takes place both within and outside a Mennonite colony, the novel addresses patriarchal violence and silencing in more general terms. Early in the novel, Irma asks herself "how do I behave in this world without following the directions of my father, my husband or God?"—the patriarchal trinity (21). To this list, one should add Diego Nolasco, the movie director who not only gives Irma an escape from her father's conscribed world but also enforces his own hierarchies, which place his film far above the well-being of Irma and Aggie. Irma, in fact, gets caught between two equally compelling and all-consuming obsessions that historically have kept women in their place: religion and art. Single-minded and zealous, Julius travels "from campo to campo imploring people to continue with old traditions even though the drought" is harming the community (10); he has killed one daughter, shunned another, and viciously whips Aggie for not obeying his strict dogma. Similarly, Diego speaks of "guerilla film making" and tells his crew that, "if you're not prepared to risk your life, then leave now" (44). The similarity between the two men is best exemplified by Irma's comment that "arguments between two visionaries are lengthy," for each man refuses to compromise his belief system (117). Although readers might be tempted to excuse the single-mindedness of Diego because he is an artist, his self-serving extremism on the subject of art has damaging consequences for Irma and Aggie, and also for Irma's husband, Jorge. Faced with the threat that Julius will disrupt production if Diego does not return Aggie to him, Diego says to Irma that "she has to go back . . . or I won't be able to finish my film," and he is adamant even though Irma insists that Aggie "can't go back" (128). Then, when Irma quits in response and asks for the money owed to her, he stalls. The production has been plagued with cash flow problems, and Diego needs to save the money that he has.

His decisions leave Irma with little choice. Desperate to save her sister from possible death, she sells the marijuana that Jorge has stashed in his barn (ironically to a *Mennonite* dealer) so that she can get the money to flee with her sister. And Toews did not make this up. As a documentary by *The Fifth Estate*, "Mennonite Connection," states, "it may seem bizarre to put the words 'Mennonites' and 'Drugs' in the same sentence, but for years some members of the God-fearing religious community [have] been smuggling narcotics from Mexico into the United States and Canada." Investigative journalist Jean Friedman-Rudovsky writes about how in the 1990s "Mexico's Mennonite community was rocked by a wave of marijuana trafficking that featured pot being smuggled into the U.S. in large cheese wheels" ("Verdict"). Jorge is eventually killed by a drug lord angry about the missing stash. Although Irma blames herself for the murders of both Katie and Jorge, she did not commit, nor even envision, such violence. Julius explicitly blames Irma when he asks her "why did you tell me she was leaving? Why did you do that?" (*Irma Voth* 237), but it was not Irma who ran over Katie with a truck. Irma also blames herself for Jorge's death because, if she hadn't stolen his marijuana, the drug lord would not have murdered Jorge. Yet she would not have stolen the marijuana had Diego allowed her to protect Aggie.

Gelassenheit

In *Women Talking* and *Irma Voth*, women are also silenced by *Gelassenheit*, which Marlene Epp defines as "yieldedness to God's will, self-abandonment, the (passive) opening to God's willing, including the readiness to suffer for the sake of God" (12). As discussed earlier, religious martyrs are often celebrated for maintaining their faith even under torture and imminent death. Although their bodies die, their spirits remain whole, and thus martyrdom can be invoked as an ultimate form of resilience in which people succeed in keeping their faith against all odds. Whether the inspirational stories are about men and women who survive being marooned at sea, or individuals who succeed despite being born into poverty and abuse, or people who remain strong under torture, humanity seems to need such stories of those who persevere. When these stories become an expectation rather than an anomaly, however, they can reveal what resilience researchers Hamideh Mahdiani and Michael Ungar call "the dark side of resilience." For example, "at-risk children" are often said to be resilient if they succeed in school or avoid becoming involved in gangs and substance abuse, but celebrating individual resilience places the responsibility for overcoming adversity on individuals rather than on underlying systems that need to be fixed (147). Mahdiani and Ungar also give the example of climate change, in which people's brave rebuilding efforts after environmental disasters can deflect attention from the need to address the conditions that caused the disaster in the first place. "Psychological resilience," they argue, "has tended to refer to how an individual's positive adaptation potentiates success rather than how a change in the environment surrounding the individual could contribute to personal transformation" (148). Stories of personal success also neglect to ask how far people would go were they raised in better conditions and did not have to fight as hard to succeed. To use the example of Nomi

Nickel in *A Complicated Kindness*, with her intelligence, compassion, and knowledge of scripture, she might find ways to conform to The Mouth's standards and remain a member of the congregation, an adaptation that her uncle would undoubtedly see as resilient. However, from an outside perspective, it is the *congregation* that needs to change, and Nomi would show more resilience by leaving than conforming. Moreover, had Nomi been raised in a community that valued her imagination and ideas rather than quashing them, she could have devoted her energies to excelling in school rather than to coping with adversity.

Sometimes, in fact, it is better to admit defeat than to persevere. Mahdiani and Ungar quote Angela Duckworth's study of "grit" in the US military and point out how "even Duckworth admits that self-selecting out of training when it became difficult was a wise (and resilient) move for soldiers who realized that the role they were training for would be a bad fit for them mentally or physically. While stories of grit or bravery are always constructed as positive, failure is also a signifier of resilience if one changes the metrics of success to include the exercise of individual preferences" (151). To return to *Gelassenheit*, then, the ideal of passive acceptance of God's will can be challenged, first, by the fact that it is interpreted through the minds of men and, second, by the fact that it might be better to leave oppressive situations than to remain resilient within them. Referencing the work of feminist theologian Carol Penner, Epp discusses how "the uplifting of suffering and submission and an ungendered emphasis on nonresistance" within orthodox Mennonite communities have "reinforced women's inability and their community's unwillingness to speak out against domestic violence" (12). One wonders, for example, if Irma's initial refusal to tell the truth about Katie's death is based partially upon her belief that obedience is built into the female lot. Their mother, whose silencing is signified by her lack of a first name in *Irma Voth*, never speaks to the authorities about Katie's death or her husband's ongoing violence. Julius quotes Luke 17:33 (KJV)—"Whosoever shall seek to save his life shall lose it. . . . And whosoever shall lose his life shall preserve it" (123)—thus highlighting his belief that surrender to God paves the way to eternal life. However, given Katie's attempt metaphorically to save her life by escaping from the strictures of home, only literally to lose her life in the process, the quotation seems to be sinister in the extreme.

It is in *Women Talking*, however, that the theme of *Gelassenheit* and the dark side of resilience are most devastatingly presented. According to the novel's premise, after the rapes are proven to have occurred and are acknowledged by the colony's leaders, Peters insists that the women forgive their assailants as a way to enter the kingdom of heaven. Although the eight women meet in the hayloft to decide whether to fight back, do nothing, or leave, August recounts how some women have already "voted to do nothing, to leave things in the hands of the Lord" (6–7), a passive acceptance of their previous, and likely future, suffering and a perverse martyrdom to serve the greater (male) good. Since the women who decide to do nothing in a way are putting the past behind them, Peters might interpret their decision as indicating resilience, but the women in the loft do not agree. One of the do nothing group once told August that, "as a Molotschnan, she had everything she wanted; all she had to do was convince herself that she wanted very little" (7), but such acceptance seems to be much like defeat.

Toews points out here and in previous works that fundamentalist Mennonite doctrine views "corporeal existence [as] a perversity" and the body as a mere vessel that will be left behind upon ascension to heaven (9). And, if the male body is unimportant, the female body is even less so. Rosemarie Garland Thomson writes that "both the female [body] and the disabled body are cast as deviant and inferior; both are excluded from full participation in public as well as economic life; both are defined in opposition to a norm that is assumed to possess natural physical superiority" (*Extraordinary Bodies* 19). In a world in which the body is secondary to the soul, and women are inferior to men, it is unsurprising that male salvation trumps female bodily (and mental) trauma. Thus, in *Women Talking*, Peters wants the perpetrators to obtain bail so that they can return to the colony and "be forgiven by the victims and in turn have the victims forgiven by God" (45). To live a Christian life, Peters believes, one must emulate Christ, who forgave his enemies even as they crucified him. But the power of his sacrifice and forgiveness comes from his having made his choices freely, for the good of humankind. The women's forgiveness is different because, as Ona asks, "is forgiveness that is coerced true forgiveness?" (26). The "opportunity" to forgive is actually an ultimatum, for, as Mariche says, "we will be forced to leave the colony . . . if we don't forgive the men and/or accept their apologies, and through the process of this excommunication we will forfeit our place in heaven" (24).

Once again Toews draws from actual circumstances in the Manitoba colony. Friedman-Rudovsky reports Minister Juan Fehr's words: "In order to go to heaven you must forgive those who have wronged you." Friedman-Rudovsky continues that, "if one woman didn't want to forgive, he said, she would have been visited by Bishop Neurdorf [sic], Manitoba's highest authority, and 'he would have simply explained to her that if she didn't forgive, then God wouldn't forgive her'" ("Ghost Rapes"). As is often the case in broader social contexts, including present-day Canada, Fehr's words suggest that the women bear part of the blame for being raped, even though they were drugged in their homes when the attacks occurred. Like their counterparts in real life, the women of the Molotschna colony in *Women Talking* are expected quietly to sacrifice their autonomy, self-respect, and safety in order to fulfill the ideal of *Gelassenheit*.

Referencing Carol Penner, Marlene Epp explains how "Mennonite perspectives on the concepts of forgiveness, obedience, and suffering have been interpreted with very gender-specific meanings for women dealing with violence in their lives. In this interpretation, biblically mandated submission became a Christian-Mennonite woman's highest virtue, even while her husband's exertion of power was an abuse of scripture" (112). Violent sexual assault hardly fits a pacifist ideology, yet the women's anger and occasional violence (Salome attacks a rapist with a scythe) receive more condemnation than the crimes themselves. Women are asked to "turn the other cheek" for the good of the community. The perceived weakness of the female mind and the inherent sinfulness of the female body are exemplified in *Women Talking* by the plight of Mina, a woman who died by suicide after a particularly vicious attack on her daughter. "At first," Toews writes, "Peters told Mina it was Satan who was responsible for the attack, that it was punishment from God, that God was punishing the women for their sins. Then Peters told Mina she was making the attack up. He repeated the words 'wild female imagination'" (57–58). His belief, again fashioned from accounts of the Bolivian rapes, that the women are not traumatized because they were unconscious when the attacks occurred (39) is contradicted by the documented distress of women sexually assaulted under the influence of Rohypnol and other "date rape" drugs. Even when unconscious, the mind can remember, and certainly the experience of waking up naked and in pain is traumatic in itself. Trauma theorist Cathy Caruth discusses how the mind shuts down during traumatic experiences: "The event is not assimilated or experienced fully at the time, but only belatedly, in its repeated *possession* of the one who experiences it" ("Introduction" 4). Faced with the unconscionable, the mind refuses consciousness, and therefore traumatic moments often recur in dreams, when the waking control of the mind lapses. Early in *Women Talking*, for instance, Ona recounts a dream in which she finds a hard candy that she wants to wash. Going toward the sink, she "was accosted by a very large two-hundred-pound pig. She screamed, Get that pig off me! But it had her pinned to the wall" (25). Her dream reflects her experience of rape, even if Ona does not consciously remember the assaults. Yet her audience interprets the dream literally: Mariche tells her that the dream is "ridiculous" because no such candy exists in Molotschna. August tells Ona that he likes her dream but that she got the facts wrong. Pigs are physically unable to look up at the sky (31–32) or, presumably, to stand on their hind legs. The dream shows, however, that her unconscious mind is processing her trauma, even though Ona was not "awake" to it at the time.

As Katrina Onstad points out in her interview with Toews, "In *Women Talking*, and in news reports of the trial, the phrase 'wild female imagination' is deployed to erase the rapes, reminiscent of other he-said-she-said dismissals of female experience, such as 'hysteria'" ("Miriam Toews: 'I Needed to Write'"). But, as Steffler remarks, in the prefatory note to the novel, Toews "strikingly refers to her novel as 'an act of female imagination,' appropriating the phrase used by members of Manitoba Colony to dismiss the so-called 'stories' of the victims" ("Breaking Patriarchy" 64) and, by publishing an account of what happened, subverting the silencing that the phrase was meant to induce. Victims of domestic violence often stay in their homes because they cannot imagine a way out; the perpetrators of the violence are too powerful, and the consequences of disobedience are too severe. According to Susan Miller's work on intimate partner abuse, however, women who escape from abuse often do so after having an "epiphany" or experiencing an "incident that . . . hastened their decision" (86). The women, in other words, identify a break event that pushes them beyond compliance and suffering toward resilience and escape. They imagine a life without their oppressors, and in visualizing such a life they begin to find ways to create a new reality.

Words and the Power of Translation

Through her sustained critique of Mennonite concepts such as the quiet in the land and *Gelassenheit*, Miriam Toews shows how fundamentalist Anabaptist values can disproportionately disadvantage and repress women. Conflicting interpretations of the stories of Mina, Ona, and others bring to mind another way in which Toews criticizes fundamentalist belief systems: by examining the power behind interpretation and translation. Anabaptism was founded upon adherence to the truth of scripture, and central tenets of Mennonitism—such as the refusal to swear oaths, separation from the world, and adult baptism—are all based upon placing perceived scriptural truth above life in the world. When the primary authority is the Bible itself, what happens, Toews asks, when women are denied access to the text that rules their lives? When those telling women what to believe are the men who seek to control them utterly? In *Fight Night*, Grandma Elvira says that "she can't really read the Bible anymore because when she reads it she only hears authoritarian old men's voices" (176–77). Her experience of reading the Bible has been tainted by the tyrants who sought to use the text to control her. Although she quotes many passages from memory, she has refused the "word" when it is co-opted by fundamentalist bullies. At least, however, Elvira has a choice whether or not to read the Bible. Because the women in *Women Talking* are unable to read and write, they are dependent on two types of translation. The first type, as August reminds readers, is that some of the women's Plautdietsch idioms are untranslatable, so though he tries to be as accurate as possible, his translation will not completely convey what the women said. And, because Plautdietsch is primarily an unwritten language, August translates the women's words as he goes along, making the women's chances of ever reading the text even more remote. The women would have to learn not only how to read in the first place but also how to speak and read English.

Concerns about August's translation seem to be minor when placed next to the second type of translation: the men's vaunted ability to read and interpret the Bible itself, often in ways detrimental to the women's autonomy. But the Bible was not originally written in Plautdietsch, High German, or English, so unless the men know the original Aramaic, Greek, and Hebrew they, too, are working with a translation. Add to this that the women hear the words in the Bible only as they are selected and uttered by the colony's male members, and biblical authority has been shown to be susceptible to the preconceptions of translators and interpreters. Scholars of religion have a long history of debating the merits of biblical translations, and one area of contention, especially in the past fifty years, has been how gender is translated in various versions. Even though the women in the novel hear the Bible in High German, controversies over the translation of the Bible into English might shed some light on this issue.

Since the rise of feminism, various translators have sought to make the gendered language of the Bible more inclusive, whereas others have suggested that gender-inclusive translations are not true to their original source texts. For example, Ross S. Kraemer and Jennifer Eyl speak of "the perils of gender-inclusive translation of the New Testament" (295) when it ignores "the historical reality of ancient Mediterranean patriarchal cultures" (296). They conclude that "gender-inclusive translation of ancient texts should never be presumed as the default. In some cases, it is clearly warranted, when supported by the text itself. At other times, as we have endeavored to illustrate, it is clearly distorting" (318). The gendered language of the Bible reflects the sexism of the times and cultures in which it was written and translated; however, Kraemer and Eyl acknowledge that in some cases past translators have deliberately chosen male-oriented language when a more inclusive word choice might be merited. For example, "Paul's letters to Christ's followers in Rome or in Corinth are unquestionably intended for both women and men, even though much of their language presumes a male reader/auditor" (317). Similarly, Marmy A. Clason explains a controversy surrounding Today's New International Version (TNIV) of the Bible. Clason notes that the Greek word "*anthrōpos* most frequently refers to all human beings," yet the word is often translated as "man." She continues that "the NIV translated Romans 3:28 in this way: 'for we maintain that a man [*anthrōpos*] is justified by faith.' Since it is obvious that the meaning of the verse would apply to everyone, women included, the TNIV translates it as 'for we maintain that a person [*anthrō-pos*] is justified by faith'" (26).[4] Martin Mittelstadt cites the example of Ephesians 5:22, in which Saint Paul famously states "wives, submit to your own husbands, as to the Lord" (NKJV), but his injunction is usually cited "without awareness of 5:21, a plain call to locate the submission of wives to their husbands within the context of mutual submission" (47). Although some modern translators favour a more gender-inclusive approach, and thus reflect a more welcoming attitude toward the role of women within the church, others use the Bible to maintain the patriarchal status quo, even when the original source texts were more gender inclusive than their translators might allow. Those who view the Bible as the direct voice of God will see these patriarchal biases as ordained and sanctioned by an infallible power.

Women Talking explores issues of interpretation grounded in patriarchal translations and readings of the Bible and the dependence of women on men to tell them what the Bible says. "Yes," says Ona, "our inability to read or write puts us at a great disadvantage in any negotiation over the interpretation of the Bible" (158). Earlier she provokes a moment of levity in the novel's life-and-death discussion when she asks "but how are we to determine God's will, if not by thinking? and Salome answers "that's easy, Ona, Peters will interpret it for us!" (117, 118). As the primary source of *gnosis*, or knowledge, the Bible can be used by the unscrupulous to keep women in their place, a thought that the women embrace when Salome says "we, the women, do not know exactly what is in the Bible, being unable to read it. Furthermore, the only reason why we feel we need to submit to our husbands is because our husbands have told us that the Bible decrees it" (157). The faith of the women in the colony's men has been severely tested, and they now question the men's ability to interpret the Bible fairly and accurately.

Previously, the women have fallen victim to wilfully incorrect interpretations of their experiences, for the men have discounted their stories by saying that the women were dreaming, receiving divine punishment for their sinful thoughts, exaggerating, or fabricating stories to hide their sexual indiscretions. One such interpretation, that of "Narfa, or Nervousness" (*Women Talking* 3), deserves particular attention. Although August uses the term to describe his own neurotic behaviour, and Ona and Salome's father is said to have died by suicide because of it, the term, like "hysteria," with its roots in *hysteros*, the womb, is mostly reserved for women and used to discount their experiences. As writers on women and madness such as Jane Ussher and Phyllis Chesler have shown, female "madness" often arises out of repressive cultural standards in which rebellion against behavioural norms is classified as deviant and thus discounted. Ussher writes that "the madwoman, like the witch, no longer has an identity as an individual, as [an] autonomous subject, [and] she has disappeared under the enveloping label attached to her" (61).

Of the eight "women talking," the colony singles out Ona for particular disapprobation. Labelled after her father's death by suicide as "a pariah, as the devil's daughter, and God-given burden to the colony" (172), she has been deemed unmarriageable, which ironically made her a frequent victim of rape since she slept alone. Now pregnant out of wedlock, Ona has even less status than the other women. As August says, many colonists view her as a ghost "because of her Narfa, her spinsterdom, and her burgeoning belly" (137). Yet her diagnosis of *Narfa* seems originally to have stemmed from relatively minor infractions of the social order. Ona roams "about the colony, her hair too loosely covered, her dress too untidily hemmed, a suspicious figure" (3). Paradoxically, however, in an analysis reminiscent of Thomas Szasz's observation of "the case of Breuer's famous patient Anna O.," who became mentally ill after having become "an oppressed, unpaid, sick-nurse" (216) and secretly resenting her role, Ona, "the devil's daughter," benefits from the diagnosis of *Narfa*, even as she is shunned. Anna O. became ill after a long period of nursing her father, and Szasz speculates that, because it would have been unfeminine of her not to want to look after her ill father, she subconsciously sought attention and rest by becoming ill herself (216–18). Similarly, Ona's *Narfa* might seem like a sickness to the other Molotschnans, but it is actually a resilient adaptation to oppression.

Toews comments in an interview that,

> now, today, we would say somebody is suffering from a type of mental illness. Whether that is even the case with Ona or not, Ona is a person who has—either through illness or just circumstance—kind of removed herself from that society. Of course, she's still there, physically. These are her people and her world.
>
> But in a sense, she's liberated herself, because as soon as people stigmatize her with this "Narfa," she becomes somebody that they wouldn't expect anything of, really. So whatever her actions are, if they involve breaking the rules, it would almost be accepted or ignored. She has Narfa, so is considered a write-off. ("How Miriam Toews Gave a Voice")

When Ona became pregnant, for example, the colony made plans to marry her to a mentally disabled man. August recounts her rejection of this plan on the basis that the man "deserved better than a woman afflicted with Narfa and that he would be tainted with sin for marrying a woman who was not a virgin." He continues that "the elders of the colony" have therefore "concluded that Ona is beyond redemption, that her Narfa has rendered her incapable of reasoning" (*Women Talking* 49). From the reader's perspective, however, her refusal to make her ostensible shame "go away" makes perfect sense. Ona has a history of standing up to the community elders and speaking the truth. When, for instance, Peters denies that her sister Mina died through suicide, saying instead that she died from inhaling ammonia fumes, Ona rearranges Mina's kerchief "to reveal the rope marks on her neck" and says "in a loud voice to the congregation that it wasn't ammonia from cleaning the barn that had killed her" (57). As an unwed expectant mother, Ona knows that her pregnancy stands as a reminder of the rapes that the elders are trying to ignore, and when she mentions her non-virginal state as a reason for not marrying she indicts a system that values female chastity but devalues women. Ona even admits to the women talking that *Narfa* is "liberating, in a way" (124), since her status as a lesser person leaves her with more freedom to bend rules. Her *Narfa* gives her "a type of liberty to speak her mind because her thoughts and words are perceived as meaningless" (28), yet Ona is the first of the eight women to formulate a list of conditions that must be fulfilled for the women to remain in the colony: "Men and women will make all decisions for the colony collectively. Women will be allowed to think. Girls will be taught to read and write. The schoolhouse must display a map of the world so that we can begin to understand our place in it" (56). Although the other women quickly discount her list as impossible, her ideas are "mad" only within the context of extreme patriarchy.

As Toews shows in *Women Talking*, diagnoses such as *Narfa* or hysteria serve to discount women's rebellions against the status quo: if the patriarchal system is "sane," and male-dominated systems use interpretations of the Bible to prove that it is, then any questioning of male prerogatives and authority is "insane." Thus, when Agata says that "we're all nervous. We can't avoid nervousness" (185), she highlights the precarious position of women in the colony. Peters and others might "diagnose" the women with *Narfa*, but the women have every right to be nervous. They have been raped while unconscious, beaten and put down while awake, and subject to excommunication if they dare to think for themselves. In other words, the women recognize that for women in the Molotschna colony, *Narfa* is inherent in being female.

Who gets to interpret the world and why are also central concerns in *Irma Voth* as the main character moves between three languages and four worlds (Canada, her father's farm, the movie set, and Mexico City). The question of biblical interpretation comes up in a scene in which Julius tells Diego to leave the *campo* and Diego replies that he has a right to stay on the property that he has legally rented. Julius responds by quoting Christ's prophecy in Luke 17:34 (KJV) about his second coming: "I tell you," Julius intones, "in that night there shall be two men in one bed. The one shall be taken and the other shall be left" (*Irma Voth* 123). Diego asks Irma what her father means, for he does not recognize his speech as a reflection of how the righteous (Julius) will go to heaven while the sinner (Diego) will remain behind. Julius knows, as Irma likely does, that in Luke 17 Jesus also mentions Noah's flood and the destruction of Sodom and Gomorrah, two cataclysms in which the majority of people were destroyed and only the righteous survived. Diego and Julius speak in different registers because they inhabit different worlds. Julius relies on the primacy of the Bible, whereas Diego is committed to the primacy of art. Although Diego eventually understands that he must return Aggie to her father if he wants to complete his movie, he likely misses how thoroughly he has been condemned. Julius believes that he speaks the word of God; Diego thinks that he is dealing with a particularly nasty crank.

For all their differences, however, the men agree that what Aggie does is up to them. Diego knows that Julius will "fuck up the production" (128) if he does not get his way, and Julius, who has already beaten Aggie so severely that her back is covered in blood and bruises, thinks that he is saving her soul. Faced with the men's certainty, Irma thinks "I've run out of words. I have nothing. I've failed" (130). Even when she prays at the feet of her father, he remains unmoved since his interpretation of Aggie's staying in Diego's house must be more accurate than his daughter's. Irma realizes that her interpretation of Aggie's present and future suffering means little to men who view the world through the higher realms of religion and art.

Although words fail Irma here, in another sense she is well aware of the power of language. Because she can speak Plautdietsch, English, and Spanish, Diego hires her to act as a translator for his film. Although he tells Irma that "it's very important that your translation of my words is precise" (26), often she deliberately mistranslates them, both to soften his words and to counter his assumptions about female submissiveness. When Diego tells the crew that they must be prepared for work at all times, for example, and "if you're not prepared to risk your life . . . then leave now," Irma translates to Marijke that "he wants us all to have fun, relax and be brave" (44). Meanwhile, Marijke questions why the character that she is playing "would be serene all the time. Was she in a depressive fog or not quite human or just plain stupid?" (43). Diego, however, has bought into the stereotype of the subservient and long-suffering Mennonite wife. Speaking of an upcoming scene between Alfredo, the man who plays the cheating husband, and Marijke, who plays his wife, Diego tells Irma that "Alfredo will tell Marijke that he has to go to town on some kind of business and Marijke will indicate through her body language that she does not believe him but that she will accept what he is saying for the sake of peace in the home. Alfredo will take a few steps then come back and put his hand on her shoulder and tell her that he loves her. Marijke will tell him that she loves him too. Okay? he said. It's simple, right?" (50). In the Reygadas film, as in the fictional version here, the wife eventually dies from a broken heart, worn down by anguish at her husband's infidelity, which makes this scene less "simple" than it seems. Irma expresses her disdain for Diego's version of silent suffering by asserting her own translation. She instructs Marijke to "tell him [Alfredo] quietly that you're tired of his bullshit. In fact, no, not tired, but very close to being *defeated* by his bullshit" (50). Magdalene Redekop reports that mistranslation was also part of the film *Silent Light*. When a group of Mennonite women watched a screening of the film, they "could not watch *Stellet Licht* without laughing constantly, in large part because of the absurd mistranslations in the subtitles" (*Making Believe* 107). Irma's intentional mistranslations are one of the funniest aspects of the novel. They are also a profound comment on how received interpretations should be questioned, for Irma gives the character that Marijke plays much less *Gelassenheit* than Diego wants. Irma can do so because he does not understand Plautdietsch, and Marijke does not understand Spanish. Although Irma essentially rebels behind Diego's back, her "secret" rebellion might give her more confidence later to reject his and her father's privileging of their own agendas.

Early in the novel, Irma "trie[s] quickly to remember the meaning of the word *samizdat*" (48), which translates from Russian as "we publish ourselves": "By the thousands and tens of thousands of frail, smudged onionskin sheets, samizdat spreads across the land a mass of protests and petitions, secret court minutes, Alexander Solzhenitsyn's banned novels, . . . [and] all sorts of sharp political discourses and angry poetry" (Parry). Interestingly, Toews also uses the word at the conclusion of *Women Talking* when August Epp writes that, "when a man's dream becomes for us the truth, when Menno Simons' fevered vision is the word, when Peters' angry interpretation is our narrow path and facts are in the world, the world we don't belong in, or can't belong in, or perhaps do belong in, and they are kept from us and the real facts take on mythical importance, awe, they are gifts, samizdat, currency, they are the Eucharist, blood, forbidden" (198–99). Irma's diary, her wayward translations of Diego's movie dialogue, and August's minutes are all forbidden texts: *samizdat* produced in spite of injunctions from fundamentalists, such as Peters or Julius Voth, who would eradicate dissent. Like Russian writers who risk their lives and freedom to produce texts that challenge state authority, the women create a forbidden text when they ask August to record their deliberations, and Irma creates subversive texts when she undermines Diego's high art with rebellious mistranslations and when she writes in a diary that she knows her father would destroy if he found it.

Both *Women Talking* and *Irma Voth* highlight the subversive power of language. After Irma flees to Mexico City, she finds herself living near "a refuge for exiled writers" who have been "forced to leave their own countries" (213). Although the ways in which they escaped differ, all of them left "with unfinished business and a broken heart," an apt metaphor for her own exile from her home and what can happen when creative individuals speak back to a repressive state. Like the "women talking," Irma knows that "freedom has its price" (214) in terms of homes and families lost, ostracism, and the risk of imprisonment or death. Yet silence is a worse fate than banishment, and sometimes voicing a problem can bring it into focus and help to create change. At the beginning of the novel, Irma thinks about how she sometimes talks to the Sierra Madre mountains: "I compliment them on their strength and solidity, and by hearing myself talk that way I am reminded that those words exist for a reason, that they're applicable from time to time. It's comforting" (7). Irma contemplates the words *strength* and *solidity* in order to find resilience in a world that has undermined her at every turn, for she understands that words can reify concepts, both positive and negative. When we formulate a concept through words, we can help to bring it to life.

In fact, Toews's concern with freedom of speech highlights a paradox that Grace Kehler, Di Brandt, and Magdalene Redekop have all addressed. Kehler notes that "church and state authorities ordered that the tongues of Anabaptists be cut out, burned, or screwed down, prior to their public deaths, preventing them from verbally attesting to their faith and to their willing acceptance of martyrdom" ("Representations" 172). As Kehler also mentions (167), Brandt gives a compelling reason for why a community that gave up so much for freedom of speech and belief has become, in extreme cases, so intent on silencing dissent among its own members. Brandt reminds her readers that "before the persecutions" the "women of [her] culture had voices and power and freedom" and spoke out for their beliefs. However, "the violence of the persecutions got internalized in our psyches and we began inflicting them on each other, the same violent subjugations of body and spirit the Inquisitors visited upon us" (*So This* 3). Turning their trauma inward, some Mennonites began to silence themselves. Toews's characters are often shown writing or, in the case of *Women Talking*, commissioning writing, as a way to speak their own truths. Yes, their audience will be limited, or even non-existent, but the writing helps to clarify their thoughts so that they can make plans for the future. To use the words of Ona, believing that their discussion is valuable enough to be recorded helps the women to "think for themselves" and thus enables them to make a choice.

Trauma and the Politics of Choice

Trauma often paralyzes those who experience it, making resilience almost impossible to contemplate. In *Irma Voth*, Toews provides an apt analogy for the power of trauma and the strength needed to recover from its effects. Once Irma reaches Mexico City, she encounters Noehmi, a young female artist who quotes from the book that she is reading: "*Katherine compared the energy of trauma to a cobalt bomb with a radioactive half-life of one hundred years*" (175). When Irma asks Noehmi what she thinks the author means, she replies that "maybe it meant that every trauma presents a choice: paralysis or the psychic energy to move forward" (175).[5] Her analysis is both accurate and reductive. Not all people in abusive relationships, for instance, have the psychic power to escape from them. Both a victim of violence and a witness of violence against her children, Irma's mother, for example, stays with Julius even though he has murdered her eldest daughter, banished Irma, and severely beaten Aggie.

Furthermore, the victims of rape in the real Manitoba colony did not leave their community. In *Women Talking*, Scarface Janz and others who vote "to do nothing, to leave things in the hands of the Lord" (7), will leave themselves and their daughters—according to the other women's analysis—open to more attacks, yet they decide to stay. In a way, the women of the real Manitoba colony, Irma's mother, and Scarface Janz "choose" to stay, but one wonders whether choices made from limited options are really choices. Women who remain in abusive relationships often do so because they believe that they have no choice: they are traumatized by repeated abuse and usually isolated from community resources that could assist them to change their lives. Add to this that one of the symptoms of trauma is recurring flashbacks to the traumatic event, images that many would prefer to forget, and Noehmi's statement in *Irma Voth* becomes even less persuasive. In *Women Talking*, August tells the women that humans "completely replac[e] their outer skin every month," but "Neitje interrupts [him]. Except for the scars" (37). Some experiences cannot be glossed over and remain present in the skin and the soul. Paralysis, in other words, is not a choice but a symptom.

Still, Noehmi's words hold truth for Irma Voth and the eight women talking. The novels show that trauma is indeed like radiation, with a "half life" that continues through generations. Irma mentions at both the start and the end of *Irma Voth* that her father witnessed the murders of his family members in Russia (13, 251), and his trauma bookends her description of her own trauma. Although in no way excusing his violence, the slaughter of his Russian family might help to explain it. When, in *Women Talking*, Peters reads a headline—"*In 2011 the Devil Appeared, in the Shape of Seven Ghosts, to the Girls and Women of the Molotschna Colony*"—Heinz Gerbrandt, who has since left Molotschna with his wife and children, reports to August that Peters said "dump men in the middle of nowhere, confine them, abuse them, suspend them in limbo, and this is what you get." Heinz and August then wonder how Peters "can carry on here as the bishop of Molotschna, the way he does" (100). But, as Ona suggests, it is "perhaps not men, per se," who prevent the women's emancipation "but a pernicious ideology that has been allowed to take hold of men's hearts and minds" (66). The men might have experienced or witnessed abuse as children and, like many abusers, have been conditioned to see violence as "normal" behaviour. In a sense, the men are victims of their ability to victimize.

In cases in which people have the wherewithal and resilience to choose, perhaps trauma presents a choice between death and life, stasis and change. In *Literature in the Ashes of History*, Cathy Caruth discusses "Freud's enigmatic move in the theory of trauma from the drive for death to the drive for life, from the reformulating of life around the witness to death to the possibility of witnessing and making history in creative acts of life" (5). Caruth explains that, when Freud began to treat patients traumatized by war, he had to revise his previous theory on dreams as wish fulfillment, for the soldiers repeatedly had nightmares that took them back to the very things that their conscious minds wanted to avoid. Caruth focuses on how in *Beyond the Pleasure Principle* (1920) Freud juxtaposes the nightmares of the returned soldiers with a young child playing a game of *fort* and *da* (gone and here) when his mother leaves his company. At first, Freud speculates that the child makes up the game to reassure himself of his mother's "joyful return" (qtd. in Caruth 4), but, as Caruth describes, Freud contradicts his first explanation when he says that the child focuses more on the loss than on the return. Caruth writes that "the creative activity of the child's game, Freud recognizes with surprise, does not ultimately involve a symbolic representation of the mother's pleasurable return, but repeats, in a kind of stammer that interrupts its story, the painful memory of her departure. Like the soldiers' dreams, the game thus reenacts the memory of a painful reality. What is most surprising in the child's game, however, is that this reenactment of reality in the game places repetition at the very heart of childhood, and links the repetition to a creative act of invention" (4–5).

In Caruth's reading of Freud, the trauma for the soldier and the child rests in their inability to process the shock of their experiences: "The breach in the mind—the psyche's awareness of the threat to life—is not caused by a direct threat or injury, but by fright, the lack of preparedness to take in a stimulus that comes too quickly" (6). Thus, when the child and the soldier return again and again to the moment of their trauma, they are trying to prepare themselves more fully for the fact of *life*: "And as such the trauma is not only the repetition of the missed encounter with death but also the missed encounter with one's own survival. It is the incomprehensible act of surviving—of waking into life—that repeats and bears witness to what remains ungrasped within the encounter with death" (6).

Applying Caruth's analysis, then, *Irma Voth* and *Women Talking* are about resilience, "waking into life," as much as they are about trauma and patriarchal violence, and it is here that Toews's discussions of art in both novels come to the fore. Although the theme is more consistently delineated in *Irma Voth*, both novels highlight how Mennonite patriarchs suppress art because they think it sinful and full of temptation. August's father, for instance, was excommunicated partly for "sins pertaining to the storage of intellectual materials and to the dissemination and propagation of said materials, even though the materials were art books, photographs of paintings that my father had found in the garbage behind a school in the city" (*Women Talking* 13). Art's importance as inspiration comes up at the conclusion of the novel when the women discuss whether photographers and painters know what their final images will look like before they begin. When August replies that "the photographer might possibly have a better idea of what the work will look like than the artist, Michelangelo, would have of the final expression of his art," Ona concludes that "we, the women, are artists." Although Mariche undermines Ona's conclusion by saying that the women are "artists of anxiety" (165), their decision effectively to recreate their religion and embark into the unknown has a flair of artistry about it. Historically, women have been more often models and muses for male artists than artists in their own right, but these "artists of anxiety" have refigured their trauma and pain into new ways of being. When Ona suggests that "the women can create their own map" (84), she implies that creativity is a way forward in a world that has thwarted the women's every thought. To borrow words from *Irma Voth*, the women need to "just begin" (253).

Paul Tiessen writes of how Irma experiences a series of epiphanies through her encounters with art. The first occurs when she finds Aggie weeping in front of Diego Rivera's mural *México a través de los siglos* (Mexico through the Centuries). "Aggie begins to discover for herself, and helps Irma to begin to discover, the very idea of herself as a person with capacities of her own" ("'It Was Like Watching'" 68), a particularly important insight for Irma, who tends to think of herself as a failure at living. The second occurs when Aggie discovers Irma's homesickness and decorates their room to resemble night at the *campo*: "In return for her gift of art, Irma gives Aggie the gift of truth, letting go of the story about the hidden moments in her family's past back in Canada six years earlier, the dark moments that continue to stalk and implicate her and, especially, her father" (68). And the third occurs when Irma goes to see the movie that Diego has made and realizes that art is more than the sum of its parts. The movie, which Irma undermined by changing Marijke's lines and which seemed, during filming, to be nothing but a jumble of unrelated scenes, allows Irma a catharsis. Her father has told Diego that "art is a lie" (*Irma Voth* 18, 253), and to a certain extent his accusation is confirmed by Diego's assurance that "by making this film we can help to preserve your culture and prevent it from disappearing" (70), only later to tell his audience at the film screening that "it's not about Mennonites, that much I'll say" (245). In addition, Irma thinks of how art can misrepresent reality when Aggie, afraid that Diego's dog, Oveja, has been killed, sees him on the screen and says "he's alive!" Irma thinks that Aggie's certainty "was interesting in its way. In the way that it might not actually be true but that it seemed true in that very moment" (240). Even though Irma has witnessed the filming and knows the tensions and truths behind Diego's stylized portrayal of Mennonites, when she sees her world represented on screen she is struck by the emotional truth of art: "All the pictures strung together and people in them, walking, talking, kissing, dying. I felt so happy. Or maybe it wasn't happiness. There was something that I was beginning to understand but I didn't know what it was. It was like watching my own life. It was a pathway into myself" (239). Irma recognizes how art creates and encourages empathy. Tiessen points out how she sees the movie as "one coherent song" (*Irma Voth* 237): "Again, Toews makes us aware of the sense of the moral vision and the perseverance of an artistic creator ordering the chaos" ("'It Was Like Watching'" 68).

Diego's film prompts Irma to review painful memories—Katie's preparations for leaving, Jorge's departure, even her father's trauma "as a little boy on a road in Russia"—and she says that "I was trying to get to the bottom of things. I was trying to formulate a thought. Or a cure" (*Irma Voth* 251). Her thought process sharpens when she hears Ximena's anguished cries after Ximena "bit[es] into a live electrical cord." Irma thinks that "she was in real pain. She had suffered a serious shock. . . . She was surprised and hurt. She was fragile after all, a helpless baby." As Irma realizes that Ximena has entered the world of sudden shock and unexpected pain, a world prone to trauma, Irma begins to formulate a new plan:

> The gathering storms in my head disappeared and I had figured
> out the solution to my own problem. I understood what it was to
> want someone to stay. And I knew what to do next. And I knew
> the answer to my own question: if this was the last day of your
> life what kind of a story would you write?
>
> YOU MUST BE PREPARED TO DIE!
>
> I read over the original heading in my notebook, the one that
> Diego had given me a long time ago to record my thoughts and
> observations. I pondered his dark advice. I scratched out the
> word DIE and wrote LIVE. (251)

What Tiessen calls Diego's "dangerous gift of a notebook and a pen" prompts Irma to "learn to occupy more than one world" ("'It Was Like Watching'" 65) and to formulate new ways to respond to the wrenching trauma of Katie's death and its aftermath. As Irma contemplates her notebook at the conclusion of the novel, she feels the pull of her pen. As she recounts, "I opened my notebook again thinking that I had all sorts of ideas and things to write about but now I'm not sure. I heard my mother's voice. Irma, she said, just begin" (*Irma Voth* 253). Her mother first gives

Irma this advice when, two weeks after Katie's death and the family's relocation to Chihuahua, Irma believes that she is dead and her mother and father cannot "convince [her] of the truth" (14, 16). Since Irma's Cotard's Syndrome[6] is clearly brought on by the trauma of Katie's murder and Irma's guilt for having "caused" it, her mother's advice could be reformulated as "just begin to live again after your life has been torn apart."

Remapping the Mennonite Path: A Way Forward

The first epigraph to this chapter indicates the centrality of Romans 12:2 to Mennonite belief. The verse provides an impetus for the non-conformity at the heart of Anabaptist tradition (Epp 181) and, ironically, sets a precedent for the women talking and Irma Voth to find the means to interpret their religious teachings anew. Miriam Toews says that "there are ways of being Mennonite in the world that are about equality and have female ministers that are open to the LGBTQ+ community and are loving and tolerant. They do exist, and my mom belongs to one of those churches. So, these [conservative] pastors and leaders have choices" ("Women Will Write"). Thus, when the women in *Women Talking* discuss how God might interpret their leaving the colony not as an act of disobedience, which the men surely would find it, but "as a time for love, a time for peace," August silently interjects that "I am struck by a thought: Perhaps it is the first time the women of Molotschna have interpreted the word of God for themselves" (159). Given Salome's previous angry denunciation of teenage boys who give them orders, their ensuing conversation about what to do if their sons refuse to leave is again revolutionary. As Mariche says, they "can't carry fourteen-year-old boys on [their] back[s]," and Agata replies that "we will try to *influence* our sons" to decide for themselves to leave the colony with their mothers (162). Agata claims her rightful status as an "elder" whose opinions should matter and whose influence should be respected.

Admittedly, this discussion about sons foreshadows the one sour note in the women's decision to leave the colony: their departure is not completely non-violent. Autje and Neitje use the belladonna spray to incapacitate the

Koop brothers, who, they fear, will betray them, and Salome sedates and kidnaps her son Aaron when he refuses to leave the colony with her. She also sprays Scarface Janz, who threatens to tell the men that the women are leaving (206). In spite of these acts, the conclusion of the novel uplifts the reader by showing that the ideals at the heart of Mennonitism are not dead as long as strong women and gentle men can interpret them anew. The women have been told that the "good and acceptable and perfect will of God" demands their obedience to the patriarchal trinity of God, father, and husband, but in keeping with the origins of Anabaptism, they decide to think for themselves and reframe the doctrine previously used to control them. As the women debate whether to stay at home and fight or to leave the colony for an uncertain future in a world that most of them have never seen, they arrive at three key demands: "We want our children to be safe. We want to keep our faith. And we want to think" (120).

In addition, the women benefit from the "social ecological" model of resilience. Although they have been denied access to outside help, their strong bonds with each other give them the power to resist their oppression. Each has individual strengths that she brings to the meeting. Salome is "a fighter, an instigator" (31), Ona has eccentricity and intelligence, Agata and Greta have the experience of age, Mariche and Mejal bring their questions and conflicting perspectives, and Autje and Neitje have playfulness and youth. The women support each other as a community and recognize their united strength, making it possible, in the words of Ona, to envision "a new religion, extrapolated from the old but focused on love" (56).

Rather than obey Peters's dictum of forgiveness, the women decide what they value most, and obedience is not on their list. After all, how can one justify obedience when it amounts to condoning sin? Greta reframes the concept of forgiveness when she suggests that it comes from meditative searching of the soul: "Leaving will give us the more far-seeing perspective we need to forgive, which is to love properly, and to keep the peace, according to our faith. Therefore, our leaving wouldn't be an act of cowardice, abandonment, disobedience or rebellion. It wouldn't be because we were excommunicated or exiled. It would be a supreme act of faith. And of faith in God's abiding goodness" (110). Her radical theology reveals a new assertiveness. Were she to stay in the colony, Greta reasons, she would be forced to fight ongoing male violence, but her religion values non-resistance. Not resisting rape, however, would further defile the women and lead the men to sin further, to the detriment of all of the colony's souls. If the women stayed, according to Agata, then "we would turn Molotschna into a battlefield" (104).

Referring to the Mennonite history of migration, Greta asks the other women "how many times will we pack our bags and disappear into the night?" (153). In choosing to leave the colony, however, the women remain true to the centre of the Mennonite religion: freedom of worship and pacifism. They follow the same path that their ancestors took when they left Prussia for Russia, when they left Russia for Canada, and when they left Canada for Mexico. Although it could be argued that some of those moves stemmed from parochialism and fear of outside influences, the women's exodus from the Molotschna colony is based upon the need to love freely and without fear. Since the early Mennonites also insisted on the importance of *choosing* to believe—hence the tenet of adult baptism— the women return to this ideal when they reject the doctrine of enforced forgiveness and decide that they can interpret the Bible for themselves. As Grace Kehler puts it, "given such horrific abandonment of a peace practice, the women's leave-taking of the colony signals a paradoxical and parabolic act of *returning* to lived faith as a homeland" ("Miriam Toews's Parable" 41). Agata expresses the resilience and hope that her ancestors might well have felt: "We have ruled out staying and fighting because our faith consists of core values, one of them being pacifism, and we have no homeland but our faith, and we are servants to our faith, and by being such we are assured eternal peace in heaven" (*Women Talking* 151). Toews includes a clear signal of new belief systems when August says of Ona "and the gates of hell shall not prevail against her" (198), echoing Christ's words to Peter in Matthew 16:18 (KJV).[7] To August at least, Ona will be the inspiration for a new church, one that emphasizes the power of love and life.

Irma Voth's eponymous protagonist, too, must reconcile a traumatic past and present with hope for the future. Like the women of Molotschna, Irma chooses to leave her family, first by marrying Jorge against her father's wishes, then by associating with people whom her father deems corrupt when she works on the movie set, and finally by moving herself and her two sisters to Mexico City. Although in some ways Irma is better off than Ona and the other women in Molotschna—at least Irma knows some geography and can read and write—she is still taking a leap of faith. She saw what happened to her sister Katie when she decided to leave, and Irma herself has experienced her father's physical violence. Although she could have decided to remain at the movie set and ignore Aggie's plight, at the young age of nineteen she finds the resilience to make a home for herself without violence. Travis Kroeker shows how Irma rejects her father's renunciation of worldly life, as defined in Mennonite doctrine, when she explains that "our motto is from the 'rebuke of worldliness,' which is from the Biblical book of James: *Whosoever will be a friend of the world is the enemy of God*" (*Irma Voth* 12; Kroeker 90). As represented by her father, the patriarchal order condemns, shuns, and destroys life. Julius, after all, is literally a murderer in the name of keeping his eldest daughter from sinful ways.

In one of Toews's characteristic double endings that show a character's dream scenario followed by a rebuttal, Irma decides to return home to attempt a reconciliation with her father. At first, she describes how she returns home to the joyful embrace of her mother and younger brothers, but then she contradicts herself by describing how she hears her family behind the door but has not yet knocked on it. Thus, like *Women Talking*, *Irma Voth* ends at a moment of hope and uncertainty. Whereas the women talking decide to leave their community, Irma briefly returns to hers so that she can see her family and offer her father forgiveness. She plans, however, to return to Mexico City and the new life that she has established there. The novels are alike in that their main characters have decided to move on and accept the unknown and to express resilience in the face of great trauma. According to Toews, "*wild* is a word used to discount and discredit what women do and say. . . . But the wild female imagination is also the stuff of art" ("I Needed to Write"; emphasis added). Against all odds, the women in these two novels assert their right to talk, to create, and to be free. They imagine an alternative to being treated as less than fully human, and in the process they create the possibility of a new future. In the face of extreme trauma, the women exemplify resilience. "Perhaps," as Ona says in *Women Talking*, "the women can create their own map as they go" (84), a map that values the core principles of the Mennonite religion but returns women to their central place in their lives and communities.

Unfortunately, however, as Toews knows all too well from her own life, not all individuals find the means to move toward a better future. In both *Swing Low* and *All My Puny Sorrows*, which I discuss in the next chapter, she centres her examination of resilience on what happens when loved ones, because of incurable mental illness, are unable to thrive. Toews turns her attention to how those who survive the suicide of a loved one must find ways to be resilient when faced with those who reject the very possibility that resilience exists. A loved one's death through suicide is a devastating blow that, ironically, requires survivors to find ways to overcome loss and, as Irma says, "prepare to live" even when they have seen how resilience sometimes fails.

"COMING FOR TO CARRY ME HOME"

Autofiction and Reparation in
Swing Low: A Life and *All My Puny Sorrows*

There are no windows within the dark house of depression through which to see others, only mirrors.
—MIRIAM TOEWS, SWING LOW (217)

I'm sometimes up and sometimes down,
Comin' for to carry me home,
But still my soul feels heavenly bound,
Comin' for to carry me home!
—"SWING LOW, SWEET CHARIOT" (TRADITIONAL SPIRITUAL)

When we write we offer the silence as much as the story. Words are the part of silence that can be spoken.
—JEANETTE WINTERSON, WHY BE HAPPY WHEN YOU COULD BE NORMAL? (8)

"Suicide is a death like no other, and those who are left behind to struggle with it must confront a pain like no other," writes Kay Redfield Jamison, an expert on bipolar disorder and the author of *Night Falls Fast:*

Understanding Suicide (292). In addition to the pain caused by the death itself, suicide survivors[1] must cope with feelings of rejection, self-recrimination, anger at loved ones for taking their own lives, and the stigma that sometimes prevents death by suicide from being acknowledged or discussed openly. In *Swing Low: A Life* and *All My Puny Sorrows*, Miriam Toews uses autofiction as a reparative strategy to address the referred pain of suicide. Just as an injury to one part of the body can be felt in a part not directly affected by the injury, so too the torment that the person contemplating suicide seeks to end through death can be transferred to those left behind. By examining theories of suicide survivorship, I show in this chapter how Toews tells the stories of her father and sister in an attempt to lessen the stigma associated with suicide, advocate for the rights of the mentally ill, and address her own bereavement. On one level, suicide can be understood as a failure of resilience or, perhaps more accurately, a loss of belief that resilience is possible. Suicide survivors, then, must find ways to reaffirm resilience after having received the message that recovery was not possible, at least for the person who lost their life to suicide. Toews sustains her own resilience by writing of the family members whom she lost. Hers is a reparative movement that celebrates the lives of her sister and father and examines how, once "the cataclysm has happened," according to D.H. Lawrence, those left behind can "start to build up new little habitats, to have new little hopes" (qtd. in *All* 317, 318). Toews builds one such "habitat" through her writing itself.

I mentioned Toews's autobiographical impulse in previous chapters, and in this chapter I address two books in which this impulse is the strongest, *Swing Low*, the fictionalized autobiography of her father, Mel Toews, and *All My Puny Sorrows*, her elegiac novel based upon the suicide of her sister Marjorie. An examination of other works by Toews shows that she consistently bases characters on aspects of her own past and that certain scenarios are repeated from book to book. Reminiscent of Mel, for instance, diffident, silent, and withdrawn fathers appear in *A Boy of Good Breeding*, *Summer of My Amazing Luck*, and *A Complicated Kindness*. As Toews said about *Summer*, "even though that book isn't a Mennonite book, it's still there, it keeps coming up, the father who's distant and doesn't speak" (interview with Reed). She also said that August Epp in *Women Talking* "is really a character modelled on my father" (interview with Reed). Furthermore, in *The Flying Troutmans*, Min's depression is based upon that of Marjorie, and *Fight Night* refers to the suicides of Swiv's grandfather and her aunt Momo. Although Toews does not make the connection explicit, her previous discussions of the suicides of her father and sister allow readers familiar with her work to make a connection between Swiv's grandfather and aunt and Toews's own family.

And it is not just her family that receives autobiographical attention. Magdalene Redekop notes that "the words of Diego, the fictive director in [*Irma Voth*], are almost verbatim quotations of actual comments made by [Carlos] Reygadas," the real-life director of *Silent Light* (*Making Believe* 114). In some ways, the novels by Toews act as paratexts for each other, and she adds to this sense of synchronicity through interviews and comments about correspondences between her life and the lives of her characters. This is particularly true of *Swing Low*, *All My Puny Sorrows*, and *Fight Night*, which refer, with various degrees of fictionality, to the suicides within her family. As her clearest statement on resilience so far, *Fight Night* has a focus different from that in either *Swing Low* or *Puny Sorrows*; whereas they describe the suicides of Mel and Marjorie Toews, *Fight Night* occurs after the suicides have happened, and the people left behind are finding ways to heal from them. I will therefore address *Fight Night* separately in Chapter 5.

Fiction versus Non-Fiction: The Problem of "Voice"

Although Toews refers to *Swing Low* as a work of non-fiction and *All My Puny Sorrows* as a work of fiction, neither book fits easily into either category, for each reveals true events alongside imagined situations and characters. In *Swing Low*, Toews writes a memoir about her father's life, but instead of writing a traditional biography or a personal memoir, which would refer to her father using the third-person pronoun *he*, she writes all but the introductory and concluding pages of her narrative in his voice. Toews writes as if she *were* her father, using the first-person pronoun *I* of the autobiographical subject, even though Mel lost his life to suicide in 1998, two years before *Swing Low* was published. Although he lived a very successful life on the surface, becoming an admired and inspirational teacher, marrying, and raising two daughters, Mel lived a double life in which he was energetic and outgoing in public but silent and reclusive at home. *Swing Low* begins with his hospitalization for mental illness and describes how Mel attempts to fit together the events in his life that have led to his breakdown. His thought processes become progressively more disturbed until the end of the narrative, when Toews concludes her father's story by describing how, in 1998, Mel died by walking in front of a moving train.

Toews says that "I think of *Swing Low* as non-fiction even though obviously it is in this grey area, and it's hard to slot or label." Moreover, she insists on the verifiability of her account: "Everything that happens in the book really did happen. *Every* single thing. His thoughts at any given time are based on what people *told* me about that he had said about what he was thinking. So in the book when I say *he's* thinking this or that, it's based on something that somebody had told me he had said." To ensure veracity, Toews ran her narrative "past a whole bunch of people" before it was published, which usually she does not do ("It Gets under the Skin'" 123). However, group recollection or confirmation does not necessarily ensure truth, especially about the thoughts of a man who Toews admits habitually hid his deepest self from others. Since autobiographers themselves sometimes get their details wrong, there is likely some factual slippage in her account of her father, translated through the remembrances of his friends and family members and then through the medium of her authorial voice. No matter its verifiability, Mel's narrative voice is a fiction because Toews must project herself into his psyche and create what she *assumes*, based upon her own experiences and the memories of others who knew her father and reported what he said or would have thought.

Although *All My Puny Sorrows* tells the thinly veiled story of Toews's sister Marjorie, who died by suicide in 2010 after a long experience of mental illness, the novel does not use the actual names of the people involved. When asked by a reviewer if "this new novel is actually fiction," Toews replied that "it's a combination of things that happened, conversations that happened, but I call it fiction because not all of it is verbatim. . . . This is a cliché, but in fiction I feel it is easier for me to get to some sort of truth, some kind of more honest writing" ("Profound Despair"). *Puny Sorrows* describes two sisters, Elf and Yoli Von Riesen, and their ongoing struggle over whether Elf, a long-term sufferer from depression who wants to end her life through physician-assisted death, should be allowed to do so. Since at the time the novel was written, and as is still mostly the case today, mental illness is not considered a legal ground for MAID (medical assistance in dying), Elf pleads with Yoli to take her to Switzerland, where the law allows severely depressed individuals to opt for assisted death. When Yoli cannot comply with Elf's wish, Elf responds in the same way that her father, Jacob (and Mel Toews), did: she walks in front of a moving train. After her death, the novel turns to how Yoli and her mother, Lottie, move to Toronto, purchase a house, and rebuild their lives, much as Miriam Toews and her mother, Elvira, did after Marjorie's death.

Autofictional works exist in a liminal space in which they are neither entirely fiction nor entirely non-fiction. Instead, in autofiction, the artistic distance afforded through writing provides the psychic space for an author to reframe the past. Thus, Toews, who experienced the deaths by suicide of her father and sister, mediates the emotions common to many suicide survivors—grief, guilt, anger, depression—through the discipline of her art. Since a book is a "made" artifact, the act of writing about trauma provides some distance by forcing the writer to reframe the experience in a way that is accessible to readers and organized by artistic decisions on language, narrative strategy, and what to include and exclude. As Jeanette Winterson, herself a writer of autofiction, remarks, "reading yourself as a fiction as well as a fact is the only way to keep the narrative open—the only way to stop the story running away under its own momentum, often towards an ending no one wants" (*Why Be Happy?* 119). Trauma circles back on itself and can inspire endless recriminations, fears, and terrors, but for Winterson, as for Toews, autofiction allows writers to grasp the difficulties of their lives, examine those difficulties from the perspective of art, and refine responses to them.

Vulnerable Subjects: The Author and Her Stories

When it comes to writing of the pain of others, however, autofiction can be morally complex, and this complexity should be addressed particularly in the case of *Swing Low*, in which Toews writes in the voice of a man who preferred to keep his inner life private. Many have discussed the tension that exists regarding how much authors should reveal in autobiographical writing: honest reporting versus protection of others' privacy. As Leigh Gilmore[2] argues in *The Limits of Autobiography: Trauma and Testimony*, we demand autobiography's "separateness from fiction" (8), and we judge life writing according to the accuracy of its testimony.[3] In a well-publicized case, when James Frey falsely portrayed *A Million Little Pieces* as an autobiographical account, Oprah Winfrey said that he had "betrayed millions of readers" who had trusted the veracity of "his" life story (qtd. in Wyatt A1). Toews herself has weighed in on this controversy. When asked by Melissa Steele whether she had any sympathy for Frey, Toews replied that "I don't have any sympathy for him. He was passing something off as something that it wasn't." She explained how all that Frey and his publisher "needed was a line that said some elements of the book had been fabricated" ("'Authentic'" 9). In another interview, Toews said that, "especially when it comes to memoir; as we've seen in the past, when you tell the reader, 'This is true. This all happened' and then it didn't—you get into a lot of trouble. They hate that. They feel betrayed, and ripped off, and angry. And that makes sense. It's lying in a way. It's a moral thing" ("Rumpus Interview").

Yet, as Paul John Eakin asserts, "life writers are criticized not only for *not* telling the truth—personal and historical—but also for telling too much truth" (3). Since our lives are lived in relation to others, telling our own stories might mean revealing secrets that expose friends and family members to scrutiny that they neither profit from nor desire. It is one thing, after all, to discuss one's own mental illness, conviction for shoplifting, or extramarital affair, but when a writer reveals the secrets of others it can be interpreted as violation and betrayal. So strong is the expectation of the right to privacy that even authors of fiction have been chastised for coming too close to actual people and events. Robert Thacker, for example, discusses how the inhabitants of Wingham, Ontario, were unhappy when they saw aspects of themselves in Alice Munro's short stories (45, 76–78, 159). Nor is the linking of fictional characters with their supposed real-life counterparts a recent phenomenon. Charlotte Brontë, for instance, received censure when some readers thought that the Reverend Brocklehurst in *Jane Eyre* was an unfair depiction of the Reverend William Carus Wilson.[4]

Because it implicitly references biographical details, autofiction can have ethical dilemmas similar to those of life writing, including debates about the status of what life writing and disability studies theorist G. Thomas Couser calls "vulnerable subjects." As Couser writes, "deliberation on the ethics of life writing entails weighing competing values: the desire to tell one's story and the need to protect others, the obligation to truth and the obligations of trust" (*Vulnerable Subjects* 198). In his definition, vulnerable subjects are "persons who are liable to exposure by someone with whom they are involved in an intimate or trust-based relationship but are unable to represent themselves in writing or to offer meaningful consent to their representation by someone else" (xii). Examples include parents of children with severe developmental disabilities or adults who narrate the story of a parent's decline into dementia. In each case, the individual subject cannot offer a response or provide clarification. In the case of commercially success-ful works such as John Bayley's *Elegy for Iris* (1999), the writer profits from a tale that the vulnerable person might not have wanted told. Using that book as an example, Couser summarizes that "the very cause of subjects' vulnerability to exploitation may seem to make them invulnerable to certain kinds of harm—such as psychic pain or harm to reputation." Even though subjects are incapacitated, however, their privacy is still violated since their infirmities are co-opted into a story not only of their own losses but also of the losses of those who write about them. "Ironically," Couser continues, "the assumption of their invulnerability to harm may make them all the more prone to abuse" (23). Deceased or without a voice, vulnerable subjects cannot speak back to what is written about them.

One could argue that those who die before writers tell their stories are no longer vulnerable. Couser, however, counters this rationalization by saying that "*death* would not seem to qualify as a state of dependence;

indeed, it might seem to suggest utter invulnerability to harm; but I would argue that it entails maximum vulnerability to posthumous misrepresentation because it precludes self-defense" (*Vulnerable Subjects* 16). Often told to loved ones ahead of time, final instructions left by the deceased prove that on some level the living believe that their bodies retain their identities even after their brain waves have ceased or, for the more religious, their souls have left their physical bodies. Why else would it matter that their ashes are spread at a particular place or that they are buried in an expensive coffin? As Couser writes, "we trust that after we die our corpse will be treated with respect, that our 'will' will be honored, and that secrets we may have divulged will be respected. . . . In this regard, death may be the state of ultimate vulnerability and dependency" (16). The lengths to which some will go to honour the deceased's wishes imply that many believe that, though a person has died, his or her memory and desires live on.[5]

Swing Low, especially, calls into question the interplay between the author's compulsion to tell her father's story and the vulnerability of those who, because of their close connection to the author, are necessarily exposed in the telling. Toews attributes writing in her father's voice to her desire to commemorate her father, who concealed his mental illness and considered himself a failure, but his very reticence about his personal life calls into question her decision to write as if he were speaking. As Magdalene Redekop noted in an early review of *Swing Low*, "some readers will find this appropriation of voice an unforgivable transgression" (244). She continues that "the fact remains that the father, being dead, cannot make this 'life' an authorized version and this is the painful open secret of this book" (245), raising the question of when, if ever, a writer can be excused for speaking in another's voice, especially when the writer reveals secrets that the subject wanted to keep private. Redekop tempers her critique by describing *Swing Low* as part of Toews's grieving process, as "personal therapy" (245), and as an expression of her love for her father.

Grace Kehler expresses similar concerns when she writes about teaching *Swing Low* during graduate seminars: "While we never achieved a feeling of ease regarding Toews's act of speaking for and as another (and arguably should not have been able to achieve that), collectively we came to appreciate her attention to pain as a '*pedagogy of expressive possibility*'" ("Transformative Encounters" 167).[6] In part, Kehler and her class explain Toews's disregard of her father's wish for silence by framing Toews as part of a long Mennonite tradition of standing up to violence. "Toews," Kehler writes, "frequently highlights the violence of stigmatizing and silencing non-conformists within the Mennonite community—though she indicts as well other institutions like medicine that similarly pride themselves on refraining from harm" (161). Mel was a believer with perfect church attendance, so theoretically he would have been safe from his community's censure. However, as Toews describes in "A Father's Faith," she believes that censure is built into the religion itself. When every action or thought "gets you closer to or farther away from eternal life," and "to be human, basically, is to be a sinner," one can become so caught up in perfecting the self that one ends up full of "self-loathing." Fundamentalism can foster internalized violence and hence depression. When one considers that some Steinbach Mennonites, according to Toews, construed "depression or despair . . . to be the result of a lack of faith" (195), one could say that self-loathing invites even more self-loathing. In writing in the voice of her father, Toews insists that his life had value, even if he never believed that to be so.

Two other theories shed light on Toews's authorial decisions in *Swing Low*: Couser's conception of collaborative autobiography and Eakin's description of "relational lives." "The ethical difficulties of collaborative autobiography," writes Couser, "are rooted in its nearly oxymoronic status" (*Vulnerable Subjects* 35). Although the word *collaborative* suggests cooperation between two or more people, the prefix *auto* suggests one self, and this highlights the power differentials that can result when one person writes another's story. Couser delineates a range of power relations that can occur in collaborative autobiography, from ethnographic collaboration in which subjects might have little control over how they are portrayed (42–44) to the opposite power differential in the "as-told-to" celebrity autobiography, in which the celebrity "assumes or is given more credit for the writing than is legitimate" (49) and gets to dictate the "spin" placed on the life story.

Although ideal collaboration posits equal partnership, it is difficult to achieve this goal when one person has control of the "pen" and the other control of the narrative. Hospitalized for severe depression, confused, and forgetful, Mel Toews had control over very little. In fact, as Toews tells readers in her "prologue" to *Swing Low*, his very helplessness made him ask her to "write things down for him, words and sentences that would lead him out of his confusion and sadness to a place and time that he might understand" (3). As Toews continues, "soon I was filling up pages of yellow legal notepads with writing from his own point of view so he could understand it when he read it to himself. After his death, when I began writing this book, I continued to write in the same way. It was a natural extension of the writing I'd done for him in the hospital, and a way, though not a perfect one, of hearing what my father might have talked about if he'd ever allowed himself to. If he'd ever thought it would matter to anybody" (3–4). Toews, then, frames *Swing Low* as a continuing dialogue with her father, a kind of therapeutic elucidation of his essential self.

Depression, after all, can be hidden in a way that physical challenges often cannot. Some depressives take on a typical stance, slumping forward and avoiding eye contact, whereas others cannot muster the energy to get out of bed, wash, or eat. Still others, like Mel before he retired, are high functioning, hiding their symptoms successfully from everyone but close family members. In *All My Puny Sorrows*, Elf is similarly able to trick hospital staff when, after two non-fatal suicide attempts, she twice convinces her carers that she has recovered enough to be sent home. In the first instance, Elf cuts her wrists and drinks bleach two weeks after she leaves the Psychiatric Ward. Hospitalized once again, she eventually convinces doctors to give her a day pass to celebrate her birthday, only to use that opportunity to step in front of a moving train. As a long-time mental health patient, Elf knows what staff need to hear to discharge her from the hospital. Yoli, who has heard Elf tell "the nurses and the doctors [before] that she's feeling good, positive, not suicidal, not at all," compares her performance as a recovered patient to "giving a rehearsed speech at the Oscars" (108). Elf hides her ongoing depression under assurances of recovery, only to turn around and embrace self-destruction. Although one must take care when comparing a fictional character with her real-life counterpart, one might speculate that, if Marjorie Toews were as good at hiding her pain from others as her father was at hiding his, Toews has constructed narratives that attempt to understand her father and sister more clearly, even as they themselves found ways to hide their deepest thoughts from others.

Toews's description of her writing process is also evocative of Eakin's concept of relational lives: that is, autobiographies that have as their main subject not the author of the work but a relationship that the author deems essential to his or her formation of self. "Narrative structure in these cases," Eakin says, "is telling us something fundamental about the relational structure of the autobiographer's identity, about its roots and involvement in another's life and story" ("Relational Selves" 71). In one of the cases that Eakin mentions, *Maus: A Survivor's Tale* (1986, 1991) by Art Spiegelman, "the autobiographical act is doubled, for the story of the other, of the informant (Art Spiegelman's father Vladek, for example), is accompanied by the story of the individual gathering this oral history (Art Spiegelman himself)" (70–71). As Eakin also points out, Spiegelman tells "the story of the story" (72), exploring how his life is intertwined with his father's experience. Spiegelman mitigates his use of his father's voice by highlighting that he, the son, is telling and interpreting his father's narrative.

Toews also tells "the story of the story." She writes using her father's imagined voice, but occasionally she reminds the reader of what she is doing, often writing into Mel's inner dialogue passages that remind the reader of his daughter's role as amanuensis. When Mel recounts, for instance, a confrontation between his daughters and hospital staff, he ends the episode by saying that "one daughter shushes other daughter. They will soon come into my room with their lies and their smiles and their hugs and kisses. We'll write things down together in big block letters (I haven't the heart to tell them I'm not blind) and I hope they don't leave too soon" (*Swing Low* 22). In a later passage, Mel narrates that "you should have seen my face light up when my daughter brought these notepads in to the hospital. . . . I tried to write down what I thought were the pertinent points. I often asked her to repeat them" (48). Moira Farr astutely writes that this passage "really would have more comfortably read, 'You should have seen his face light up when I. . . .'" The awkwardness of the passage gives the reader a sense of Mel watching himself or, more accurately, of Toews watching/writing Mel. Farr continues that "it seemed more likely to me that it would be a writer-daughter noting the irony of a silent father choosing 'Oh for a Thousand Tongues to Sing' as his favourite hymn than the devout churchgoer himself. In spots like these, the reader feels the strain of the imagined voice, and perhaps wishes the daughter-author could somehow unmask herself." When Toews uses anaphora in her description of how Mel came to ask her to record his thoughts, the effect is more literary than the ramblings of a confused elderly man: "But towards the end I was going in circles. Towards the end I was going in circles. Towards the end I asked her to write it down for me" (*Swing Low* 48). Passages such as this remind the reader of the artifice involved in recreating Mel's narrative voice, that it is Mel's *daughter*, already a published author, who translates his words onto the page and organizes them into a volume. Farr sums it up well when she says that what Toews does in *Swing Low* is "a kind of literary high-wire act that few would dare to try."

As the daughter of a father who almost never spoke at home, Toews, as is true of a relational life, also writes herself into his thoughts by including descriptions of the love that he felt for her but rarely expressed. Growing up with a father as depressed as Mel would have been difficult and, judging from her accounts of him and similar fathers in her other works, could result in hurt and estrangement. After forcing Miriam to mow the lawn in the very afternoon that she is leaving home for a post–high school graduation adventure, Mel hears her "asking Elvira [her mother] why I had to be that way, why I was the way I was, and Elvira saying nothing but I don't know, honey, I don't know" (*Swing Low* 195). Mel also describes his strained relationship with his adolescent daughters: "I didn't know how to be with them, other than as a teacher, and the odd time I made an effort to interact casually and affectionately as I felt a father should, it felt forced and artificial and I knew they sensed it too, and I became self-conscious. I retreated into my bedroom, reassuring them with a few words of my love and concern, and smiling at them often like a distant relative, unsure how to proceed from there" (171). In such passages, Mel's thoughts intersect with his daughter's need to have him *think* them. In effect, Toews writes in the assurances of her father's love that were not forthcoming during his lifetime.

As Toews writes in *Swing Low*, "words couldn't save my father" (227), but through imagination and empathy she can save herself and create works that live on in the minds of those who need hope and inspiration in order to continue with their own lives. *Swing Low* and, to a lesser extent, *All My Puny Sorrows* document the negative effects of silence in Mel's life and suggest an additional reason for Toews's disclosures about her father's and sister's deaths. As a child, Mel watched as his depressed father withdrew when faced with emotional conflict, and thus he learned the importance of silence and denial. While hospitalized for his first mental breakdown at age seventeen, Mel confessed his family situation to a psychiatrist, and consequently his mother and father rebuked him for destroying the family honour. In response, he resolved never to speak of his family to anyone. The fictional Mel describes how he "was prisoner and warden simultaneously, longing to free myself with words while going to every effort to prevent the words from escaping the darkness of my mind" (86–87). Toews recounts the cognitive dissonance that she and her sister felt when they entered their father's grade six classroom and discovered an enthusiastic and outgoing man with a "booming" voice (2). But Mel paid for his energetic classroom persona by shutting down completely when not in public. Toews relates that "there was only one thing" that she, her mother, and her sister "missed, and that was hearing him speak" (2). An extrovert in the classroom, Mel collapsed into withdrawn silence while at home. By writing *Swing Low*, Toews broke that silence by acknowledging her father's mental illness, bringing into the open what Mel and certain members of his family worked so hard to hide. In an interview with Dave Weich, Toews explained that, "when somebody you know and love has [died through] suicide, it's so hard to understand. You just don't know how it could have happened. You want to be inside that person's head so you can figure out why this person made this choice. Was it rational? Irrational? *Let's put everything together and see.* I wanted to be inside his head, and in order to do that I had to become him" ("Miriam Toews Breaks Out"). Her formulation here, however, begs the question of whether the resilient and resourceful daughter—or for that matter anyone—can truly get inside the head of another person. Kehler names the voice in *Swing*

Low a "hybrid voice" ("Transformative Encounters" 170), a term that aptly underlines how daughter and father are a combined presence in the text.

Kehler also notes that "Toews's writing bears witness to Mel's traumas, which lead to silence, while the historical-imaginative voice of Mel bears witness to the impact his silences had on the family members he loved but for whom he could not always be present. He ruminates on *their* hurts as well as his own" ("Transformative Encounters" 169–70). Thus, when Toews recounts her father's inner monologue about his daughters, and particularly about his relationship with her, she makes a reparative gesture not only with regard to Mel but also in relation to herself. In *Swing Low*, Toews the writer has her imagined father (in the sense that she is writing using his voice) recount several instances when he was close to her: a Ferris wheel ride at Walt Disney World (192), "exchang[ing] fatalistic grimaces" with her as they sat in the back seat of a car winding its way up the side of a mountain (186), Miriam hanging upside down and looking in his bedroom window (139). Mel also writes of consoling Miriam after she gets in trouble at school and recounts how "this rare connection between the two of us sustained me for days" (173). Since, as *Swing Low* recounts, Miriam often "baffled" Mel with her rebellious behaviour such as smoking cigarettes, drinking beer, hanging out with French boys, and especially twice getting pregnant out of wedlock (191–92, 201), she now restores their relationship.

Were it not for the many explanatory interviews that Toews gave around the time that *All My Puny Sorrows* was published in 2014 and the numerous correspondences between it and *Swing Low*, her account of her sister Marjorie's life and death in *Puny Sorrows* could rest under the mantle of fiction, in which the author's life is considered raw material for, but not an exact rendition of, elements from "real life." For readers familiar with Toews's work, however, *Swing Low* serves as a paratext for the later novel. There are simply too many correspondences between Toews's account of her father's life and those details recounted in *Puny Sorrows*. Elf and Yoli are not exact replicas of Marjorie and Miriam, yet the correspondences between *Swing Low* and *All My Puny Sorrows* seem to be more prominent than the differences. Both Elf and Marjorie are said to have inherited their father's beautiful green eyes (*All* 28; *Swing Low* 159), and Elf is six years older than Yoli (as Marjorie was six years older than Miriam). In *Swing Low*, Mel talks about how he remained silent at home for an entire year, speaking only in public (135), and Yoli refers to the same incident in *Puny Sorrows*: "Sometimes my sister stops talking. Our father did it too, once for a whole year" (25). Similarities also exist in how Toews describes herself as intervening in her father's care, asking for Mel to be seen by a psychiatrist and for his illness to be taken seriously (*Swing Low* 16, 21). After a lifetime of dissimulating and denying his illness (63, 218), Mel can fool hospital staff into thinking that he is more stable than he really is, to the frustration of his daughters. Miriam and Marjorie beg the staff to "make sure he isn't discharged" (51), but in the end Mel walks out of the hospital to his death. As Miriam's fictional counterpart in *Puny Sorrows* writes, "how many times would I beg hospitals not to let my people go? Elf and I begged and begged and begged the hospital in East Village not to let our father go but they let him go anyway and then he was gone for good" (225). Such a scenario plays out in *Swing Low* as well as the daughters argue that their father is pretending to be better in order to be allowed to go home (22).

In yet another example, *All My Puny Sorrows* begins with Elf, Yoli, and their parents watching while their old house is moved away to make room for the expansion of a car dealership (1–2, 6–8). This event traumatizes their father, who sold the house only because he was too fragile to withstand the dealership owner's pressure. In her writing, Toews places particular weight on this incident, blaming it for the mental collapse of her father. The 1996 edition of *Summer of My Amazing Luck* (though not the 2006 revised edition), *Swing Low*, *Puny Sorrows*, and several of her other works mention the literal loss of this home: the so-called pink house that Geoffrey Van Alstyne/Mel Toews/Jacob Von Riesen built early in their married lives. "In 1976," Toews writes, the "small world" of her father "turned upside down when [he] lost [his] home again and this time for good." It was a major project for him to build a house "from scratch" for his family, but as the town expanded the house was in the way of the car dealership, whose owner needed more land to grow his business (*Swing Low* 176). "Business was next to godliness in our town," Toews explains in another description of the incident ("Peace" 16), and Mel's right to personal property was deemed less important than a business owner's financial interests. According to Toews, her father was hounded by the car dealership's owner and a real estate agent and made to feel that he was wrong to stand in the way of commerce. Fearing confrontation, Mel sold his pink house, but he never recovered from losing his special place. As Toews commented,

> I see now, as an adult looking back, that it was very pivotal in my father's life, for sure, and maybe in my mother's life. I mean my mom is so resilient, she bounces around, and she does her thing. And I think part of the reason it was pivotal for me as a kid was because I saw how, I saw for probably the first time, you know, I was twelve, and I was getting older, you know, wiser, . . . how devastated my dad was, and the reaction, how he reacted to it, and the effect that it had on him, and I remember thinking, oh, this was a *dream* for him. This was a house that he built, that he designed, that he loved. . . . So I witnessed all that for the first time, seeing how much my dad suffered. And it was all associated with that house. (interview with Reed)

This quotation highlights several important ideas about home as well as Toews's continued framing of the loss of the house as a study of the comparative resilience of her mother and father. Her mother was able to recover from personal setbacks, whereas her father was devastated when the house was taken away. Having the internal strength that her husband lacked, Elvira Toews, whom Toews describes in an interview with Shelagh Rogers as "the most resilient person I've ever known" ("Why a Nine-Year-Old"), was able to continue with her many projects and other interests, but Mel, for whom the loss of the house was the loss of a dream of safety, never fully recovered. Toews mentioned that resilience is "hard to define in relation to mental illness because of course it's an illness and requires treatment, medicine, therapy, whatever. But life itself, aside from the added weight of illness, 'requires' resilience, strength, and courage" (email to the author, 8 August 2021). Her resilient characters can recover from even the most devastating threats to home, whereas those who suffer from mental illness often cannot.

Other events, though not appearing in *Swing Low*, correspond to biographical incidents that Toews has recounted in interviews. In *All My Puny Sorrows*, for example, Yoli tries to get her sister seen by the attending psychiatrist, who rarely shows up and is dismissive when he does (173–74, 213). Like Miriam did with Marjorie, Yoli tries to convince hospital staff to keep Elf in care, but instead they give her a day pass. Elf uses the pass to walk to the train tracks and take her own life, just as Marjorie did (Medley; *All* 261–63). In *Puny Sorrows*, Yoli and Elf's cousin Leni died by suicide three years after her uncle Jacob. Toews had a similar experience when "a very very close cousin" died by suicide "a couple years after [her] dad did" ("Miriam Toews Breaks Out"). *Puny Sorrows* also narrates a conversation in which Yoli tells Elf "it's time to fight now" and Elf replies "I've been fighting for thirty years" (240). Toews asserts that "my sister said that to me" ("Author Miriam Toews"). Like Yoli, Miriam, at the request of her sister, researched taking Marjorie to Switzerland for a physician-assisted death (Medley). Toews said in an interview that, "in my case with *AMPS*, I can say it's a novel—and it is. That gives me the freedom to make stuff up. But I can also say it's the most autobiographical novel that I've ever written, and people who know me who are familiar with what my family experienced will say, 'Oh, that happened, and that happened, but that didn't happen'" ("Rumpus Interview").

Given how closely Toews aligns the stories of Marjorie's and Elf's deaths by suicide in *All My Puny Sorrows*, readers might ask, as others have regarding *Swing Low* and Mel, how much of her experiences would Marjorie have wanted her sister to share? *Puny Sorrows* describes how Elf and her family value her privacy. Her partner, Nic, for instance, is "furious because a neighbour of theirs saw Elf being loaded into the ambulance covered in blood and told a few other neighbours and now a reporter has called Nic asking about Elf's condition" (147). Her agent, Claudio, protects her reputation by telling reporters that Elf "bail[ed] from her tour due to exhaustion" and that "her family has asked for privacy." Yoli's reply—"we did? . . . Is anyone talking to them [the reporters]?"—indicates that Yoli, too, wants to shelter Elf from the press in need of a juicy story (195). The ensuing conversation between Nic and Yoli indicates the conflict between acknowledging a stigmatizing condition and wanting to protect an already vulnerable individual from further harm. Learning that a fellow musician went to visit Elf in the hospital, Yoli and Nic talk:

> Oh, so everyone's gonna know now, I said. Did he talk to her?
>
> It doesn't really matter, said Nic. I mean the truth is the truth.
>
> I just want . . . I was hoping to protect her.
>
> You have been, I said. You've been protecting her. You've always protected her. (196; ellipsis in the original)

Elf, a famous concert pianist, is more vulnerable to her situation becoming news fodder than a less famous person would be, yet the underlying distress that "everybody is going to know" suggests that vulnerable subjects have a right to privacy and to control how and when their experiences are disclosed. Her fame makes Elf vulnerable to excessive attention and gossip-mongering. In the case of Marjorie, her sister's status as a famous Canadian writer means that, once committed to novelistic form, Marjorie's struggle with mental illness will be known and discussed by many readers who otherwise would not even know her name. Yet, as Nic says, "the truth is the truth," and the more people disclose their mental illnesses, the more likely those illnesses will lose their stigma.

In a nuanced essay, "Friendship, Fiction, and Memoir: Trust and Betrayal in Writing from One's Own Life," Claudia Mills outlines the tension between the writer's need for material and friends' and family members' preference for privacy: "To be a writer is to be committed to telling the truth, sometimes the literal truth (for writers of nonfiction), sometimes a 'deeper' truth which is more than mere factual accuracy but a kind of fidelity to what *is*. Writers can write only the truths that they know, which are often the truths drawn from their own friendships and family relationships" (104). In speaking of her sister, Toews justifies her revelations by saying that

> I wouldn't want to expose the deep secrets or the sort of very personal intimate details of anybody that I knew. I'm willing

to expose my own, but you know in this case my sister's gone, my father's gone, and I feel that their story, if I'm able to tell it in a way that is useful to other people, then I am willing to tell that story if it can generate a discussion about mental illness, about suicide, about coping with suicide after the fact. Then I'm willing to do it. To draw these things, drag them, into the light. ("Miriam Toews Brings")[7]

Toews clearly feels the tension between her social responsibility as an author and her sister's status as a vulnerable subject, but she justifies her disclosures as service to the larger public good of destigmatizing mental illness.

Suicide Survivorship and the Need for Narrative

Toews's authorial decisions may well be influenced by her status as a survivor of the violent deaths of her father and sister, for, as studies of suicide survivorship have shown, suicide can make survivors themselves vulnerable subjects. "It has been suggested that for every suicide death a minimum of six individuals are deeply affected by this traumatic event" (Begley and Quayle 26), and some place the numbers much higher (Levi-Belz and Lev-Ari 1). In addition to the loss of a loved one, suicide survivors must cope with the social stigma associated with suicide, including guilt that they did not do more to help prevent the death, feelings of rejection, and realization that they might not have known the deceased as well as they thought. Toews, for instance, wrote in a published letter, "Do you feel guilty for not having prevented your dad from killing himself? (Yes.) Do you feel you need to atone for his death? (Yes.)" ("On Studying Psychology"). Such feelings of grief and guilt are a common reaction to a loved one's suicide. Moreover, those close to a victim of suicide statistically are more likely to consider suicide themselves (Begley and Quayle 27; Jamison 169; Jordan 680; Ratnarajah and Schofield 618; Sheehan et al. 331) or to experience "adverse health effects" at a greater rate than the general population (Rostila, Saarela, and Kawachi 919).

When Toews published *Swing Low* in 2000, she did not know that her sister would die by suicide in 2010, but Marjorie's death confirms how suicide survivors themselves can be vulnerable to psychological illness either because of the hereditary nature of some mental illnesses or because of the trauma of losing a loved one. The autofictional works of Toews can be understood as her attempts to reassess her relationships with her father and sister, understand them in the light of suicide, and reconcile herself to their deaths. As Toews writes in *Swing Low*, "by dragging some of the awful details into the light of day, they became much less frightening. I have to admit, my father didn't feel the same way, but he found a way to alleviate his pain, and so have I" (4). The lasting damage accruing to suicide survivorship necessitates acts of healing that can include intimate disclosures about the primary vulnerable subject—the person who has died by suicide—by the secondary vulnerable subject—the suicide survivor. Resilience might sometimes necessitate, therefore, a betrayal of confidence as the suicide survivor finds a way to cope with intense and ongoing loss.

Edwin Shneidman writes that "the person who [dies by] suicide puts his psychological skeleton in the survivor's emotional closet" (qtd. in Rostila, Saarela, and Kawachi 919; see also Sanderson 33). Traditionally, the metaphor of the skeleton in the closet refers to a secret that, if exposed, will damage the one who holds it. In the sense that suicide reveals the psychological anguish of those who take their own lives, it exposes the skeleton in the closet, but as Shneidman implies, the damage caused by the revelation affects suicide survivors as well. Richard K. Sanderson asserts in "Relational Deaths: Narratives of Suicide Survivorship" that suicide "is more than a deliberate act of lethal self-destruction: It is also a *communication*, an interpersonal or 'dyadic' act, a self-dramatization performed before an audience consisting of the suicide and of *other* persons, usually members of the suicide's family" (35; emphasis in original). After the suicide of a loved one, survivors might perceive the "deeply wounding message—life is not worth living" (35)—and feel saddened because the deceased person's longing for death was stronger than love for those left behind.

Sanderson perceptively points out how survivors need to "decipher" (36) the suicidal act in order to give it meaning in their own and the deceased person's lives. First, the survivor looks to find what caused the suicide and to assign blame. Second, the survivor tries to give the suicidal act meaning so that "the suicide, in the old cliché, 'will not have died in vain'" (36). Survivors might portray writing about suicide as a reparative act in which the writer helps others to recognize the signs of potential suicide, lobbies for improved mental health care, lessens the stigma attached to death by suicide by talking about it directly, and, perhaps most importantly, comes to terms with the suicide and finds peace (36–37). To return to Shneidman's metaphor, survivors might need to exorcise the skeleton in the closet by talking about it openly. Sanderson concludes that "as an act of self-definition, as a communication that both gives shape to one's life and expresses a yearning for a different life, suicide bears a certain resemblance to autobiography itself. If killing himself or herself is the suicide's 'autobiographical act,' then retelling that death in a published (auto)biography is, for some survivors, a way to regain control over the family story and over their own lives" (44). *Swing Low* and *All My Puny Sorrows*, in Sanderson's sense, are autobiographical acts of healing. Toews uses the liminal space between autobiography and fiction to dramatize and to process her father's and sister's violent deaths.

Like Lottie in *All My Puny Sorrows*, who resists the funeral director's kind impulse to spare her the sight of Elf's damaged face, Toews looks at the suicides of her father and sister directly. In doing so, she counters not only the cone of silence around such deaths but also a cultural impulse to control bereavement in general. In "A New Model of Grief: Bereavement and Biography," Tony Walter writes that "in the classic texts [on bereavement] there is a major theme emphasizing detachment achieved through the working through of feelings, and a minor theme emphasizing the continued presence of the dead and a continuous conversation with and about them. Because of a largely secular and individualist culture, both the authors of these texts and their readers have typically underplayed or ignored this minor theme—creating the clinical lore of bereavement counseling" (8)[8]—that encourages detachment from the deceased and views prolonged remembrance of the dead as "complicated" grief requiring therapeutic intervention. Mardi Horowitz and co-authors suggest a diagnosis of complicated grief if, a year after the death of a loved one, the client is still experiencing "intense intrusive thoughts, pangs of severe emotion, distressing yearnings, feeling excessively alone and empty, excessively avoiding tasks reminiscent of the deceased, unusual sleep disturbances, and maladaptive levels of loss of interest in personal activities" (904).[9] In contrast, Walter proposes what he calls "a new model of grief" (7) that encourages the bereaved to "construct an enduring and shared memory of the dead" (14). By talking to others about the deceased and by constructing joint biographies, the bereaved can find continuing places for the dead in their own lives and move toward peace by not forgetting the dead but celebrating their ongoing roles in the lives of the living. "In other words," writes Walter, "bereavement is part of the process of (auto)biography, and the biographical imperative—the need to make sense of self and others in a continuing narrative—is the motor that drives bereavement behaviour" (20).

In a response to Walter's "new model of grief," Arnar Árnason takes Walter's point a step further: "We need to emphasize that the stories of the bereaved are creative achievements of 'emplotment'—the construction of plots—and characterization; they are stories rather than history" (189). The bereaved use story not only to tell what happened in the deceased's life but also to give that person a continuing role as the bereaved individual moves forward. As Árnason points out, bereavement stories contextualize the deceased in the survivor's life narrative, and in this sense they are subjective rather than objectively accurate. They are not so much about what happened as they are about how what happened fits into an ongoing story of life without the deceased (195–96). Differentiating between "grief," the raw and immediate pain that survivors feel in the aftermath of a loved one's death, and "mourning," a healing experience that moves the mourner forward into consolation and acceptance, Margaret Steffler contrasts the rawness of Toews's memoir of her father with the "fiction-elegy" for her sister in *All My Puny Sorrows* ("Writing through the Words" 120). "It is through intense grief" that Yoli Von Riesen is "able to create presence out of absence, successfully drawing mourning out of grief, consolation out of mourning, and transforming backward glances into forward movement" (121). If one thinks of Árnason's and Walter's arguments about the importance of creating stories that reflect the lives of the deceased in the minds of the living, then *Puny Sorrows* shows Toews further along in the process of mourning—perhaps because she knew her sister better than she knew her father, a cipher to her while he was alive. In some ways, Toews has to "create" her father before she can mourn him.

"Narrative Wreckage"

Toews, however, recreates her father's life through an artistic reordering of the materials available to her, changing what Arthur W. Frank calls a "chaos narrative" into a profoundly moving account of her father's long struggle with mental illness. In *The Wounded Storyteller: Body, Illness, and Ethics*, Frank describes how illness challenges the concept of a coherent self. "The illness story," he writes, "is wrecked because its present is not what the past was supposed to lead up to, and the future is scarcely thinkable" (55). The narrative break, or wreckage, caused by illness can be counteracted through the creation of a new story—one that tells how illness was encountered, cured, or accepted and especially how illness changed the individual's sense of self. Frank divides illness narratives into three main "types": the restitution narrative, the chaos narrative, and the quest narrative.

Concerned with recovery, the restitution story focuses "on sickness as interruption, but this interruption is finite and remediable" (Frank 89). Such narratives often see illness as an anomaly that can be fixed through the interventions of modern medical technologies. As Frank suggests, however, chronic illness challenges the restitution narrative, for many illnesses, such as Alzheimer's or Parkinson's, can be palliated but not yet cured. "When restitution does not happen," Frank states, "other stories have to be prepared or the narrative wreckage will be real" (94).

The other two types in his taxonomy occur primarily when an illness proves to be chronic or produces a death sentence. The chaos narrative, in many ways, is not a story at all, for he calls it an "*anti-narrative*" that "imagines life never getting better" (98, 97), much as is the case, incidentally, with the clinical depression described in the two works under discussion here.

Frank writes that, "in telling the events of one's life, events are mediated by the telling. But in the lived chaos there is no mediation, only immediacy. The body is imprisoned in the frustrated needs of the moment. The person living the chaos story has no distance from her life and no reflective grasp on it. Lived chaos makes reflection, and consequently story-telling, impossible" (98). To expand his thesis, suicide can be interpreted as the ultimate statement in a chaos narrative, for the person who experiences suicidal thoughts may believe that restitution, the potential for a cure, is impossible; that medicine, our modern panacea, does not always work; and that the future, which could hold the possibility of a successful quest for wholeness, is without hope.

Unlike the chaos narrative, the quest narrative takes illness and turns it into a story of overcoming, of finding some meaning or spiritual fulfillment. The writer of such a narrative steps back from his or her experience and recognizes the overall meaning that has been gained, the insights raised, by being ill. Even though narrators might have lived through chaos, they perform a redemptive action in writing their tales. In retrospect, the illness assumes purpose and meaning. In *Swing Low*'s moving first-person portrayal of the life, manic-depressive illness, and eventual suicide of her father, Toews takes his incoherent, largely silenced personal story, his unspoken chaos narrative, and makes it into a quest story. The power of this work comes from the interplay between Mel's chaos and Miriam's resilience.

"Nothing accomplished," Mel's first words in *Swing Low*, his daughter recounts, were "two hopeless words, spoken in a whisper by a man who felt he had failed on every level" (1). Significantly, Mel spoke these words the day before his death by suicide, and thus they serve as his final verdict on his life. His conception of biography, mentioned several times throughout *Swing Low*, supports his self-assessment that his life has been meaningless, for Mel views biography as the province of "famous men and women, mostly politicians and journalists," whose "life stories help to give [his] own a little context, and also inspiration" (47). His daughter, however, believes that his story is worth telling, and thus the following pages can be interpreted as her quest to bring meaning to her father's life. Her accomplishment in *Swing Low* is both to recount Mel's chaotic and broken thoughts and to show

how much Mel actually achieved. She overlays his sense of chaos with her own sense of discovery and hope. As we learn in the prologue, for instance, Toews got very few of the stories that she tells about her father's life from Mel himself: "I became obsessed with knowing all that I could about his life, searching, I suppose, for clues that would ultimately lead me to the cause of his death. With the help of my mother and my sister and Dad's friends, colleagues, and relatives, I've managed to put a few pieces of the puzzle of his life together" (3). Her metaphor of the "puzzle" of her father's life highlights making order out of chaos, since it takes time and effort to put together an image from a pile of individual pieces. Her structure gives order to what Toews perceives as her father's success in being a responsible citizen, husband, and father despite the depredations of mental illness.

Writing in her father's voice, Toews consistently uses metaphors of chaos and confusion. In the present time of the story, for instance, Mel has been hospitalized for what his doctors call "a psychotic breakdown" (10). Because of his tendency to wander out of the hospital and around town searching for his "lost" wife and home, Mel has been fitted with a "wander guard" (8), but even as a child he had the urge to run from a home that was really no home: a house with a silent, mentally ill father, who like Mel himself retreated for long periods into his room, and a verbally abusive mother who showed love for two of her children but only dislike and anger toward Mel. Just as later he would walk compulsively around town until he developed bleeding blisters on his feet, as a young man he ran all over town without any destination, seemingly an attempt to escape from his circumstances. Mel calls walking his "second-favourite chaos-dispelling activity" (9), yet his wandering itself is chaotic because it has no destination and is usually in search of a stable home that seems to elude him. He continues to "dream of homelessness two or three times a week" (137).

Mel's favourite "chaos-dispelling activity" is writing, and once again writing illustrates his need for order and his failure to achieve it. The fictional Mel recounts how he kept "records of everything, every transaction, every purchase, every drawing my children ever made, every notebook they filled as students. Everything. But they're not doing me much good now" (7). He keeps all of this paper—ranging from household receipts, to casual notes left by his family, to airplane seating plans during family vacations—in an attempt to stay grounded, but finally Mel's compulsive document collecting is not enough to ensure stability. As Toews writes, "in the end, words couldn't save my father" (227). After a lifetime of writing notes to himself on index cards, on the day of his death "the yellow cards that fell out of his pocket and onto the tracks were blank" (227). Toews's great accomplishment in *Swing Low* is to reflect her father's chaos narrative while producing a work that reconstructs his thoughts and celebrates his achievements during his life.

"Autobiographical reconstruction," writes Anne Hunsaker Hawkins, "is often described as a process of selective remembering, ordering those memories into a narrative form, and in so doing discovering—or imposing—meaning" ("Writing" 117). In *Swing Low*, the fictional Mel critiques his attempts at autobiography by saying that "I had intended to review my life as a movie but I can see now that it's not fitting nicely into that format. It has all the structure of a bamboo hut in a hurricane and I must apologize for this lack of cohesion" (26). At one point, Mel admits that "it is interesting that I have used the word 'myself' three times in the last two paragraphs and have no idea what it means anymore" (25). If, as Thomas Couser attests, chronic disability often "annihilates selfhood" (*Recovering Bodies* 5), then it is up to Toews to define her father's selfhood in order to preserve his memory. Mel's comment reminds readers that, though Mel— the book's first-person "I"—ostensibly tells his life story, it is his daughter who creates and "imposes meaning" on the text; in doing so, she juxtaposes her overall artistic organization of *Swing Low* with her father's confusion.

To solidify the book's bittersweet message, Toews ties her account to references to the famous spiritual "Swing Low, Sweet Chariot." Mel's favourite television show was the CBC classic *Hymn Sing*, so it seems to be fitting that Toews should use a religious song as her controlling metaphor, especially since the song's promise of a successful journey to heaven counteracts her father's endless wandering while confirming the faith that sustained Mel during his life. Some people consider suicide a sin. In *All My Puny Sorrows*, for example, Lottie exclaims after one of Elf's non-fatal suicide attempts that Elf "doesn't need forgiving. It's not a sin," and Yoli replies "but fifty billion people would disagree with you" (40). Yoli later condemns the "Mennonite busybodies who tell me in sanctimonious sing-song and with bland pat-a-cake faces that my father's suicide was *evil*" (173). Thus, Toews's insistence that her father has been "carried home" to God is an act of defiance against those who might believe otherwise. "Swing Low, Sweet Chariot" might serve as a hope for both Mel and Marjorie. Fittingly for two people who died by stepping in front of a train, the *chariot* in the song's title is a code word for the underground railroad: the secret network that helped enslaved people to flee oppression. As *Swing Low* shows, Mel was "sometimes up, and sometimes down," so it is consoling to think that "still [his] soul feels heavenly bound," that he will have a chance to establish a new life. In the face of her father's depression, which Toews labels "a clinical, profoundly inadequate word for deep despair" (3), she suggests a counternarrative that affirms her father's Mennonite faith in redemption through God's love. She concludes *Swing Low* with a message of hope and forgiveness: "Dad, you've earned your rest. Schlope schein" [Sleep well] (228).

In a similar way, *All My Puny Sorrows* concentrates on Yoli's movement from a chaos narrative to a quest narrative. To return to the concept of primary and secondary experience of suicide, *Swing Low* focuses on the primary vulnerable subject, the person who commits the act, whereas *Puny Sorrows* focuses on the secondary vulnerable subject, the person who, because of the long-term damage that can accrue to suicide survivors, can experience emotional or even physical illness that also needs to be addressed. Through Yoli, Toews shows the upheaval that mental illness causes even before the suicide as well as the devastation experienced by survivors after it. In contrast to *Swing Low*, *Puny Sorrows* tells the story of the suicide survivor's emergence from the pain created by another's mental illness and death.

In speaking about *All My Puny Sorrows*, Toews states that "writing helps me to create order out of chaos, and make sense of things. It helps me to understand what I've experienced, what I've felt and seen, so it becomes a little easier to handle" ("Author Miriam Toews").[10] Whereas *Swing Low* takes the "chaos" of her father's life and gives it meaning and purpose, Toews's work in *Puny Sorrows* can be said to reclaim a version of her own life, disrupted as it has been by two suicides within her immediate family. Using fictional licence, Toews exaggerates Yoli's unruly home life compared with her own. During the novel, Yoli's apartment becomes progressively run down. Yoli is plagued with mice, carpenter ants, broken appliances, and other domestic disasters. As she fights to keep her sister alive, she flies "back and forth, back and forth, from the west to the east to the west to the east" (269), from her home in Toronto to the hospital in Winnipeg, and as her sister deteriorates Yoli spins more and more out of control. "Listen!" she wants to shout at Elf. "If anyone's gonna kill themselves it should be me. I'm a terrible mother for leaving my kids' father and other father. I'm a terrible wife for sleeping with another man. Men. I'm floundering in a dying non-career" (111). She even keeps losing her manuscript novel, a work that, like her life, seems to have no forward motion and no structure. Meanwhile, Elf is a renowned concert pianist, lives in an ideal house with an ideal partner, and even has a perfect cleaning lady.

Yoli achingly describes the gaping hole left by her sister's death, her mourning, and her deep sense of loss. However, at Tina's funeral Yoli gets a lesson of sorts. While one of Tina's many relatives delivers an anecdote about the deceased, the woman's small son has "a heyday playing with his great-grandma's remains" (253). Momentarily nonplussed by her son's naughty behaviour and ash-covered face, the woman sees her husband remove their son from the scene of the crime and continues to speak, leading Yoli to think that "just because someone is eating the ashes of your protagonist doesn't mean you stop telling the story" (254). In a similar way, Yoli and Lottie must continue with their lives, even as their hearts are breaking, and ironically it is Elf's death that paves the way for the resolution of her mother's and sister's chaos narratives. Lottie, like Elvira Toews in *Swing Low*, is "totally burned out from trying to keep Elf alive," as is Elf's partner, Nic (45). Yoli, in the process of divorcing her husband of sixteen years, has a precocious fourteen-year-old daughter in Toronto, and considerable money troubles, exacerbated by not being able to work on her writing because she is flying back and forth to be with her sister and give Lottie a much-needed break.

While no one wanted Elf to die, her death allows family members to get on with their lives. Elf bequeaths Yoli enough money for her to buy a house, albeit a very run-down one, as well as "a monthly sum of two thousand dollars for the next two years so that [she] can stay at home, in a room of [her] own, and write" (271). At first, both Yoli and her new house are "wrecked." Lottie eventually has to tell Yoli to stop getting drunk and making prank calls to the hospital in retaliation for the medical staff who gave Elf a day pass that allowed her to kill herself. And, to put it mildly, the house that Yoli buys "needs work": "The roof needs replacing, the foundation is full of holes, the yard is overrun with weeds, and skunks live under the deck." The house is also surrounded by a ditch full of sludge, and every morning Yoli picks up used condoms from around her property (275). However, as Lottie, Yoli, and her daughter, Nora, settle into the house, things begin to fall into place. Lottie joins a progressive Mennonite church, and "the church people have come around and planted things in our hideous front yard. Flowers, shrubs, perennials, some decorative rocks" (287). *All My Puny Sorrows* begins with the Von Riesen family's home being carted away, but it ends with a home rising out of the rubble, reclaimed from the chaotic mess around it. Each incremental step requires great effort, yet each step, once made, proves that additional steps are possible.

"What about Zurich?" Physician-Assisted Death

Some argue, as an acquaintance of Yoli's does after Elf's death (277), that suicide is a selfish act since it deprives loved ones of the suicide's presence, but one could also assert that keeping an individual alive against her will, or even preventing her from availing herself of the solace of death, constitutes selfishness in the loved other. Thus, literary critic Amy Rushton identifies a progression in *All My Puny Sorrows* from Yoli's early stance of keeping Elf alive at all costs to a more nuanced understanding of her suffering: "Elf asking Yoli to take her to Switzerland to die is the turning point for Yoli: after years of tearfully, furiously, bullyingly imploring her elder sister to stay alive, she seems to comprehend how *exhausted* Elf is by continuing to live" (204–05). Grace Kehler perceptively describes how

Yoli's behaviour toward her sister mimics elements of the judgemental certainty that the Mennonite elders have exhibited about the Von Riesen family: "Indeed, like the very institutions Yoli deplores, she finds herself quantifying suffering—Elf's should be more livable than her own, given Elf's successes—and advocating conformist narratives of the decent and the good, narratives in which the patient enters into life-sustaining practices through an exertion of reason and will—or becomes the enemy" ("Making Peace" 345). Like the Mennonite elders, Yoli expects Elf to follow a preordained path to happiness. Like the medieval sinner who succumbs to *accidie*, Elf is guilty, according to Yoli, of not recognizing the good in her life and instead focusing on the bad.

Yoli sees Elf's depression, at times, as a personal rejection of her family. "Listen," she says to Elf. "Don't you think that mom has suffered enough with dad and all that shit and now, what, you love the perverse idea of a fucking encore?" As Yoli continues, "if you were perfect you'd stick around. See how life goes, how the kids do, do you ever think about Will and Nora and what this all means to—." As Elf says to her sister, such accusations are "cruel" (*All* 164) because they make her seem like a selfish narcissist who would get better if only she loved her family more. Early in the novel, Yoli identifies the "major problem" in her relationship with Elf: "She wanted to die and I wanted her to live and we were enemies who loved each other" (37–38). But when, the novel asks, is the sacrifice of staying alive too much to bear?

Whereas some people condemn suicide as a failure of love, others celebrate the romantic idea of the suicidal artist as the epitome of creative sensitivity. As a young woman, for instance, Elf, like Nomi Nickel, can be read as a rebel whose mental illness represents a much-needed response to the stultifying environment in which she lives. Elf, Yoli recalls, was once "free and therefore dangerous" (15), a young woman who defied the town's conventions and was totally committed to her art. Yoli remembers with admiration "the moment Elf took control of her life" (14) by defiantly playing Rachmaninoff's Prelude in G Minor, Opus 23, when the "alpha Mennonite" and "his usual posse of elders" (11) showed up at her parents' house to complain about Elf's plan to attend university. Brad S. Born elaborates how Toews writes against the stereotype that mental illness creates great art: "Regarding her sister Elf's mental illness, adult Yoli very clearly separates her fond reminiscence of her sister's loudly voiced romantic rebellion from her internalized, largely silent, suicidal depression. Elf's depression halts her concert piano tour. Her suicide attempts silence her music." Instead of playing passionately on the world stage, a depressed Elf feels as if she has a glass piano lodged inside her body, and she can hardly breathe for fear of breaking it. As Toews says in an interview with Anna Fitzpatrick, "I think there are people who view that artists are—that a certain type of mental illness, or a certain type of pain, like internal psychic pain is the thing that creates questioning, and creates good art. Sometimes it does, but it's certainly not necessary, I don't think[.] In my books I hope not. It's a misunderstanding, I think, too, for people who have experienced it, I don't think that it's easy to focus on the craft, you know, on making art when you're just in the grip of this really dark despair" ("'No Wonder'"). If the piano represents the artistic soul of Elf, and her great gift as a pianist seems to be her ability to translate her deepest emotions into her playing, then her soul and her art are now trapped within her. According to Born, Yoli "refuses to dignify mental illness as an expression of noble defiance." Toews sees depression as a state that cuts one off from oneself and others, not as a conduit to artistic expression.

Nic recounts that for Elf "there is no delivery from the torment of the days" (*All* 98), and thus in one sense keeping Elf alive is a violation of her autonomy. The language of the hospital, in fact, often echoes the language of imprisonment. At the hospital after her second non-fatal suicide attempt, for instance, Yoli recalls how, when Elf earlier made a "furtive attempt to disappear by starving herself to death," she pleaded with Yoli to let her die, but Yoli called an ambulance instead, and Elf ended up in the hospital (36–37). When Yoli visits her sister after her second attempt, this time by taking an overdose of pills, Elf asks her if "somebody is being shackled out there in the hallway." The sound, which Yoli identifies as dishes crashing, reminds Elf of Bedlam, an institution notorious for keeping the "mad" in chains (30). At one point, her hands are "tied down with cotton ribbons" (39), and after her third non-fatal suicide attempt, in which she drinks bleach, she is unable to talk because of a tube stuck down her throat to help her breathe. Seeing her sister in the hospital, Yoli is torn between wanting to spare Elf the humiliation of treatment and keeping her safe from self-harm. Given Toews's religious background, Yoli's comment on begging hospital staff to keep her father or sister safe—"how many times would I beg hospitals not to let my people go?" (225)—reflects a well-known spiritual with the chorus "Go down Moses / Way down in Egypt's land / Tell old pharaoh, / Let my people go." In a paradoxical formation, therefore, Yoli wants to save Elf by keeping her in "bondage," yet Yoli becomes increasingly aware of how keeping her sister alive is a violation of her personal freedom. Although it would be an insult to the historical horrors of slavery to compare it to the plight of one mental health patient, Elf is restrained against her will, and in her desperation she takes ever more violent action to free herself.

In her examination of the complex web of relations between family members and the suicidal "other" who is both loved for herself and resented for not being well, Toews takes on not only her own reluctance to condone the death of a much-loved sister but also the Canadian justice system's infantilization of the mentally ill. When Toews published *All My Puny Sorrows* in 2014, it was illegal in Canada for an individual to consent to his or her own death or for any person to assist in such a death. On 6 February 2015, the Supreme Court of Canada released a unanimous decision, *Carter v. Canada*, which overturned section 241(b) of the Criminal Code, "which prohibits assisting suicide, and section 14, which provides that no person may consent to death being inflicted on them," declaring that "s. 241(b) and s. 14 of the *Criminal Code* are void insofar as they prohibit physician-assisted death for a competent adult person who (1) clearly consents to the termination of life; and (2) has a grievous and irremediable medical condition (including an illness, disease or disability) that causes enduring suffering that is intolerable to the individual in the circumstances of his or her condition." The Supreme Court ruling gave the Canadian government one year, later extended by four months, to bring legislation in line with this decision. Thus, "Bill C-14, legislation on medical assistance in dying, received royal assent on June 17, 2016" (Government of Canada, Department of Justice). According to *Globe and Mail* writer Sandra Martin, Toews "admitted she had 'no words,' only 'endless tears of gratitude' for the Supreme Court ruling on physician-assisted death." Martin continues, however, that "it is too soon to say whether the decision will translate into a law that would have helped Ms. Toews and her family, but she said it is 'an amazing day' nonetheless."

Toews's relief at the ruling did not, in fact, translate into a law that would have helped Marjorie end her life. Bill C-14 limited medical assistance in dying to those whose "natural death has become reasonably foreseeable" and whose illness is "serious and incurable" (qtd. in Dying with Dignity Canada 4). As Dying with Dignity Canada asserts, "the law's eligibility criteria effectively exclude most, if not all, Canadians whose primary under-lying medical condition is a mental illness" (7) because of two factors: the mentally ill are not deemed competent to make decisions regarding their own deaths, and death from mental illness is not "reasonably foreseeable" in the sense that the legislation means. Further changes to the law, introduced on 17 March 2021, give future hope for those who, like Elf, feel that life is unbearable; however, as Canada's MAID website states, those who have "a mental illness [as their] only medical condition . . . are not eligible to seek medical assistance in dying" until 17 March 2023. The intervening time will be used, according to the website, to investigate "safeguards" to prevent a vulnerable population from being exploited by others. Toews's discussion in *All My Puny Sorrows*, then, is still relevant in spite of her early optimism that changes to Canadian law would soon allow the clinically depressed to opt for physician-assisted death.

In a critique of MAID legislation, Graeme Bayliss, a writer who has documented his own struggles with depression, believes that "more subtle and more invidious is the idea that the mentally ill—that uniform mass of derangement and dissociation—are, by definition, incapable of decid-ing rationally to kill themselves." Individuals contemplating suicide are presented with "a Catch-22: I don't want to live, but the very fact that I don't want to live means I can't possibly consent to die." Alexandre Baril goes even further when he writes that, "based on the sanist silencing of suicidal subjects through the injunction to life and somatechnologies of life, suicidal people constitute an oppressed, stigmatized group whose claims remain unintelligible within society, law, medical/psychiatric systems and anti-oppressive scholarship" (203). Although Baril believes that "attempting to destigmatize and recognize suicide as an option, albeit one that requires considerable critical reflection," can save lives by allowing people to speak openly of their desire for self-destruction and thus allow greater opportunities for harm reduction, he also asserts that, "regardless of physical condition or imminent death, all people who wish to die, including suicidal people, should have access to medically assisted suicide" (212).

Because Elf knows that that option is not available in Canada, she asks Yoli to take her to Switzerland, where, as Yoli finds out through her research, medical professionals acknowledge a condition that they call "'weariness of life' and [the mentally ill] have the same rights as anybody else who wants to die according to Swiss law. You can argue that she [Elf] is dying. She's weary of life, that's for sure" (*All* 232). In a conversation with Yoli, her friend Julie holds out hope that Elf, like many before her, will recover and go on to lead a happy and productive life. When Julie says that "my gut instinct is that you shouldn't do it" (i.e., take Elf to Switzerland), Yoli replies "but she'll do it anyway. That's *my* gut instinct." Julie avers that "there might be some change" (156), and thus she underlines how hope is one of the main reasons for denying those facing suicide the right to die: clinical depression is not an irreversible illness such as A L S or some forms of cancer. Physically, the organs of the body function within acceptable parameters, so there is always a desperate hope that mental illness will resolve itself.

There is even a corollary about the difference between terminal physical illness and mental illness in *All My Puny Sorrows*. Lottie is understandably committed to keeping her daughter Elf alive, yet Lottie allowed her father to die. As we learn, he spent nine years incapacitated by a stroke. In the final days of his life, he could be kept alive only by constant suctioning of the fluid collecting in his lungs, but Lottie, a trained nurse, "decided not to." Far from being upset at her actions, her brother-in-law Frank called this decision the "best thing she could have done for him" (245). Her father was in the end stage of life when Lottie decided not to continue the treatment necessary to keep him alive (244), yet for Yoli the death of Elf also has a certain inevitability and therefore the potential for an easing of suffering at its end. On the one hand, Yoli agrees with Elf's agent, Claudio, who exhorts Yoli to "keep her alive. You must try everything. Everything" (171). On the other, Yoli wants to end her sister's pain, and since nothing else seems to be working maybe death is the only option.

More than once Elf tells Yoli that "I'm afraid of dying alone" (149, 213), for there is always the spectre of their father's violent death. Elf raises this possibility when she implores their mother "to take her to the train tracks" so that she can complete the suicide attempt that Lottie interrupted (131). As Yoli begins to understand Elf's position, she wonders whether suicide could be considered a rational act: "So if the problem is life and its unlivability then a rational, working brain would choose to end it" (151). Given that Marjorie, like her fictional counterpart, died by walking in front of a train, Miriam never got a chance to test her resolve to help her sister, if it was even possible to do so, but Toews has said that she regrets how her sister died: "Going back to my own experience and seeing my sister in such agony, and thinking of her having to die violently and alone; that there were no other options for her . . . made me really think of the idea of assisted suicide, of providing a peaceful, good death to people who have decided for themselves that's what they want and that's what they need to get rid of the pain" ("Author Miriam Toews"). Toews indicates that, knowing her father's suicide and its aftermath, she should have allowed her sister a merciful end.

All My Puny Sorrows echoes her guilt at not having done enough to save her sister and at not having assisted her to end her life in a gentle manner. In a poignant description of the aftermath of the suicides of both her father and her sister, for example, Yoli reflects that "somehow his glasses didn't break, maybe they flew off his face into soft clover, or maybe he had carefully removed them and put them down on the ground, but when she [Yoli's mother] took them out of the plastic bag they crumbled in her hands. . . . His wedding rings were bashed and nearly all of his two hundred and six bones broken" (48). Similarly, the funeral director tries to convince Lottie that "she should perhaps just look at her [daughter's] hand" (271) rather than her "smashed-up face" (270), presumably because of the devastation caused by Elf's mode of death. But that was not her first choice as a method of dying. "What about Zurich?" Yoli wonders. "She would have died peacefully and not alone. That's all she wanted. I had failed" (296). The novel's concluding dream sequence describes their imaginary trip to Switzerland and final meal together as they anticipate Elf's "early appointment the next morning" (321), a vision of what might have been had Yoli been able to honour her sister's plea to die in a family setting.

Control, the Mental Health System, and the Conundrum of Compliance

"If you have to end up in the hospital, try to focus all your pain in your heart rather than your head" (*All* 219), decides Yoli after comparing the care received by her aunt Tina, admitted to the hospital for heart problems, and that of Elf in the psych ward. In *Swing Low* and *All My Puny Sorrows*, and to a lesser extent in *A Complicated Kindness* and *The Flying Troutmans*, Toews presents the mental health–care system as a fraught triangulation among mentally ill individuals, their families and friends, and what Michel Foucault calls "psychiatric power." Although Toews acknowledges that deficiencies in the mental health–care system arise partly from underfunding and overwork, she also accuses the system of placing mental health patients in what might be called a conundrum of compliance. The diagnosis of mental illness allows health-care professionals to discount "difficult" patients for playing "silly games" (*All* 174) or "acting like a child" (*Swing Low* 77) while expecting them to be rationally compliant with a doctor's orders. Lottie exclaims in exasperation at how the hospital treats Elf that "she's a human being." Lottie, Yoli elaborates, "couldn't bear to see Elf in the psych ward. That prison, she said. They do nothing. If she doesn't take the pills they won't talk to her. They wait and they badger and they badger and they wait and they badger" (*All* 205). This is a far cry from the ideal health practitioner whom Yoli has imagined earlier, who says "I am here for you and I will work very hard to help you. I promise. If I fail it will be my failure, not yours. I am the professional. I am the expert. You are experiencing great pain right now and it is my job and my mission to cure you from your pain" (176). Yoli asks for compassion rather than condemnation, but the system censures non-compliant behaviours rather than addresses what might have caused them.

With regard to censuring non-compliance, the practices described above have elements in common with religious fundamentalism. As in *A Complicated Kindness*, in which Nomi talks about the "complicated kindness" (46) that both condemns her to hell and wishes to save her, Toews tempers her critique of fundamentalism by acknowledging the huge role that faith played for her father and the solace that she believes it gave him "in those last violent seconds he spent on earth" ("Father's Faith" 197). Yet Toews also highlights an unforgiving Mennonite patriarchy, with its "squad of perpetual disapprovers," in *A Complicated Kindness, Irma Voth, Swing Low,* and *All My Puny Sorrows* (251). *Puny Sorrows*, for instance, questions the pious certainty of a Mennonite minister who visits Elf in the hospital: "He told her that if she would give her life to God she wouldn't have any pain. She would want to live. And to deny that was to sin egregiously" (222). Toews asserts in *Swing Low* and in interviews that such condemnation intensifies the stress of the sufferer (as it did for her father). As Yoli says in *Puny Sorrows*, "you can't go around terrorizing people and making them feel small and shitty and then call them *evil* when they destroy themselves" (181).

Metaphorically, shunning is an extreme manifestation of a tendency within fundamentalist communities: a focus on getting merit points for the next life leads to harsh censure of perceived sins and misdemeanours in this one as well as lack of compassion for those who struggle and fail. Toews connects the shame enforced by religious groups that "you've sinned and you've veered from the straight and narrow and you need to be punished or forgiven" with attitudes among the public and some health-care professionals toward mental illness. She continues that "there's this notion that you're responsible for your own illness, and that you've misbehaved" ("'No Wonder'"). All too often the mental health–care system forgoes compassion in order to exercise control, and in this sense it blames the mentally ill for not cooperating in their treatment. However, as Lottie says in *All My Puny Sorrows*, "is co-operation even a symptom of mental health or just something you need from the patients to be able to control every last damn person here with medication and browbeating?" (214). Toews's novels illustrate that, just as there are kind and compassionate Mennonites, so too there are many excellent health-care workers, such as nurse Janice in *Puny Sorrows*, but her novels also demonstrate that overarching systems, both faith based and psychiatric, demand that people obey the rules and do as they are told. Elf, for example, refuses to eat in the hospital cafeteria or to talk to her psychiatrist, and she is shunned by some of the hospital staff. After the first visit in which she refuses to express herself verbally, her psychiatrist walks away, saying that "I'm not interested in passing a notebook back and forth between us and waiting while she scribbles things down. It's ridiculous. . . . If she wants to get better she'll have to make an attempt to communicate normally" (174). Rushed and overtaxed health-care workers cannot always spare the time for patients' eccentricities. However, Elf is caught in a loop in which her mental illness manifests as non-cooperation, and her lack of compliance leads to withdrawal of the very thing that might make her less mentally ill. Ironically, when Elf, like Mel in *Swing Low*, is most desperate to die, she can pretend to be well enough to be discharged by following hospital rules: eating her breakfast, talking to staff, and taking her pills (*All* 106).

Amy Rushton discusses how Toews's novel "is not simply a space of grief but of righteous anger at a system and society that could not help her sister in any meaningful, long-lasting way." Rushton further argues that *A Little Life* (by Hanya Yanagihara) and *All My Puny Sorrows* "question the ethics of survival at all costs and add an empathetic viewpoint on debates about the right to die for those suffering psychological distress" (198). Neo-liberalism, says Rushton, pays lip service to the crisis in mental health care by promising to combat the "stigma" of mental illness. But focusing on stigma hides a deeper problem: the lack of funding within the health-care system (199). In contrast to "the neoliberal fixation on individualism and demands for self-responsibility," *Puny Sorrows* indicts a health-care system that focuses on the bottom line rather than on patient care and places the sole responsibility for wellness at the feet of patients and their families (196). As Rushton puts it, "the anger in *AMPS* stems from frustration of institutions which demand that Elf remains alive at any cost—as long as that cost falls under that year's budget for mental health care" (203–204).

Swing Low also addresses these issues. Mel, for instance, overhears his daughter saying that "this is the second time my father has been in this hospital without receiving any type of care whatsoever. Where is the psychiatrist?" She is told that the psychiatrist retired that very afternoon (21–22). Care for Mel is complicated by his ability to pretend that he is well, often to the point where he speculates that medical professionals "felt sure that my wife and daughters [have] been overreacting, that perhaps they were just tired of the inconvenience of having to be with me" (222). For both Elf and Mel, however, the system's lack of staff leads professionals to focus on superficialities instead of deep care. When Mel and Elf pretend to be better, they give the system what it desperately needs, a bed for another patient. The lack of time and the demands on an overtaxed system prevent carers from delving deeply and perhaps preventing tragedy.

All My Puny Sorrows also refutes neo-liberal models that equate economic success with happiness, since Toews reverses the relative success of the two sisters, making Elf an internationally recognized concert pianist, whereas Marjorie—though she had substantial musical talent—did not perform at an elite level. Meanwhile, Yoli, Toews's counterpart in *Puny Sorrows*, is the author of the mildly popular Rodeo Rhonda series, something of a comedown from Miriam's own success as a well-established Canadian writer who has won many literary accolades, including the Governor General's Literary Award for *A Complicated Kindness*. Yoli says to Elf that "you have this amazing guy who loves your ass off, an amazing career that the whole world respects and gives you shitloads of cash for" (162), whereas "everything in [Yoli's] life is embarrassing," from her failed relationships and attempts to find happiness in casual sex to her attempts to write a novel that "nobody wants to publish" (161). Freed by fiction from sticking strictly to "the facts," Toews reverses the relative success of the two sisters to make a key point: suicidal thoughts and depression can affect anyone, not just those whose lives seem to justify sadness. As she comments in an interview, "a lot of times people think that it doesn't make sense for people to be depressed when they have everything, a loving husband, a successful career, fame and fortune. . . . I wanted to make this point that profound despair can strike anybody" ("Profound Despair"). Perhaps, as well, Toews subconsciously wants to counter her father's verdict on his life—"nothing accomplished" (*Swing Low* 1)—by showing that even the most "accomplished" individuals can suffer from depression.

Toews's change to the characters' family history also raises the notion of inherited and collective trauma. Lottie, for instance, speaks of how "suffering, even though it may have happened a long time ago, is something that is passed from one generation to the next to the next, like flexibility or grace or dyslexia" (*All* 18). Drawing from the work of Cathy Caruth and others, Robert Zacharias gives an insightful summary of how inherited trauma can affect future generations. Speaking of the "break event," which he sees at the heart of Canadian Mennonite narratives, Zacharias writes that "the argument that a collective imaginary can be structured or 'coloured' by a single historical event clearly presupposes that something of the impact of that key experience of displacement can be passed on across generations" (*Rewriting* 145). When asked in an interview about her recurring references to the Mennonite flight from oppression in early-twentieth-century Russia, Toews said that growing up in Steinbach "there were always stories, always stories, and so relatives of ours (not my parents) and friends, they would have stories of how they escaped in the '20s and even in the '40s. . . . So it was always like this narrative that was always there" (interview with Reed). In *All My Puny Sorrows*, Yoli raises the issue of inherited trauma when she asks Julie "do you think you're still suffering from your grandparents being massacred in Russia?" Julie answers that "just" her grandmother died. Even though she shrugs when Yoli asks "do you think that all that stuff can still affect us even now?" the fact that she asks the question indicates the power of collective memory and inherited trauma (103).

With Elf in the hospital and her father and cousin Leni dead by suicide, Yoli also asks "are Mennonites a depressed people or is it just us?" (135). But a few pages later she considers her mother, "a Rubenesque bundle of flesh and scars, a disciple of life, and my sister a wraith," and she asks herself "how does one give birth to the other?" (138). Elf, perhaps, takes after her father, whereas Yoli has inherited her mother's resilience. Family dynamics also seem to contribute to Elf's depressive personality. When, for instance, Jacob Von Riesen attempts to educate the Canadian public by selling placemats containing historical information, his efforts are met with scorn or uninterest. Characteristically, he comes home disheartened, goes straight to his room, and shuts the door. Whereas Yoli, who goes with him on his "sales" trip, makes people laugh by telling "a colourful story of our time on the road," Elf immediately empathizes with Jacob's pain, going into his room and sitting with her father for hours (143). Elf even says to Yoli that "I had to be perfect so you could fuck up and you were more than happy to do it. One of us had to show some fucking empathy . . . towards dad and all his acres of existential sadness" (162). One can attribute Elf's and Jacob's depression to historical trauma, "family dynamics" (163), genetic inheritance, or even, as Rushton avers, alienation from neo-liberalism, but Toews suggests that mental illness is too complex to be attributed to one cause. Elf can sympathize with her father because she has inherited his genetic predisposition toward depression (nature), or she can develop depression because she plays the role of her father's comforter within the family dynamic and is therefore more affected by his moods (nurture).

Sisters and Not-So-Puny Sorrows

Margaret Steffler has described how Toews's novels often feature pairs of sisters who exhibit varying degrees of resilience ("Presence of Absence"). Often one sister tries to save the life of the other, as happens in *The Flying Troutmans* and *All My Puny Sorrows*. Or, as in *A Complicated Kindness* and *Irma Voth*, a much-loved older sister leaves behind objects and memories that serve as touchstones for their younger siblings. Given the depth of the sister bond in *Puny Sorrows*, it is fitting that the title of the novel comes from a poem by Samuel Taylor Coleridge that references two sister bonds: that between Charles and Mary Lamb and that between Coleridge and his deceased sister Anne. Coleridge wrote the poem, which he titled "To a Friend," to help console Charles when his sister suffered a bout of "delirium in the winter of 1794–5," one of the early manifestations of the mental illness that would plague Mary for the rest of her life (Appignanesi 15). Lamb's worries about his sister's health prompted Coleridge to remember his own dear sister. In the excerpt of the poem printed in *Puny Sorrows*, Yoli reads

> In fancy (well I know)
> From business wand'ring far and local cares,
> Thou creepest round a dear-lov'd Sister's bed
> With noiseless step, and watchest the faint look,
> Soothing each pang with fond solicitude,
> And tenderest tones medicinal of love.
> I too a SISTER had, an only Sister—
> She lov'd me dearly, and I doted on her!
> To her I pour'd forth all my puny sorrows
> (As a sick Patient in his Nurse's arms)
> And of the heart those hidden maladies
> That shrink asham'd from even Friendship's eye.
> O! I have woke at midnight, and have wept,
> Because SHE WAS NOT! (237)

When Yoli finds the passage in a book of Coleridge's poetry, she exclaims to herself "I had found Elf's Coleridge poem! The one she'd taken her signature AMPS from" (237). Wanting to leave her mark on a town that she was already in the process of rejecting, the teenage Elf paints "AMPS" (all my puny sorrows) on public property throughout East Village, yet as a symbol of rebellion it is both powerful and cryptic, much like Elf herself. Given the never-ending rules that the townsfolk are supposed to follow, spray-painting red letters on public spaces is provocative. However, on Yoli's advice, Elf removes her initials, EVR, from the original design "because everyone in town will know whose they are and then the fires of hell will raineth down on us, et cetera." In a town that stands "against overt symbols of hope and individual signature pieces," Elf's graffiti symbolizes her rebellion (9). However, that rebellion is circumspect because no one but Yoli knows that Elf painted the letters, and the message itself is undecipherable. One can imagine the town authorities correctly interpreting Elf's graffiti as an act against the status quo, but for what purpose? Is "AMPS" a reference to electricity? Why? What do the letters mean? All Mennonites Prefer Sandwiches? After Many Pretty Sunsets? Like so much about Elf, the acronym is not readable without a key, and she is reluctant to provide such insight even to her mother and sister or perhaps even to herself.

The words *all my puny sorrows* are themselves a puzzle. In Coleridge's poem, they refer to "And of the heart those hidden maladies / That shrink asham'd from even Friendship's eye," the kind of troubles that a boy or young man would tell only the person to whom he is closest, but likely they are problems that pale compared with the greater sorrows in the world at large. Yet those who remember their adolescence know that, though the sorrows experienced in one's teens might be insignificant in retrospect, they can seem like an all-consuming tragedy at the time. In the context of Coleridge's life, the death of Anne at age twenty-four[11] was far from a "puny sorrow," and for Lamb, to whom the poem is addressed, Mary's mental illness manifested in a deeply tragic way when, a couple of years after Coleridge wrote his poem, Mary murdered her mother during a severe mental breakdown.

Toews's title achieves full irony when one considers that the sorrows experienced by Elf and those who love her are wrenching, unsettling, soul destroying, and intense—anything but "puny." Seen from the outside, the severely depressed can seem to be upset about "nothing," self-indulgent, or even, as Yoli at one point accuses Elf, wilfully ignoring their perceived "perfect" lives. Yoli never really knows why Elf is so drawn to the words that she takes as her "signature." Did she choose them in protest against how the Mennonite elders in her town belittled the weak and the disenfranchised? Did Elf see them as ironic given that, as a creative person, her frustrations at living in a town that distrusted creativity were not "puny" at all? The acronym AMPS, in other words, highlights how language both explains and obfuscates, allows for multiple interpretations, and often fails to reveal the depths of people's experiences, thus making the quotation a fitting title not only for Elf but also for Toews's novel.

Toews says of writing *All My Puny Sorrows* that "this was like bleeding onto every page. It took everything I had. I feel as though I'm just in the process of rebuilding and regrouping and regaining my energy and equilibrium and then figuring out what I want to do" ("*All My Puny Sorrows*"). Suicide survivors are often met by two types of silencing: that which comes from the stigma attached to the act and a general model of grief that encourages the bereaved to put mourning behind them and get on with their lives. But, as Lottie pithily says, one cannot "tie off grief like a used condom and toss it in the garbage" (*All* 294). For Toews, writing provides an opportunity to commemorate events and people who otherwise would be silent, to leave a lasting record of their places in her life and the lives of others. A lifelong obsession with words could not save Mel Toews from mental illness, and in spite of her love of reading, books do not save Elf.

In fact, she uses her need for books as a pretense to get Nic out of the house so that she has the time to get to the railway tracks. "Books are what save us. Books are what don't save us" (*All* 267), Yoli reflects after Elf's death when she sees all of the books that her sister left behind. However, though books could not save Elf, she helps to save her sister by providing her with money to buy a house and, "à la Virginia Woolf, a monthly sum of two thousand dollars for the next two years" (271). By providing Yoli with both the means to write and a home in which to write, Elf sets her sister on the path to resilience, giving her both the physical safety and a means to speak about her pain. Leigh Gilmore writes about a contradiction at the heart of trauma studies: theorists "assert that trauma is beyond language in some crucial way, that language fails in the face of trauma, and that trauma mocks language and confronts it with its insufficiency. Yet, at the same time language about trauma is theorized as an impossibility, language is pressed forward as that which can heal the survivor of trauma" (6). In *All My Puny Sorrows* and *Swing Low*, two avid readers take their own lives, but it seems that, by writing "relational lives" about her father and sister, Toews might have eased her own pain. Yoli speaks of "trying to crack Elf's secret code, the meaning of life, her life, the universe" (*All* 44), but in the end there are no grand revelations other than that life must go on, even in the face of intense sorrow.

One can think of *Swing Low*, *All My Puny Sorrows*, and *Fight Night* as movements in a tripartite discussion of resilience in the aftermath of familial suicide. *Swing Low* ends with a brief mention of Mel's suicide and his daughter's decision to create a fictionalized autobiography in order to deal with her grief and understand her father better. *Puny Sorrows* takes resilience a step further by describing not only Elf's suicide but also its aftermath as those left behind after her death build new lives for themselves in a new city. In *Fight Night*, the suicides of a father and a sister are mentioned but in retrospect. They are not documented in the novel itself, and this creates additional reparative distance between the trauma of suicide and the need for resilience among survivors.

In addition to the timelines of the three works moving further away from the "chaos narrative" of Mel's final months in hospital, the works show a movement toward stability in the form of homes.[12] In *Swing Low*, Mel begins his story with the loss of his beloved pink house, and he spends much of the book wandering in search of the home that he lost. Since he is hospitalized for depression and dementia in the present timeline of the novel, in a sense Mel dies without a home, unless one considers that he had a home in his faith. In *All My Puny Sorrows*, her home crumbles around Yoli, and in spite of her increasingly frantic efforts she cannot keep Elf alive. However, the novel goes beyond Elf's death by suicide to show that one's home can be re-established and one's community regrown. The final events in *Puny Sorrows* show three individuals: Yoli, her mother, Lottie, and Yoli's fourteen-year-old daughter, Nora, renovating a derelict house and growing stronger as it takes shape. In *Fight Night*, the third of what might informally be called Toews's "suicide trilogy," Grandmother Elvira, her daughter, Mooshie, and the novel's narrator, nine-year-old Swiv, live together as they cope with the aftermath of Elvira's daughter Momo's death by suicide a year before the story opens. There is also a reference to the earlier suicide of Momo and Mooshie's father. Even characters' names echo through the three novels. Toews's mother, Elvira, shows up in fictional form through the name of Swiv's irrepressible grandmother, and here as well the three books show a pattern of increased celebration of Elvira Toews and her character. Elvira does not appear in the present setting of *Swing Low*, for she is resting in the city after exhausting herself caring for her husband. Mel says that he "would like to apologize to someone for killing [his] wife" (42), even though his daughters remind him many times that she is still alive. *Puny Sorrows*, in contrast, shows Lottie as a resilient character who keeps moving forward even after the deaths of her husband, daughter, and sister. In fact, the end of the novel has a clear tribute to her resilience as Yoli rethinks her assumption that she was taking care of her mother by bringing her to Toronto to live in the new house. "I have just realized something," Yoli says. "It's not me who's survived, who's picked up and gone on, who's saved my mother by bringing her to Toronto, it's my mother . . . and she's taken me with her" (292; ellipsis in the original). In her most powerful description of resilience yet, Toews writes a tribute to her mother and her ability to continue on in the face of the deaths of two family members by suicide and her own health problems. Thus, it seems to be fitting to end my book, with its discussions of home and resilience, with a consideration of *Fight Night* and the power of one elderly woman to inspire community, hope, and redemption.

CONCLUSION

The Fight against the Night

She said what makes a tragedy bearable and *unbearable is the same thing—which is that life goes on.*
—MIRIAM TOEWS, *FIGHT NIGHT* (66)

Instead of art aspiring towards lifelikeness what if life aspires towards art, towards a creative, controlled focus of freedom, outside of the tyranny of matter? What if the joke about life imitating art were a better joke than we think?
—JEANETTE WINTERSON, *ART OBJECTS* (59)

A brilliant novel in its own right, Miriam Toews's *Fight Night* (2021) also confirms the paratextual elements in her oeuvre and her continuing preoccupation with the themes that I have discussed in this monograph. Once again, for example, we have a novel that references two sisters, six years apart in age (66). Here, as well, the older sister and her father have died by suicide, and once again the remaining family members struggle to find their equilibrium after devastating grief. *Fight Night* even contains an extended trip to California, a continuation of the "road trips" in *The Flying Troutmans* and *Summer of My Amazing Luck*. Although Toews never mentions Mennonites by name in *Fight Night*, readers familiar with her work will pick up on references to a town cowed by a fundamentalist tyrant, the protagonist's references to her grandmother's "secret language"

(13), the Plautdietsch phrases that Grandma uses throughout the novel, and her references to her "town of escaped Russians" (106). Although the events in *Fight Night* take place after Grandma has left her repressive town, the novel critiques fundamentalism and its tendency to enforce belief through domination and threat rather than love. As in *Irma Voth* and *Women Talking*, however, *Fight Night* also shows that much good can be salvaged from religious faith. In addition, *Fight Night* continues Toews's interest in the home as a place unsettled by old griefs and continued irritations and upsets yet a central place in which resilience can begin and grow.

Fight Night opens, as Toews's novels so often do, with a family in crisis. Nine-year-old Swiv,[1] her youngest narrator to date, has been expelled from school for fighting, and her elderly grandmother Elvira has taken over Swiv's lessons in a very unconventional way. They practise spelling by playing Boggle, and Elvira teaches Swiv Latin words by translating the instructions on pill bottles (45, 21). Swiv's mother, Mooshie, is in her third trimester of pregnancy, often angry and depressed, and Swiv's alcohol-dependent father has left the family without providing a forwarding address. Emotionally, Grandma Elvira is a strong and resilient woman, but her health is failing, and it falls to Swiv to care for her and manage the house while Mooshie is at work. Swiv makes sure that Grandma takes her pills, she is ready with the nitro spray when Grandma has an angina attack, and she helps Grandma to dress and put on her compression stockings.

Midway through the novel, Elvira decides to visit relatives in California, and Swiv goes along in the role of grandchild/caregiver. Near the end of the trip, Elvira dances for the residents in a care home that she is visiting, falls, and breaks her arm. Then she gamely ignores her pain until she can return to Canada and avoid American hospital bills. In the conclusion of the novel, Grandma collapses during her plane ride back to Toronto and is hospitalized at about the same time as her daughter Mooshie goes into labour. Mooshie gives birth to a daughter, something of a shock to Swiv, who has named the baby Gord while it was in utero. As Swiv's new sister enters the world, Grandma Elvira prepares to leave it. After a long life of fighting for herself and others, Grandma writes to her nurses *"my friends, I'd like to negotiate my surrender!"* (247). She refuses heroic measures, asks that the tube be removed from her throat, and dies as Swiv and Mooshie sing her favourite song. As Swiv writes to her absent father, "here's a question for you, Dad. If three people go into a hospital and one of them dies, how many people will leave the hospital? If you're our family, it's still three" (249). While Swiv mourns the loss of her beloved grandmother, she also celebrates her ongoing life with her mother and her baby sister. Her grandmother has taught her valuable lessons on not only the need to fight but also the time to surrender. Most importantly, Grandma has provided Swiv with the example of her own life, one so full of resilience and strength that Swiv can persevere in spite of her beloved grandmother's death.

Grandma Elvira says that "joy ... is *resistance*" (197), by which she means resistance to tyranny in any form, whether religious, medical, or social. And for Elvira resistance often equates to resilience. As a woman who cares little about how others judge her, she resists societal expectations about where so-called little old ladies should go, how they should dress, and what they should or should not do. More significantly, her freedom comes from a lifetime of speaking back to the fundamentalist beliefs with which she was raised. Concerning what she later calls "*the awful reign of Willit Braun*" (209), her town's religious leader, Elvira exclaims that "they took our life force. And so we fight to reclaim it . . . we fight and we fight and we fight . . . we fight to love . . . we fight to love ourselves . . . we fight for access to our *feelings* . . . for access to our *fires*" (160; ellipses in the original). Readers who know Toews's works will undoubtedly see parallels between Willit Braun and The Mouth in *A Complicated Kindness*, Julius Voth in *Irma Voth*, Bishop Peters in *Women Talking*, and the Mennonite elders who make the Von Riesen family's life difficult in *All My Puny Sorrows*. In these works, fundamentalism is a soul-destroying refusal to allow for personal interpretations of God because those who claim authority impose their strict readings of scripture on others, often to the detriment of independent thought. As Grandma Elvira implies here, the danger of fundamentalism is how it reduces people to their transgressions. Rigid religious systems stress how people violate the rules and impose labels of sinfulness that can easily lead to self-hate. Elvira insists that she and her family fight to love and be loved, that they leave the extreme judgementalism of the religious elders behind them.

The comedian and the crusader exist side by side as Toews uses humour to underline the absurdities inherent even in the most tragic situations and to challenge institutions and individuals who take themselves too seriously. As readers have come to expect from her work, *Fight Night* is hilarious as well as poignant, and much of its humour comes from the interactions of Swiv with her mother and grandmother. Toews captures the excruciating embarrassment of a young girl faced with a mother who makes confrontational comments to strangers and a gregarious grandmother who goes out in public wearing slippers and sweat pants. In addition, humour often lightens the terrible circumstances in which Toews's characters find themselves. When Grandma gives Swiv a math problem, for instance, she employs dark humour that not only reflects her anger but also shows her ability to mock life's many injustices and absurdities. After telling Swiv the story of a friend who attempted to leave her abusive husband but then returned to him out of guilt, Elvira tells Swiv how she and her friends prayed for the husband to die so that his wife could be free. As Elvira asks Swiv, "if it takes five years to kill a guy with prayer, and it takes six people a day to pray, then how many prayers of pissed off women praying every day for five years does it take to pray a guy to death?" (31). This is definitely not the type of math problem found in school textbooks, but it provides valuable lessons on resistance, humour, and solidarity.

As David Bergen perceptively comments, Toews "goes to dark places and yet she comes out leaning to the light" (qtd. in Barber). An often uneasy wit pervades her writing, so readers might look up from one of her books laughing and then perhaps feeling that they should not be. It is this edgy blend of the serious and the satirical, the ridiculous and the profound, melded with compelling characters, that makes Toews such an engaging and effective writer. As Magdalene Redekop writes, "what lifts [*A Complicated Kindness* and *All My Puny Sorrows*] above the grievances that they attack and the grief that they express is the comic vision of Toews." Redekop "imagine[s] Toews as having an inner clown whose movements are guided by this vision and who is brave enough to keep going no matter what obstacles appear" (*Making Believe* 203). One could say the same thing about the characters in any of the nine books by Toews. Even those characters who eventually stop fighting—Mel Toews in *Swing Low*, Elf Von Riesen in *Puny Sorrows*, Elvira in *Fight Night*—successfully combat the obstacles placed in their way by mental or physical health crises until they finally succumb to them.

Like so many of Toews's works, *Fight Night* is deeply autobiographical yet an imagined story. "Everything is fodder. Everything is fuel," comments Toews. "The brain never stops struggling to reshape every experience and feeling into a coherent narrative. A writer doesn't live 'in the moment.' A writer steals the moment and stashes it away to gnaw on later in the day, in a dark and lonely room" (qtd. in Bethune). In a conversation with Tom Power about *Fight Night*, Toews comments on her blend of autobiography and fiction by saying that in this work, as in her other works, "the protagonist has a consciousness of her own, or his own, that is different from mine," a distance that allows her to move away from the personal to express what she calls "a more universal truth" ("Miriam Toews on Her New Novel").[2] Jeanette Winterson, who also uses autofiction to discuss her past and find resilience through the reparative act of writing, makes a valuable point that can apply to Toews's use of humour and autobiographical material. Discussing Gertrude Stein's *The Autobiography of Alice B. Toklas* and the ethics of revealing the lives of others, Winterson writes that "the question is an ethical one only if we assume that fiction is a copy of actual life." She goes on to say, however, that this is not what Stein is doing in her work. She is creating a heightened reality, a reflection of her era, rather than a faithful likeness of her partner Alice B. Toklas or even of herself (*Art Objects* 59). Toews consistently transforms elements of her own life narrative to express key emotional truths, and so do her characters.

In her fictional universes, her protagonists often write out their experiences, transforming their pain into artifacts that express their individualism and abilities. One thinks, for instance, of the letters that Elf and Yoli send to each other in *All My Puny Sorrows*, Nomi's extended letter to Mr. Quiring in *A Complicated Kindness*, and the diary that Irma keeps in *Irma Voth*. *Women Talking*, on one level, is August's self-conscious reflection on the writing process, and *Fight Night* is an epistolary novel in which Swiv writes a letter to her absent father, and her mother and grandmother are assigned the task of writing letters to the unborn "Gord." These personal communications give the characters emotional immediacy as they work to make sense of the disturbing elements in their lives. Elf, Yoli, Nomi, August, and Irma have a freedom of expression in these "private" modes of writing that might be denied if they spoke in the open. Characters who write through letters, diaries, and in Mel's case fictionalized autobiographical recollections create verisimilitude while also making readers aware of Toews's artifice. The humour, the arrangement of details, and the emotions expressed by her characters show her ability to make her subjects immediate and real, yet that very immediacy highlights the art that has created these unforgettable voices and stories. If, as Winterson suggests, "the joke about life imitating art were a better joke than we think," then Toews's writing allows others to find freedom and to address their own demons—in other words, to find solace in the stories created by her art. Her humour, one of the most memorable aspects of her writing, transcends the ordinary and shows us the absurd. We laugh even as we have cause for deep sorrow. Even at its most devastating, there is a playfulness in Toews's work, a willingness to deal honestly with messy lives and uncontained conclusions. There are births and deaths, as *Fight Night* underscores, with their joys and sorrows.

Writing Pain

Obviously, art is not a universal panacea. His love of words did not save Mel Toews, and Elf Von Riesen dies by suicide in spite of her passionate commitment to playing the piano. Nomi Nickel's words might end up in Mr. Quiring's wastepaper basket, and August Epp's account of the women's conversation in the hayloft might never be read by anyone else. However, for others, art is a way to fight and to win. In Mom's letter to Gord in *Fight Night*, Toews expresses a philosophy of writing supported by her characters in the novel, but it can also stand as an expression of her belief in the power of writing in general. Mom writes to Gord that "I remember reading an interview with a writer once and she said that she was writing *against* death, that the act of writing, or of storytelling, that every time she wrote a story I mean, she was working through her own death. She didn't care about impermanence. She didn't care if anybody read her stories. She just wanted to write them down, to get them out of her" (89–90). Even if a story is never published, the act of recording it helps the writer to clarify ideas and provides some distance from the events being discussed. Sometimes just getting the story out is a release and relief in itself.

Although Elaine Scarry speaks mainly of the experience of bodily pain, her book *The Body in Pain: The Making and Unmaking of the World* lends insight into how Toews translates excruciating and tragic experiences into fictions that transcend the pain that inspired her to write. Scarry's influential work describes how people in extreme pain lose their ability to speak and are able to express their pain only in agonized sounds rather than in language. To be in extreme pain, she suggests, is to be without the ability to speak about that pain, for pain reduces the mind to one focus: the pain itself.

Although many have come up with scales that allow people to quantify and describe what their pain feels like—Ronald Melzack's "The McGill Pain Questionnaire: Major Properties and Scoring Methods" is a good example—there is always slippage between what the sufferer experiences and how much the sufferer can "explain" the pain so that others will understand it. "Intense pain," writes Scarry, "is also language-destroying: as the content of one's world disintegrates, so the content of one's language disintegrates; as the self disintegrates, so that which would express and project the self is robbed of its source and its subject" (35). Words such as *throbbing*, *cramping*, and *burning*—all used in the McGill questionnaire—can help someone to understand what the subject is enduring, but the interlocutor cannot *feel* what the person in pain feels. There is a gap at the heart of pain that makes it solely the sufferer's experience. For Scarry, therefore, pain is the only human experience that does not have an object. People are hungry for food, they love an object or another individual, or they fear a certain event or entity, but pain exists only as itself. As Scarry puts it, "pain is not 'of' or 'for' anything—it is itself alone" (162). In a sense, people do not experience pain *for* a hammer; they experience the pain of being hit *by* the hammer, and once the hit occurs the pain is felt only as itself.

Scarry goes on to say that, just as pain represents the only thing in human experience that does not have an object, so too "the imagination is remarkable for being the only state that is wholly its objects" (162). She states that "it is impossible to imagine without imagining something" (162). With the possible exception of the Hebrew YHWH, whose name cannot be pronounced and whose being, contradictorily, is beyond knowing yet omnipresent, imagination involves creating an object, a scenario, or a feeling that exists in relation to lived experience (164). When we imagine someone's pain, we rely on our memories of our own pain. The word *burning* has meaning because most of us soon learn the feeling of touching something too hot and can reconstruct what it is like to be burned. Through metaphor and empathy, imagination is at the heart of understanding the pain of others and allowing a version of that pain to be heard and experienced. To counter the negative emptiness of pain, in which we can live only in the moment of agony, we create artifacts and ideas that insist on something more. If pain is an inarticulate state without an object, then speaking of pain is the source of many an inspirational work of art.

In *Irma Voth*, for example, Toews shows how Ximena's anguished cries after biting into an electrical cord not only give Ximena her first taste of the risks that come with our "fragile" bodies but also give Irma some insight into her own condition. Irma tries to block out the cries of her baby sister but cannot, and soon she "figure[s] out the solution to my own problem" (251). Irma empathizes with the inconsolable crying of her sister; however, instead of lamenting the horrors in store for Ximena in a world that Irma knows is full of setbacks and losses, she reconsiders her life and decides to live it. In the clarity brought on by Ximena's pain, Irma's imaginative epiphany says that there is more to life than its limitations. Irma must be prepared to "LIVE" (251).

The worst pain in Toews's works, however, is psychic rather than physical. "Ho!" says the irrepressible Grandma in *Fight Night*. "Are you kidding me? It's only pain. We don't worry about pain. It's not life-threatening" (40). With the exception of Ximena and Nomi's nightly face aches in

A Complicated Kindness, Toews's characters do not spend much time talking about physical pain. Even Grandma's "Triple Scoop Sundae" of "gout, trigeminal neuralgia, [and] angina" (*Fight Night* 40) fades in significance beside the pain of losing both a husband and a daughter to suicide. Toews's most depressed characters—Min in *The Flying Troutmans*, Elf in *All My Puny Sorrows*, and Mel in *Swing Low*—are largely silenced by the psychic pain that they suffer. These characters' wordless anguish provides insight into how Scarry's point that "physical pain is not only itself resistant to language but also actively destroys language, deconstructing it into the pre-language of cries and groans" (172), can be applied to the mind. In severe depression, the distinction between psychic pain and physical pain can be said to collapse. As William Styron eloquently says, "the gray drizzle of horror induced by depression takes on the quality of physical pain. But it is not an immediately identifiable pain, like that of a broken limb" (50). Toews recounts how her sister convinced her that "psych pain is as real as any physical pain, and it was manifesting itself as physical pain as well as psych pain" (qtd. in Rinehart). Thus, Toews's silent depressives exhibit a loss of language analogous to that found with physical pain. In response to the pain of others and her own grief at the suicides of her sister and her father, Toews creates imaginative acts that transcend her grief and bring what has been silenced into language. Imagination can be a curse when an individual envisions horrors and slights that might never come, but it is also a vehicle for resilience. Whether writing about the imposed silence of religious fundamentalism, the internal and external silencing of the mentally ill, or the agonizing throes of grief and trauma, Toews performs resilience by moving pain into language and artistic expression.

"Rage, Rage against the Dying of the Light"

Toews's use of Dylan Thomas's poem "And Death Shall Have No Dominion" early in *Fight Night* (9) also evokes his more famous words, "Rage, rage against the dying of the light." The title *Fight Night* is evocative, with multiple implications. It could be a call to fight the dark night of the soul (fight the night), or it could describe, as the end of the novel implies, an actual "fight night" in which Grandma fights to stay alive and then decides to forgo medical interventions that might prolong her life. However, while Elvira is dying in one ward, her daughter Mooshie gives birth to a child in another. As noted in the epigraph to this epilogue, a tragedy is both "bearable" and "unbearable." Swiv reports her mother's comments in *Fight Night*, "she said what makes a tragedy bearable *and* unbearable is the same thing—which is that life goes on" (66). On the one hand, tragedy makes people feel that life is not worth living, that they cannot go on because the pain is too great. On the other, it is a consolation to know that life continues in spite of loss and that sorrow may ease over time. At one point in *Fight Night*, Elvira speaks of how tragedy and comedy are linked: "Do you know Shakespeare's tragedies? People like to separate his plays into tragedies and comedies. Well, jeepers creepers! Aren't they all one and the same? So, King Lear fails to connect with what's important in life and loses his mind . . . who hasn't? There is comedy in that, don't kid yourself. That's life! And life doesn't necessarily make sense. We're human!" (158; ellipsis in the original). In tragedies such as *King Lear*, there is much remorse and regret for actions taken or not taken. If Cordelia was not executed through Edmund's treachery, however, then the play would end with rising action, the good rewarded and the bad punished. Nahum Tate's famed bowdlerization of the play (1681) is a case in point, as Tate produced a version which supported his belief that audiences wanted a morally appropriate ending where good characters were rewarded. Cordelia and King Lear both lived in his revision, effectively turning Shakespeare's tragedy into a comic work (Foakes 85).

When Elvira goes on to postulate a new drama with bits of *As You Like It* and *King Lear* rolled into one, she says that such a work should be "mainstream," not part of a Fringe Festival (159). Tragedy contains elements of comedy and comedy elements of tragedy. Anomalies of timing, personality, and willpower make all the difference. As shown in *Fight Night*, tragedy, indeed life itself, becomes more bearable when one fights back. One needs to "rage against the dying of the light," a metaphor that in the context of the novel could stand not only for physical death but also for emotional coercion, loss of happiness, and depression.

What does it mean to fight? Swiv's adult responsibilities began when neither her mother nor her grandmother could cope with losing Swiv's aunt Momo. After Momo's suicide, Grandma tells Swiv that "we were in shock," mourning Momo's death, but Grandma and Mooshie failed to realize "that [they] didn't pay close enough attention to [Swiv] during that whole time" (143). To make matters worse, Mooshie accepted an acting job in Albania, so she was not only mentally but also physically absent from her daughter. Swiv, therefore, as Grandma admits, was "running the household" (146), with far more responsibility than a nine-year-old girl would normally have. One of Toews's most endearing characters, Swiv is an odd combination of adult understanding and childhood feelings and spontaneity. Her embarrassment at anything to do with sex and her desire to censor her mother's and grandmother's exuberant behaviour show her youth. Swiv thinks that her "family should never be out in the world" (110) because of their tendency to talk to strangers on buses and generally act in ways that make her want to become invisible. "Why can't we just do things normally!" Swiv exclaims in frustration, though readers might wonder how bored she would be if her eccentric mother and grandmother suddenly became "normal" (166).

Her behaviour at school and home shows negative and positive ways of fighting. Swiv is obsessed with playing King of the Castle, fighting "even grade six boys" for domination of the schoolyard. Coming home with torn clothes, bruises, and missing clumps of hair, Swiv gets a lesson from her mother, who says that Swiv's obsession with being king of the castle "was definitely a fight, but not exactly the kind of fight she was talking about" (69). Giving an example of how, after the suicide of her father, Mooshie had a panic attack and drove herself to the hospital without waking up her husband, she says that "there were fights and then there were fights. She said it was like me playing King of the Castle at school. (I don't *play* King of the Castle.) Lonely" (70–71). Swiv's indignant interjection that King of the Castle is not play shows her independence of thought and perhaps her desire to control one small aspect of her life in which she can end up on top. But Swiv has also been isolated both at school and in her family. As Grandma says to her, "you needed your mom. You needed your dad! You needed me. You needed Momo. You needed someone! I guess that was basically the beginning of your . . . you know . . . sort of fractured relationship with school" (145–46; ellipses in the original). To her mother, however, Swiv risks loneliness when she fights by herself for something relatively unimportant. Echoing Michael Ungar's concept of "social ecological" resilience, Mooshie says that "we need teams. We need others to fight alongside us" (71), a message Elvira also gives to Swiv later in the novel (158). "Lonely fights are the worst," Mooshie continues (71–72). In spite of how embarrassing Swiv finds her elders, she, her mother, and her grandmother are definitely a team, and there are greater fights than winning a playground game.

Grandma helps Swiv to understand that, though non-violence is preferable to conflict, fighting is a lifelong activity. She tells Swiv that "people sometimes have to be punched in the face to get the message to leave you alone and not bully you, but only after double-digit times of trying to use words to no avail and only up to the age of ten or eleven" (26). Grandma also writes a letter to her unborn grandchild in which she tells Gord "you're a small thing and you must learn to fight" (79). As she knows all too well, the bigger and more powerful among us often abuse their power, so she tells Swiv and Gord to stand up against bullies and learn to fight back. Grandma learned to do this when she was young, especially when she confronted the joy-hating fundamentalism of Willit Braun, a self-proclaimed king of the castle if ever there was one. "Those Willit Brauns," says Grandma. "So smug. So certain. And they caused mass-scale tragedy" (159) by their bullying of those under their pastoral care. She continues "our love . . . our resilience! Our madness . . . we go crazy, of course! We lose ourselves. We're human. They took all those things and replaced them with evil and with guilt" (160; ellipses in the original). For Grandma, fighting involves resisting those whose judgement and intolerance oppress others, who take away "agency" and replace it with "obedience" (160). Resilience, then, comes from fighting to regain the "life force" that bullies of all stripes seek to drain away. Grandma echoes the novel's title when she comments on how important it is "to find joy and to create joy. All through the night. The fight night" (159). People, as Toews comments in her interview with Power, "get stuck in the dark and they die in the dark," yet for those who can "go to the dark places" and then find their way out again there is a "feeling of elation, of life, of joy" ("Miriam Toews on Her New Novel"). Like her other works, *Fight Night* gives us the joy and the sorrow of being alive, and it tells us to keep going.

As in *Irma Voth*, the bullies whom one confronts in life are not solely religious. Like Diego, the director of the movie that Irma works on in Mexico, in *Fight Night* the director of the movie that Mooshie acts in while in Albania "lecture[s] everyone about preparing to die. They needed to be ready to die! he said. To die for his film, to die for art" (152). Like Diego, the Albanian director intimidates his cast and insists that he be obeyed. When Mooshie refuses to "take her clothes off for a scene," for example, he asks her "didn't she understand art? Didn't she understand cinema?" (154). When she still refuses, he isolates her on the set, and her fellow workers stop talking to her. The director even prevents her from leaving the set, much as Diego tried to get Irma to stay on *his* set. Once again, Toews asks us to consider links between art and fundamentalism, both of which can be used to bully others into compliance for the sake of a higher power. Belittled and abused by the director, Swiv's mother returns to Canada depressed, exhausted, and overwhelmed by guilt for having an affair, but she makes a choice between continuing to decline or "rebuilding." As Grandma tells Swiv, "she started to rebuild! She fought her way back to life" (156). Mooshie has her own brand of resilience as she fights two kinds of death. First, after the deaths of her father and sister, she fears that she has inherited a tendency toward depression. "Her *genetic legacy*" (147) makes her fear that she will go the same way, but when she gets to Albania and thinks that she might die instead from a combination of inadequate food, vicious dogs, and isolation she decides to fight "her way back to life" (156). Grandma tells Swiv that "she realized she didn't want to die." "She was fighting, fighting, fighting . . . to stay alive. To get back to you" (158; ellipsis in the original). Mooshie has some way to go before she regains her equilibrium completely, but the birth of her second daughter, whom she names Elvira in celebration of her mother, cements her commitment to living.

Each of the three main characters in *Fight Night* is writing (or fighting) against death. Swiv, who as Grandma says is also a survivor of Momo's suicide, experiences the loss of her father and the mental breakdown of her mother yet fights to keep her grandmother alive and to maintain the household. Swiv pointedly asks her grandmother "what happens to a kid if everyone in her family is insane?" Grandma astutely answers that such a child would have "quite a bit of anxiety," often be "scared," and sometimes be "angry" (95). Although often exasperated by the antics of the older people in her family, Swiv has a gentle curiosity about the world around her and a great capacity for love, even while she picks up her grandmother's pills and hearing aid batteries when Grandma accidentally and repeatedly drops them on the floor.

Grandma has multiple attacks of angina and has been hospitalized regularly for cardiac events. She literally fights death every time she uses her nitro inhaler and takes her many pills. But she is also, as Toews says of her mother in the acknowledgements to *All My Puny Sorrows*, a "Life Force." "Everybody loves to hang on to Grandma," says Swiv in *Fight Night* (186), because her positivity and humour are infectious. Nearly every speech that she makes ends with an exclamation mark because Grandma is excitable, lively, and passionate about her ideals. She loves pretty much everyone whom she meets, and she exclaims that "peoples' stories are so *interesting*!" (130). Having survived many heart attacks, life in a repressive town, and the suicides of her husband and daughter, Grandma continues to influence the world around her for the better. She says, after all, that when she thought about how she could "survive grief" her "answer was Who can I help?" (15). Despite her poor health, therefore, she decides to take a trip to California to see her nephews because one of them is "suffering" (presumably from the family illness of depression), and she thinks that she can help him (174). Unlike the characters in *Summer of My Amazing Luck* and *The Flying Troutmans* who embark on road trips because they do not feel strong enough to cope on their own, Grandma, in spite of her physical weakness, travels because she knows that she has the inner strength to help others. Her enthusiasm for life makes all of the mishaps during her and Swiv's journey to California seem humorous rather than frustrating. Swiv describes how her grandmother "just sat there looking into the distance and vibrating with joy and wonder the whole time like she'd never been in a car before" (172). Like Thebes Troutman, she sees the world "with fresh eyes" (*Flying* 187). Where others might cry or get angry, she laughs.

Her enthusiasm finally gets the better of Grandma when, during her time in California, she visits a retirement residence that houses many of her former townsfolk, refugees from the *"officious little dictator"* Willit Braun (192). After spending hours cheering up her many friends and relatives, Grandma does a dance and kicks too high, only to fall down and break her arm. Even so, she insists on getting back to Toronto before she sees a doctor because she does not want to incur a giant hospital bill in the United States, a decision that likely contributes to her death when the stress of travelling with "her broken arm and petering-out heart" causes her to collapse on the plane and be taken to the hospital in an ambulance (225).

But Grandma's death is also a lesson in when to stop fighting and illustrates that surrender, too, is an option. One of the remarkable things about *Fight Night* is its resistance to the narrative of the failed battle with mental illness. As Anne Hunsaker Hawkins shows in *Reconstructing Illness: Studies in Pathography*, "metaphors of battle and journey are ubiquitous in pathography" (61). People describe their "battles" with cancer, they "win" their fights against drug addiction, or they "lose" their struggles and succumb to illness. The metaphor of battle implies a foreign force that enters the mind or body in an attempt to destroy it, and thus the metaphor echoes paradigms of "the struggle between light and darkness, life and death, good and evil" (62). Since each of these dichotomies has a moral aspect, ill people who do not fight can be blamed for partaking in their own destruction, even though the illness that has overtaken them might be too strong to fight successfully. In addition, Hawkins says, the metaphor can be detrimental when it "functions in such a way that the sick person becomes the battlefield, or the energies of both doctor and patient are displaced onto fighting the disease rather than helping the human being who is sick" (66). Such situations arise with Min in *The Flying Troutmans*, Elf in *All My Puny Sorrows*, and Momo in *Fight Night*, in which "clueless" (*Fight Night* 140) health professionals condemn the women for their failure to do what is necessary to get well. In these cases, the needs of the patients are ignored because the women are not seen to be fighting in the right way. As Hawkins writes, "the military myth connotes power and aggressive action and, thus, serves as a strong contrast to the passivity usually associated with an illness" (88). For some, such a myth can give them agency and a sense of control; for those who either prefer to be passive or do not have the energy to fight, not being sick in the "right" way can lead to condemnatory actions by loved ones or health professionals.

Mel, Elf, and Momo might have lost their fights against depression, but that is only after many years of trying their best to live in the world, hold down jobs, and offer support to others. Swiv narrates her mother's comment that "we're all fighters, our whole family. Even the dead ones. They fought the hardest" (*Fight Night* 65) because they were in the grip of intractable mental illness. The Willit Brauns of the world see suicide as a sin against God, and the non-religious might see it as a surrender to forces that the ill individual should have kept on battling. However, such condemnatory stances miss the point. As Grandma says of her husband and Momo, "their suicides weren't *misdeeds*" (60) or even the craven actions of the weak. It is not a sin to lose to a powerful enemy, even if to do so is tragic. Grandma tells Swiv that "Momo fought so hard. She made all those jokes. . . . We had all been fighting hard. Momo most of all. But we lost. We lost! Did Momo make a decision to stop fighting? Was it a conscious decision? Well, we don't know. I'd say it was. I'd say it was and we can honour that" (139). Through Grandma's comments on Momo's death, Toews illustrates how ceasing to fight can also be an act of bravery, a renunciation of those who want to bully a person back to life. As she has made clear in her discussion of physician-assisted death for the mentally ill in *All My Puny Sorrows*, continuing to live might be too painful to contemplate, and options to take one's life in a way that is respectful to the individual involved should be available to all. In *Fight Night*, Grandma is still, according to Swiv, "sad and mad that Grandpa and Auntie Momo couldn't go the assisted dying route" (35) since it would have given them the autonomy to die peacefully with family members beside them. In another echo of *Puny Sorrows*, Grandma mourns that her loved ones died alone (65).

Yet *Fight Night* also acknowledges that resilience is only partially in our control. As Grandma says of Mooshie after her return from Albania, "now I think that she was getting rid of her old self. She was getting rid of the self that was vulnerable, the self that had maybe inherited this horrible disease . . . her *genetic legacy*" (146–47; ellipsis in original). And *Fight Night* ends with the scenario starting again. Swiv now has a sister, and both girls might have the same genetic inheritance as their aunt and grandfather. Since clinical depression often begins during adolescence or early adulthood, the two sisters might repeat the dynamic of their mother and aunt—or Yoli and Elf in *All My Puny Sorrows*, Hattie and Min in *The Flying Troutmans*, or Miriam and Marjorie Toews—with one sister showing resilience and the other eventually succumbing to mental illness.

It seems, however, that the ability to be resilient might *also* be learned and/or inherited. Grandma talks about the "fire" that she sees in her granddaughter, and like mental illness it might be passed on to the next generation. "Bioluminescence," explains Grandma, is "one's ability to create light from within. . . . Like a firefly. I think you have that, Swivchen. You have a fire inside you and your job is to not let it go out" (*Fight Night* 23). For Grandma, surrender is not the problem; never having fought is the problem. At one point, Swiv and Grandma watch a Toronto Raptors basketball game, and the players do not seem to be trying. Athletic metaphors are also common in stories of illness since "illness is here subsumed into the conventions of a sport, where how the game is played counts almost as much as who wins" (Hawkins, *Reconstructing* 73). Grandma becomes agitated as she watches the Raptors give up, and Swiv reports that "she said that's a terrible, terrible way to lose, by not trying and not fighting. You play hard to the end, Swiv. To the buzzer. There is no alternative" (*Fight Night* 88). Being resilient means playing to the end, even when losing seems to be inevitable. And, of course, speaking about life, there is only one ending. "Life is a failed mission!" says Grandma (221).

And so *Fight Night* ends with a birth and a death. After all the times that she has recovered from heart attacks, Grandma finally requests that no medical interventions be used to keep her alive. Swiv tries to convince her that the "fire inside her" is still there, but Grandma has made her choice, which shows her courage to face death. Although Swiv is devastated to lose her much-loved grandmother, she speculates after her death that Grandma taught her "what fighting is, even when it's making peace" (249). Perhaps Swiv will learn that she does not always have to be king of the castle. Near the end of the novel, after all, she describes how "Mom and I jogged down the hallway to Grandma. Mom held her giant stomach up with one hand. I held her other hand. We were all connected to each other like a search party" (228). As Grandma fails, Swiv draws on her mother's strength, as her mother draws on hers.

The book's final scene, which takes place after Grandma's death, reminds readers of her habit of accidentally dropping pills and hearing aid batteries. If Grandma noticed that she had dropped something, she would say "bombs away, Swiv!" Swiv would "come running and drop down onto the floor and scramble around" to retrieve the lost object (22). In the concluding words of the novel, she sees "one tiny blue pill on the floor under the table where Grandma sits. Bombs away, Swiv! I heard her say," and then Swiv continues, "man, you should have seen how fast I fell to my knees" (251). Not only does she describe her grandmother in the present tense, but also she links seeing the pill to rereading "Grandma's letter to Gord" in which Grandma told her unborn grandchild *you're a small thing and you must learn to fight*" (250). The book's concluding idea, therefore, links fighting and submission, Grandma's indefatigable spirit and her surrender to death. Once when Swiv was "crawling around looking" for a lost object, Grandma told her that "she had a friend named Emiliano Zapata who said it was better to die on your feet than to live on your knees" (43). Here, it seems, fighters stay on their feet, whereas those who capitulate kneel in front of their enemies; however, in the context of the novel, in which Momo and Grandpa fought until they could fight no longer and left behind Grandma, Mooshie, and Swiv to survive in the wake of traumatic loss, there is always the possibility of standing up once more. One can remember the past, as Grandma does when she uses Momo's obituary as a bookmark (58), without being destroyed by it. Resilience is possible.

Mooshie, who in Grandma's understated phrase begins the novel with "a tiny bit of PTSD" (18), gradually recovers, helped by Grandma and by

Swiv's reported affirmation that "you're strong. . . . That's what everyone in California said" (229). Swiv, who has feared that Mooshie's anger and crying might lead to suicide, now knows that her mother is essentially "strong and happy" (229). Referring to life in the town in which she grew up, Grandma reinforces the need to fight: "We fight for our lives . . . some of us lose the fight . . . oh, it can bring a person to her knees" (160–61; ellipses in the original). We are often, as Grandma says here, brought to our knees, but resilience comes from fighting to love ourselves and others, to avoid tyranny, and to be ourselves. Perhaps Swiv has learned enough from her mother and grandmother to do the same. Swiv goes to her knees to pick up a reminder of her grandmother, the "tiny blue pill" that remains after her death, and in doing so she remembers her grandmother not only in the past but also as a continuing force in the present and an inspiration for the future.

In Toews's many explorations of resilience, readers observe Lucy Van Alstyne and Hattie Troutman, who attempt to alleviate feelings of inadequacy by taking road trips to find missing fathers, only to find that they have more resources than they originally believed. The eight "women talking" and Irma Voth find the courage to reassess patriarchal interpretations of their worth and to flee tyranny, thus saving themselves and affirming what is valuable in the religion that hitherto has been used to control them. Like *A Boy of Good Breeding*, *A Complicated Kindness* addresses how resilience is challenged by rigid definitions of home as Hosea's obsessive need to keep his town's population at exactly 1,500 people and The Mouth's focus on strict obedience to religious doctrine threaten to destroy not only their own happiness but also the lives of others. Although *Complicated* concludes with Nomi torn between staying in a community that has rejected her and leaving a home that represents her only hope of being reunited with her lost family, the novel shows her incipient resilience through her humour, her resistance to oppression, and her dreams for the future. Hosea, of course, finds resilience when he accepts that he cannot control every aspect of life in Algren. Finally, in *Swing Low* and *All My Puny Sorrows*, Toews explores how those bereaved by familial suicide can rebuild their lives disrupted by loss. In these texts, resilience comes from reframing the suicide within the personal narrative of the author. Writing the story of suicide becomes a reparative strategy.

Fight Night continues Toews's coming to terms with her past. Her works breathe compassion and anger, joy and sadness. They are empathetic in their descriptions of trauma and courageous in the way that they stand up to multiple forms of tyranny. They offer deep insights into the lives of men and women, and they are inspirational in their message that we can continue with our lives in spite of the "slings and arrows of outrageous fortune" (*Hamlet* 3.1.57). As Hamlet's famous soliloquy suggests, there are many choices in life, and one of the most important is whether "to take arms against a sea of troubles" (3.1.58) or to give up the fight. Through her continuing engagement with the theme of resilience, Toews provides us with echoes of the life that she has lived, even as she writes about lives that she has imagined and embodied in her fiction. In a way, she teams up with each of us as we read her works. We feel stronger through our exposure to her wit, intelligence, compassion, and stubbornness. Toews asserts in an interview with Shelagh Rogers, "The fight is the fight to live, the fight for happiness, the fight for connection with human beings, the fight against loneliness, against alienation. There are the other fights. We can fight authority and climate change and fascism and the Taliban. But in this case, the fight is to be able to go into your heart and to love and to experience joy, to spread joy. And that's not always easy" ("Why a Nine-Year-Old"). Being joyful is difficult—there is so much trouble in our world—but her inspirational writing shows that joy is possible in the midst of suffering. Although not all people have the capacity to be resilient, others can go forward and continue to live their lives with integrity, humour, and insight. Since Toews, like Elvira in *Fight Night*, often quotes from the Bible, perhaps a passage from Psalms is a fitting ending for this book. The Psalms are full of joy and sorrow, but, as David the Psalmist says, "Weeping may endure for a night, / But joy comes in the morning" (Psalm 30:5, NKJV).

ACKNOWLEDGEMENTS

It has been a pleasure writing this monograph on the works of Miriam Toews, and I would like to thank her for her inspiring books and her generosity. As one would expect from reading her works, she has been kind, open, and candid in answering my questions. Miriam Toews's agent, Sarah Chalfant, has also been helpful in smoothing out the permissions process.

I would also like to thank the editors and staff at the University of Manitoba Press. First, Jill McConkey has been an astute and careful editor whose suggestions have improved the original draft of my manuscript. She has read my work with attention to detail and sharp intelligence. The Press's director, David Larsen, and the managing editor, Glenn Bergen, have also been helpful in guiding me through the publishing process. Dallas Harrison, who did the copy edit for this book, also requires thanks and appreciation as does Heidi Harms, for her careful proofreading. Adrian Mather gets credit for creating the index to this monograph.

Although I do not know their names, I would be remiss in not mentioning the two anonymous reviewers who gave helpful suggestions on improving the manuscript. Both reviewers took the time to provide detailed and thoughtful responses. I especially appreciate that they did this during the early stages of the Covid pandemic, when everyone was overwhelmed by moving their work online and coping with expanding restrictions. As my first reader and a loving support in my academic endeavours, my husband, Cliff Werier, deserves special thanks.

PERMISSIONS

NOTES

1   For those who might wonder about such an odd name, Toews writes that "I thought it was kind of cool, kind of ridiculous. But I used it because I was listening a lot to Jonathan Richman in those days and he had a song I love called 'That Summer Feeling.' For some reason I just dropped the 'g' to make it sound even more goofy as a name. It struck me as the kind of name a young sort of 'rebellious' couple would give their kid" (email to the author, 1 May 2020).

2   Although Steinbach is now the third largest city in Manitoba, with a population of 17,806 in 2022 (City of Steinbach), when Toews was growing up there, the population was considerably smaller. She was born in 1964, and in 1971 the population was just over 5,000. By 1981, it had grown to over 6,600 ("Steinbach"). Toews might have called her fictional town East Village because Steinbach is the largest city in the Eastman region of Manitoba.

3   In an interview with Toews, Hildi Froese Tiessen says that "it's occurred to me that there is virtually no Mennonite presence in your fiction—except for Hosea Funk, in *A Boy of Good Breeding*, of course" ("Place" 60). A couple of other Mennonite surnames creep into the text: Veronica *Epp* and Willie *Wiebe*'s Western Wear (83). Funk is a fairly common Mennonite surname (see Wenger). See also Andrew Unger, who in 2017 listed the most common surnames in the Steinbach phone book. There were, apparently, eighty-one listings for Funk (and seventy-six listings for Toews). Of course, the *Daily Bonnet* is "your trusted source for Mennonite satire," so this is not a scientific study.

4   Since Toews was reading the novels of Nelson Algren when *A Boy of Good Breeding* was first published, she might have decided to create this odd creature because of a passage from *The Man with the Golden Arm* (1949) in which a man cadges a beer by biting a cockroach in half and then calling urgently for something with which to wash it down. Toews mentions Nelson Algren in an interview with Di Brandt ("Complicated" 20) and in an email to me (1 May 2020). The reference linking Algren to cockroaches comes from Schweid (5).

5   James Urry writes that "some Anabaptists were unwilling to wait peacefully for Christ's return and believed that in preparation they needed to establish a

New Jerusalem, destroy the godless, and defend their new order by use of force" (*Mennonites* 20). Armed conflict broke out in Münster in 1534–35. During the Russian Civil War, some Mennonites formed the *Selbstschutz*, a self-defence group that not only protected Mennonite interests but also destroyed the Mennonites' moral claim not to take part in armed conflict (Kroeger 48–49).

6   Miriam Toews usually quotes from the King James Version of the Bible (1611), but for ease of reading, I use the New King James Version in my commentary on her work.

7   Nomi's description of how East Village became more strictly religious under The Mouth's authority echoes what happened in Steinbach in the 1970s. Christoph Wiebe writes about how "at the end of the 1960s or the beginning of the 1970s . . . there was an attempt in many churches in Steinbach . . . [to] 'cleanse' the congregations through rigorous church discipline, including excommunication and avoidance." Mennonite historian Royden Loewen reports that "until 1970 there was a men's-only pub on Steinbach's main street. Once the town embraced temperance in the early 1970s, drinkers were still able to get a pint at the Franz Motor Inn, which set up a beverage room just outside the town boundary" (qtd. in Friesen). Six referendums over a thirty-year period resolved to maintain Steinbach's alcohol-free status. Then in 2003, by a narrow margin of 50.9 to 49.1 percent, town residents voted to allow alcohol to be served with food. Five years later the town council voted that a liquor store could be opened within the town limits (Friesen).

8   Written in 1912 by the Reverend George Bennard, this hymn has been a mainstay ever since.

9   Coined by Thomson, the term "normate" highlights the limitations and assumptions behind the term "normal." She writes that "the term *normate* usefully designates the social figure through which people can represent themselves as definitive human beings. Normate, then, is the constructed identity of those who, by way of the bodily configurations and cultural capital they assume, can step into a position of authority and wield the power it grants them" (*Extraordinary Bodies* 8).

10 This popular tourist attraction was established in 1967 (Goldsborough, Penner, and Goldsborough).

11 See the *Oxford English Dictionary* entries for *nostalgia* and the roots *nostos* and *-algia*. As the *OED* notes, the combination form *-algia* can be found in words such as *causalgia*, *myalgia*, and *neuralgia*.

12 See, for example, *A Boy of Good Breeding*, 42. Those who want more information on this traditional canon can reference musician and educator Walter Bitner's comments on the tune and its origins.

13 Gabor Maté's book *In the Realm of Hungry Ghosts: Close Encounters with Addiction* (2008) gives an excellent overview of how his experiences as a doctor in Vancouver's Downtown Eastside support research showing that addicts have brains that have developed differently from those of non-addicts.

CHAPTER TWO

1   According to an email to the author, Toews has "definitely read *On the Road*. and *Off the Road* by Carolyn Cassady, Neal Cassady's Wife" (19 March 2020). For more on Carolyn Cassady's memoir, see Ganser (*Roads* 46–48). Ganser also provides an extensive and perceptive analysis of Aritha van Herk's *No Fixed Address*.

2   I take my emphasis on *The Rez Sisters* and *No Fixed Address* from Macfarlane.

3   In place from 1885 to circa 1941, the pass system prevented Indigenous people on the prairies from leaving their reservations without official permission. For more on the pass system, see Williams.

4   Tom Shakespeare writes that "the social model [of disability] demonstrates that the problems disabled people face are the result of social oppression and exclusion, not their individual deficits. This places the moral responsibility on society to remove the burdens which have been imposed, and to enable disabled people to participate" (217). He points out that the social model has been an important impetus for universal design and other accommodations. However, the model has its flaws. For one thing, the distinction between disability and impairment can deny some people the right to their own ways of being. As Shakespeare puts it, "the social model so strongly disowns individual and medical approaches . . . that it risks implying that impairment is not a problem" (217–18). As well, some impairments/disabilities are not easily accommodated. "While environments and services can and should be adapted wherever possible," he writes, "there remains disadvantage associated with having many impairments which no amount of environmental change could entirely eliminate" (219).

5   Composed in 1946 by Bobby Troup and recorded the same year by Nat King Cole, the song was an instant hit, and it has since been recorded by artists as diverse as Chuck Berry, The Rolling Stones, Manhattan Transfer, and Aerosmith. See "Get Your Kicks."

6   See, for instance, *John Dillinger*; and Weir.

7   Margaret Steffler points out that in *A Complicated Kindness* Nomi lists *Lives of Girls and Women* as one of the things left behind by Tash ("Fragments" 125). Steffler makes insightful connections between the two novels.

8   Keats wrote to George and Thomas Keats, "I mean *Negative Capability,* that is when man is capable of being in uncertainties, Mysteries, doubts, without any irritable reaching after fact & reason" (261; emphasis in original).

CHAPTER THREE

1 See the four-part series "Modern Ghosts of a Horse-Drawn Scandal" (Braun); also see Friedman-Rudovsky.

2 In *Women Talking*, the colony's bishop, Peters, attributes one character's account of a particularly horrific attack to "wild female imagination" (57). Toews, however, got this term from various media accounts of the rapes. See, for instance, Friedman-Rudovsky.

3 According to Royden Loewen in his book *Horse-and-Buggy Genius: Listening to Mennonites Contest the Modern World*, there "are two sets of horse-and-buggy Mennonites linked to Canada: the first lives in Canada while the second consists of Canadian descendants who live in Latin America" (5). Those who live in Canada are referred to as "Old Order" Mennonites, while the Mennonites who moved to South America are referred to as "Old Colony" Mennonites.

4 For more information, see Clason; Grether; and Johns.

5 Toews writes in the acknowledgements printed after the conclusion of *Irma Voth* that "on page 175 I quoted from a beautifully written obituary sent to me in a letter from a friend. I know that it ran in the *Globe and Mail* newspaper but regret that I have no idea when and do not know who was being so well celebrated" (n. pag.). The quotation comes from Michael Posner, who wrote of Helen Weinzweig that "she believed something else, adds [her son] Paul. She believed that every trauma presented a choice: either paralysis or the psychic energy to move forward. 'Helen likened the energy of trauma to a cobalt bomb with a radioactive half-life of 100 years. Perhaps that's how she lived so long.'"

6 Named after Jules Cotard, who first discussed this "délire des négations" in 1880, "Cotard's syndrome is a rare disorder in which nihilistic delusions concerning one's own body are the central feature." Basically, the patient believes that he or she is dead (Debruyne et al. 198, 197). For an overview, see Debruyne et al.

7 August references Christ's words to Peter: "And I say also unto thee, That thou art Peter, and upon this rock I will build my church; and the gates of hell shall not prevail against it" (Matthew 16:18 KJV).

CHAPTER FOUR

1 As is common when discussing suicide, I use the term "suicide survivor" to refer to those who have lost a close family member or friend to suicide.

2 Kehler also applies Leigh Gilmore's theory to *Swing Low*. Gilmore believes that, especially in cases of trauma, the traumatized individual's inability to find language to describe the trauma forces some authors to write at the boundary between autobiography and fiction. As Kehler summarizes, "This kind of risk-taking is most needful, according to Gilmore, in narratives of woundedness or trauma, since no ready-made

or 'transparent language' exists in which to express self-fragmentation and to articulate the tangled affective and physical contexts out of which the individual emerges" (162–63).

3 Highly publicized cases show how readers express outrage when they discover that an author has misrepresented the facts. Rigoberta Menchú, winner of the Nobel Peace Prize in 1992, for instance, was found to have embroidered the truth when she recounted witnessing "her brother's torture and murder." The resulting "firestorm of criticism of Menchú, followed by a counteroffensive by Menchú's supporters," illustrates how some readers feel cheated when authors of non-fiction bend the truth, even though, in her case, others defended her authorial decisions (Lauritzen 25). In defence of Menchú's autobiographical inaccuracies, Paul Lauritzen points out the overall truth of her exposé on how the ruling government abused Guatemala's Indigenous people. "These truths are not in doubt" since they have been well documented by independent studies. "So whatever minor details Menchú got wrong, they pale in comparison to the larger truth to which *I, Rigoberta Menchú* calls our attention" (29). Lauritzen also describes what he calls "the genre argument": that is, Menchú wrote a *testimonio*, a South American genre that "seeks to elicit solidarity with the struggles of the poor and disenfranchised." In a *testimonio*, the author "seeks to give voice to collective experience through narrating personal experience" (26).

4 For a thorough discussion of this controversy, see Nardin.

5 Couser softened his stance in his recent essay "Illness, Disability, and Ethical Life Writing" (2018). After grappling with how to write a memoir of his father, who died in his late sixties from "depression—by way of self-medication with alcohol," Couser admits that "there is no question that [his father] would not have wanted some stories told," so Couser was "perplexed about what was fair to include." He then admits how he now "recognize[s] how easy it was to render ['pronouncements about the ethics of life writing'] from a critic's, rather than a writer's, perspective."

6 Kehler is quoting Arthur Frank here; emphasis in original.

7 In quoting from this interview, I am using my own transcription. I have made slight editorial changes to remove repetition and the "ums" and "ahs" of spoken dialogue.

8 Walter writes that "the foundations for the scientific, psychological understanding of grief are generally cited as Freud's (1913) article *Mourning and Melancholia* and [Erich] Lindemann's work three decades later (1944)" (7).

9 According to Horowitz et al., prior to the publication of *DSM-IV* in 1994, there was considerable debate about whether to include complicated grief [CG] as a separate diagnostic category (904). M. Katherine Shear stated that

> CG is not in *DSM-IV*, so there are no standard, official criteria. However there is considerable evidence that CG is a specific syndrome, different from normal grief and from other mood and anxiety disorders. The clinical picture can be understood as comprised of prolonged and intense acute grief symptoms accompanied by an array of complicating thoughts, feelings, and behaviors. Symptoms of acute grief include intense yearning or longing for the person who died, intrusive or preoccupying thoughts or images of the deceased

person, a sense of loss of meaning or purpose in a life without the deceased, and a cluster of other symptoms that interfere with activities or relationships with significant others. (122)

DSM-V (American Psychological Association) includes the category "Persistent Complex Bereavement Disorder."

10 Toews makes similar arguments in interviews with Eric Volmers, Jian Ghomeshi, and Kate Taylor. See Toews, "*All My Puny Sorrows*"; "Miriam Toews Brings"; and "Profound Despair."

11 Anne Coleridge was born in 1767 and died of consumption in 1791. Samuel Taylor Coleridge was born in 1771 and died in 1834.

12 In her article, "The Presence of Absence: Sister-Loss and Home-Loss in Miriam Toews's *All My Puny Sorrows*," Margaret Steffler speaks of "what Grace Kehler has referred to as Toews's trilogy of autobiographical fiction—*A Complicated Kindness* (2004), *The Flying Troutmans* (2008), and *All My Puny Sorrows* (2014). Steffler mentions how, in each of these novels, "first-person narrators . . . face the loss of their older sisters" in "increasingly devastating" ways (54). Critics' tendency to read Toews's books as linked may stem from Toews's autofictional approach. Steffler comments, for example, "This autobiographical material, fictionalized in detail but true in emotion, exposes the rawness of recently lived life. Such 'autofiction,' written directly out of personal suffering not yet processed, holds back very little in its deliberate and open embrace of vulnerability" ("Presence of Absence" 60).

CONCLUSION

1 The name Swiv has correspondences to Toews's other works. In *A Complicated Kindness*, Tash calls Nomi "Swivelhead" because of her tendency to "look from Trudie to Ray to Tash back to Trudie to Ray to Tash and on and on trying desperately to understand what it was they were talking about" (17). In *All My Puny Sorrows*, Yoli mentions that Elf called her "Swivelhead" or "Swiv": "Swivelhead (that was her nickname for me because I was very often looking around for solid clues to what was going on and never finding them)" (22).

2 I am relying here on my own transcription of the interview.

REFERENCES

American Psychological Association. "Persistent Complex Bereavement Disorder." In *Diagnostic and Statistical Manual of Mental Disorders*, 5th ed., 789–92. Washington, DC: American Psychological Association, 2013.

Appignanesi, Lisa. *Sad, Mad and Bad: Women and the Mind-Doctors from 1800*. Toronto: McArthur, 2007.

Árnason, Arnar. "Biography, Bereavement, Story." *Mortality* 5, no. 2 (2000): 189–204.

Austen, Jane. *Northanger Abbey*. London: Penguin, 1972. First published 1818.

Barber, John. "Miriam Toews: It's a Mennonite Thing." *Globe and Mail*, 8 April 2011. https://www.theglobeandmail.com/arts/books-and-media/miriam-toews-its-a-mennonite-thing/article4267807/ (accessed 3 February 2020).

Baril, Alexandre. "The Somatechnologies of Canada's Medical Assistance in Dying Law: LGBTQ Discourses on Suicide and the Injunction to Live." *Somatechnics* 7, no. 2 (2017): 201–17.

Barlow, Constance A., and Helen Morrison. "Survivors of Suicide: Emerging Counseling Strategies." *Journal of Psychosocial Nursing and Mental Health Services* 40, no. 1 (2002): 28–39.

Bayliss, Graeme. "It Doesn't Get Better: The Mentally Ill Deserve the Right to Die with Dignity." *Walrus*, 14 April 2016, updated 18 February 2020. https://thewalrus.ca/suicide-is-not-painless/ (accessed 12 June 2020).

Beck, Ervin. "Mennonite Transgressive Literature." In *After Identity: Mennonite Writing in North America*, edited by Robert Zacharias, 52–69. Winnipeg: University of Manitoba Press, 2015.

Begley, Mary, and Ethel Quayle. "The Lived Experience of Adults Bereaved by Suicide: A Phenomenological Study." *Crisis* 28, no. 1 (2007): 26–34.

Bennard, George. "The Old Rugged Cross." 1912. GodTube. https://www.godtube.com/popular-hymns/the-old-rugged-cross/ (accessed 12 May 2020).

Bethune, Brian. "Miriam Toews: Nudging Along a Difficult Conversation." *Maclean's*, 11 October 2014. http://www.macleans.ca/culture/books/Miriam-toews-nudges-along-a-difficult-conversation/ (accessed 12 May 2016).

Birns, Margaret Boe. Review of *A Complicated Kindness*. *Canadian Ethnic Studies* 37, no. 1 (2005): 163–64.

Bitner, Walter. "Man's Life's a Vapor." *Walter Bitner Off the Podium*. Blog Post, 7 March 2020, https://walterbitner.com/2020/03/07/mans-lifes-a-vapor/ (accessed 6 June 2022).

Born, Brad S. "The 'Disciple of Life' on Suicide Watch: Reading Miriam Toews' *All My Puny Sorrows* and Other Mennonite Women's Writing about Familial Mental Illness." *Mennonite Life* 69 (2015). https://mla.bethelks.edu/ml-archive/2015/the-disciple-of-life-on-suicide-watch-reading-miri.php (accessed 8 June 2020).

Bowen, Dawn S. "*Die Auswanderung*: Religion, Culture, and Migration among Old Colony Mennonites." *Canadian Geographer* 45, no. 4 (2001): 461–73.

Brandt, Di. Review of *Summer of My Amazing Luck*. *Prairie Fire* 18, no. 2 (1997): 113–14.

———. *So This Is the World and Here I Am in It*. Edmonton: NeWest Press, 2007.

Braun, Will. "Modern Ghosts of a Horse-Drawn Scandal." Part 1. *Canadian Mennonite Magazine*, 3 October 2018. https://canadianmennonite.org/stories/modern-ghosts-horse-drawn-scandal-part-1 (accessed 10 April 2019).

———. "Modern Ghosts of a Horse-Drawn Scandal." Part 2. *Canadian Mennonite Magazine*, 17 October 2018. https://canadianmennonite.org/stories/modern-ghosts-horse-drawn-scandal-part-2 (accessed 10 April 2019).

———. "Modern Ghosts of a Horse-Drawn Scandal." Part 3. *Canadian Mennonite Magazine*, 31 October 2018. https://canadianmennonite.org/stories/modern-ghosts-horse-drawn-scandal-part-3 (accessed 10 April 2019).

———. "Modern Ghosts of a Horse-Drawn Scandal." Part 4. *Canadian Mennonite Magazine*, 21 November 2018. https://canadianmennonite.org/stories/modern-ghosts-horse-drawn-scandal-part-4 (accessed 10 April 2019).

Bridgemon, Rondal R. "Mennonites and Mormons in Northern Chihuahua, Mexico." *Journal of the Southwest* 54, no. 1 (2012): 71–77.

Brontë, Charlotte. *Jane Eyre*. New York: W.W. Norton and Company, 1987. First published 1847.

Carter v. Canada (Attorney General) (2015), 1 SCR 331, Case Number 35591. Judgements of the Supreme Court of Canada. https://scc-csc.lexum.com/scc-csc/scc-csc/en/item/14637/index.do (accessed 11 May 2015).

Caruth, Cathy. "Introduction." In *Trauma: Explorations in Memory*, edited by Cathy Caruth, 3–12. Baltimore: Johns Hopkins University Press, 1995.

———. *Literature in the Ashes of History*. Baltimore: Johns Hopkins University Press, 2013.

Casey, Nell, ed. *Unholy Ghost: Writers on Depression*. New York: Perennial, 2002.

Cassady, Carolyn. *Off the Road*. Kindle ed. New York: Overlook, 2008. First published 1990.

Chesler, Phyllis. *Women and Madness*. Rev. ed. New York: Palgrave Macmillan, 2005.

City of Steinbach. "New Census Data Shows Steinbach Continues to Grow." City of Steinbach, 2022, https://www.steinbach.ca/notices-and-announcements/census-data-shows-steinbach-continues-to-grow/ (accessed 5 June 2022).

Clarke, Deborah. "Domesticating the Car: Women's Road Trips." *Studies in American Fiction* 32, no. 1 (2004): 101–28.

Clason, Marmy A. "Feminism, Generic 'He,' and the TNIV Bible Translation Debate." *Critical Discourse Studies* 3, no. 1 (2006): 23–35.

Coates, Jennifer. *Women, Men and Language: A Sociolinguistic Account of Gender Differences in Language.* 3rd ed. Toronto: Pearson Longman, 2004.

Cook, Elinor. "Numbers Game." Review of *A Boy of Good Breeding*, by Miriam Toews. *New Statesman* 135 (2006): 51. Literature Resource Center.

Couser, G. Thomas. "Illness, Disability, and Ethical Life Writing." *CLCWeb: Comparative Literature and Culture* 20, no. 5 (2018). https://doi.org/10.7771/1481-4374.3482.

———. *Recovering Bodies: Illness, Disability, and Life Writing.* Madison: University of Wisconsin Press, 1997.

———. *Vulnerable Subjects: Ethics and Life Writing.* Ithaca: Cornell University Press, 2004.

Cruz, Daniel Shank. "Narrative Ethics in Miriam Toew[s]'s *Summer of My Amazing Luck*." *Canadian Mennonite Journal* 5, no. 1 (2013). https://mennonitewriting.org/journal/5/1/narrative-ethics-miriam-toews-summer-my-amazing-lu/ (accessed 11 September 2019).

Debruyne, Hans, Michael Portzky, Frédérique Van den Eynde, and Kurt Audenaert. "Cotard's Syndrome: A Review." *Current Psychiatry Reports* 11, no. 3 (2009): 197–202.

Denham, Paul. "Out of Control." Review of *The Flying Troutmans*, by Miriam Toews, and *The Killing Circle*, by Andrew Pyper. *Canadian Literature* 200 (2009): 196–97.

Domosh, Mona, and Joni Seager. *Putting Women in Place: Feminist Geographers Make Sense of the World.* New York: Guilford Press, 2001.

Dying with Dignity Canada. "Challenges to Choice: Bill C-14, One Year Later." July 2017. http://d3n8a8pro7vhmx.cloudfront.net/dwdcanada/mailings/648/attachments/original/DWDC_-_Challenges_to_Choice_-_July_2017_-_final.pdf?1499808563 (accessed 11 June 2020).

Eakin, Paul John, ed. *The Ethics of Life Writing.* Ithaca, NY: Cornell University Press, 2004.

———. "Relational Selves, Relational Lives: The Story of the Story." In *True Relations: Essays on Autobiography and the Postmodern*, edited by G. Thomas Couser and Joseph Fichtelberg, 63–81. Westport, CT: Greenwood Press, 1988.

Elliott, Carl. *Better than Well: American Medicine Meets the American Dream.* New York: Norton, 2003.

Epp, Marlene. *Mennonite Women in Canada: A History.* Winnipeg: University of Manitoba Press, 2008.

Farr, Moira. "He's Come Undone." Review of *Swing Low: A Life*, by Miriam Toews. *Globe and Mail*, 15 April 2000, updated 27 March 2018. https://www.theglobeandmail.com/arts/hes-come-undone/article767186/ (accessed 3 March 2020).

Foakes, R.A. Introduction to *King* Lear by William Shakespeare, 1–151. Edited by R.A. Foakes. London: The Arden Shakespeare, Third Series, 2003. First published in 1997.

Foucault, Michel. *Psychiatric Power: Lectures at the Collège de France 1973–1974*. Edited by Jacques Lagrange. Translated by Graham Burchell. New York: Palgrave Macmillan, 2006.

Frank, Arthur W. *The Wounded Storyteller: Body, Illness, and Ethics*. Chicago: University of Chicago Press, 1995.

Friedman-Rudovsky, Jean. "The Ghost Rapes of Bolivia." *Vice*, 22 December 2013. https://www.vice.com/us/article/4w7gqi/the-ghost-rapes-of-bolivia-000300-v20n8 (accessed 4 October 2019).

———. "A Verdict in Bolivia's Shocking Case of the Mennonite Rapes." *Time*, 17 August 2011. http://content.time.com/time/world/article/0,8599,2087711,00.html (accessed 6 November 2011).

Friesen, Joe. "Dry Mennonite Community Turns to Drink." *Globe and Mail*, 23 February 2008, A5. https://www.theglobeandmail.com/news/national/dry-mennonite-community-turns-to-drink/article17981185/ (accessed 23 February 2008).

Ganser, Alexandra. "On the Asphalt Frontier: American Women's Road Narratives, Spatiality, and Transgression." *Journal of International Women's Studies* 7, no. 4 (2006): 153–67.

———. *Roads of Her Own: Gendered Space and Mobility in American Women's Road Narratives, 1970–2000*. Amsterdam: Editions Rodopi, 2009. ProQuest Ebook Central.

"Get Your Kicks on Route 66." Road Trip Journeys, 20 May 2019. https://www.theroute-66.com/get-your-kicks.html (accessed 6 January 2020).

Giesbrecht, Donovan. "Metis, Mennonites and the 'Unsettled Prairie,' 1874–1896." *Journal of Mennonite Studies* 19 (2000): 103–11.

Gilmore, Leigh. *The Limits of Autobiography: Trauma and Testimony*. Ithaca, NY: Cornell University Press, 2001.

Goldsborough, Gordon, George Penner, and S. Goldsborough. "Historic Sites of Manitoba: Mennonite Village Museum/Mennonite Heritage Village (Highway 12, Steinbach)," Manitoba Historical Society, 27 January 2022. http://www.mhs.mb.ca/docs/sites/mennonitevillage.shtml (accessed 30 July 2022).

Goldsmith, Oliver. "The Rising Village." 1825. Representative Poetry Online, University of Toronto. https://rpo.library.utoronto.ca/poems/rising-village (accessed 12 December 2019).

Government of Canada. "Medical Assistance in Dying." 6 June 2021. https://www.canada.ca/en/health-canada/services/medical-assistance-dying.html (accessed 3 August 2021).

———. Department of Justice. "Legislative Background: Medical Assistance in Dying (Bill C-14, as Assented to on June 17, 2016)." 14 September 2018. https://www.justice.gc.ca/eng/rp-pr/other-autre/adra-amsr/p1.html (accessed 11 June 2020).

Graham, Sarah. "Unfair Ground: Girlhood and Theme Parks in Contemporary Fiction." *Journal of American Studies* 47, no. 3 (2013): 589–604.

Grekul, Lisa. "Uncomplicated Luck." Review of *Summer of My Amazing Luck*, by Miriam Toews. *Canadian Literature* 195 (2007): 185–87.

Grether, Herbert G. "Translators and the Gender Gap." *Theology Today* 47, no. 3 (1990): 299–305.

Griffin, Randall C. "Andrew Wyeth's *Christina's World*: Normalizing the Abnormal Body." *American Art* 24, no. 2 (2010): 30–49.

Gundy, Jeff. "*A Complicated Kindness*: Learning, Lies, and Stories." *Mennonite Life* 60, no. 2 (2005). http://www.bethelks.edu/mennonitelife/2005June/gundy.php (accessed 21 September 2006).

Hanners, Sarah M. "Promised Lands: The Anabaptist Immigration to Paraguay and Bolivia and Its Unintended Consequences for the Environment." *University of Miami Inter-American Law Review* 48, no. 2 (2017): 186–223. http://repository.law.miami.edu/umialr/vol48/iss2/8.

Hawkins, Anne Hunsaker. *Reconstructing Illness: Studies in Pathography.* 2nd ed. West Lafayette, IN: Purdue University Press, 1999.

———. "Writing about Illness: Therapy? Or Testimony?" In *Unfitting Stories: Narrative Approaches to Disease, Disability, and Trauma*, edited by Valerie Raoul, Connie Canam, Angela D. Henderson, and Carla Paterson, 113–27. Waterloo, ON: Wilfrid Laurier University Press, 2007.

Hensley, Christopher, and Richard Tewksbury. "Inmate to Inmate Prison Sexuality: A Review of Empirical Studies." *Trauma, Violence and Abuse* 3, no. 3 (2002): 226–43.

The Holy Bible. New King James Version (NKJV). Edited by Thomas Nelson. Nashville, TN: Holman, 2013.

Horowitz, Mardi J., Bryna Siegel, Are Holen, George A. Bonanno, Constance Milbrath, and Charles H. Stinson. "Diagnostic Criteria for Complicated Grief Disorder." *American Journal of Psychiatry* 154, no. 7 (1997): 904–10.

"Hosea Meaning." Abarim Publications, 18 December 2019. https://www.abarim-publications.com/Meaning/Hosea.html (accessed 3 December 2019).

Jamison, Kay Redfield. *Night Falls Fast: Understanding Suicide.* New York: Vintage, 2000. First published 1999.

Janzen, Rebecca. "Mennonite and Mormon Women's Life-Writing." In *Education with the Grain of the Universe: A Peaceable Vision for the Future of Mennonite Schools, Colleges and Universities*, edited by J. Denny Weaver, 223–39. Telford, PA: Cascadia Publishing House, 2017.

John Dillinger: Public Enemy #1. A&E Television Networks, 1995. https://video-alexander-street-com.libproxy.mtroyal.ca/watch/john-dillinger-public-enemy-1.

Johns, Donald A. "Understanding the Controversy over Gender Language in Bible Translation." *Journal of Religious and Theological Information* 6, no. 1 (2004): 43–53.

Jordan, John R. "Bereavement after Suicide." *Psychiatric Annals* 38, no. 10 (2008): 679–85.

Kaufman, Vicki. "A Life that Says Welcome." In *Homespun: Amish and Mennonite Women in Their Own Words*, edited by Lorilee Craker, 27–32. Harrisonburg, VA: Herald Press, 2018.

Kaysen, Susanna. "One Cheer for Melancholy." In *Unholy Ghost: Writers on Depression*, edited by Nell Casey, 38–43. New York: Perennial, 2002.

Keahey, Deborah. *Making It Home: Place in Canadian Prairie Literature*. Winnipeg: University of Manitoba Press, 1998.

Keats, John. "Letter to John and Thomas Keats." 21, 27 December 1817. In *Selected Poems and Letters by John Keats*, edited by Douglas Bush, 260–61. Boston: Riverside Press, 1959.

Kehler, Grace. "Heeding the Wounded Storyteller: Toews' *A Complicated Kindness.*" *Journal of Mennonite Studies* 34 (2016): 39–61.

———. "Making Peace with Suicide: Reflections on Miriam Toews's *All My Puny Sorrows.*" *Conrad Grebel Review* 35, no. 3 (2017): 338–47. https://uwaterloo.ca/grebel/sites/ca.grebel/files/uploads/files/cgr_35-3_kehler.pdf (accessed 4 June 2020).

———. "Miriam Toews's Parable of Infinite Becoming." *Vision: A Journal for Church and Theology* 20, no. 1 (2019): 35–41.

———. "Representations of Melancholic Martyrdom in Canadian Mennonite Literature." *Journal of Mennonite Studies* 29 (2013): 167–85.

———. "Transformative Encounters: A Communal Reading of Miriam Toews's *Swing Low.*" In *11 Encounters with Mennonite Fiction*, edited by Hildi Froese Tiessen, 158–76. Winnipeg: Mennonite Literary Society, 2017.

Kerouac, Jack. *On the Road*. New York: Penguin, 2019. First published 1957.

Kersten, Mike, Julie A. Swets, Cathy R. Cox, Takashi Kusumi, Kazushi Nishihata, and Tomoya Watanabe. "Attenuating Pain with the Past: Nostalgia Reduces Physical Pain." *Frontiers in Psychology* 11, no. 572881 (2020): 1–7.

Kingsolver, Barbara. *The Poisonwood Bible*. New York: HarperFlamingo, 1998.

Kraemer, Ross S., and Jennifer Eyl. "Translating Women: The Perils of Gender-Inclusive Translation of the New Testament." In *Celebrate Her for the Fruit of Her Hands: Essays in Honor of Carol L. Meyers*, edited by Susan Ackerman, Charles E. Carter, and Beth Alpert Nakhai, 295–318. Philadelphia: University of Pennsylvania Press, 2015. Proquest Ebook Central.

Kramer, Peter D. *Against Depression*. New York: Viking, 2005.

———. *Listening to Prozac*. New York: Penguin, 1997. First published 1993.

Kreizman, Maris. "Women in a Mennonite Colony Were Raped for Years: This New Novel Tackles the Aftermath." Buzzfeed News, 11 April 2019. buzzfeednews.com/article/mariskreizman/women-talking-miriam-toews-mennonites-metoo (accessed 9 September 2019).

Kroeger, Arthur. *Hard Passage: A Mennonite Family's Long Journey from Russia to Canada*. Edmonton: University of Alberta Press, 2007.

Kroeker, Travis. "Scandalous Displacements: 'Word' and 'Silent Light' in *Irma Voth*." *Journal of Mennonite Studies* 36 (2018): 89–115.

Kroetsch, Robert. *The Lovely Treachery of Words: Essays Selected and New*. Toronto: Oxford University Press, 1989.

Lauritzen, Paul. "Arguing with Life Stories: The Case of Rigoberta Menchú." In *The Ethics of Life Writing*, edited by Paul John Eakin, 19–39. Ithaca, NY: Cornell University Press, 2004.

Leshner, Alan I. "Introduction." In *Resilience and Development: Positive Life Adaptations*, edited by Meyer D. Glantz and Jeannette L. Johnson, 1–4. New York: Kluwer Academic Publishers, 1999. ProQuest Ebook Central.

Levi-Belz, Yossi, and Lilac Lev-Ari. "'Let's Talk about It': The Moderating Role of Self-Disclosure on Complicated Grief over Time among Suicide Survivors." *International Journal of Environmental Research and Public Health* 16 (2019): 1–13.

Loewen, Harry, and Steven M. Nolt. *Through Fire and Water: An Overview of Mennonite History*. Harrisonburg, VA: Herald Press, 2010. First published 1996.

Loewen, Royden. *Horse-And-Buggy Genius: Listening to Mennonites Contest the Modern World*. Winnipeg: University of Manitoba Press, 2016.

Macfarlane, Heather. *Divided Highways: Road Narrative and Nationhood in Canada*. Ottawa: University of Ottawa Press, 2019.

Macpherson, Heidi Slettedahl. *Women's Movement: Escape as Transgression in North American Feminist Fiction*. Amsterdam: Rodopi, 2000.

Mahdiani, Hamideh, and Michael Ungar. "The Dark Side of Resilience." *Adversity and Resilience Science* 2 (2021): 147–55.

Martin, Sandra. "Families Pushing for Doctor-Assisted Suicide Reflect on a Bittersweet Victory." *Globe and Mail*, 6 February 2015. https://www.theglobeandmail.com/news/national/families-pushing-for-doctor-assisted-suicide-reflect-on-a-bittersweet-victory/article22851669/ (accessed 6 February 2015).

Maté, Gabor. *In the Realm of Hungry Ghosts: Close Encounters with Addiction*. Toronto: Alfred A. Knopf, 2008.

Medley, Mark. "Complicated Kindness: Miriam Toews Grapples with the Sister Who Asked Her to Help End Her Life." *National Post*, 11 April 2014. https://nationalpost.com/entertainment/books/complicated-kindness-miriam-toews-grapples-with-the-sister-who-asked-her-to-help-end-her-life (accessed 5 June 2014).

Melzack, Ronald. "The McGill Pain Questionnaire: Major Properties and Scoring Methods." *Pain* 1 (1975): 277–99.

"The Mennonite Connection." *The Fifth Estate*, Episode 42, 24 February 2017. Directed by Terence McKenna, Ronna Syed, and Susan Teskey. Written by Bob McKeown, Hana Gartner, and Terence McKenna. https://www.cbc.ca/fifth/m_episodes/2016-2017/the-mennonite-connection (accessed 5 December 2019).

Miller, Susan L. *Journeys: Resilience and Growth for Survivors of Intimate Partner Abuse*. Oakland: University of California Press, 2018.

Mills, Claudia. "Friendship, Fiction, and Memoir: Trust and Betrayal in Writing from One's Own Life." In *The Ethics of Life Writing*, edited by Paul John Eakin, 101–20. Ithaca, NY: Cornell University Press, 2004.

Mittelstadt, Martin W. "Miriam Toews's *Women Talking*: A Call for Artistic Prophethood." *Canadian Journal of Pentecostal-Charismatic Christianity* 10 (2019): 37–49.

Moodie, Susanna. *Roughing It in the Bush, or, Life in Canada.* Edited by Carl Ballstadt. Ottawa: Carleton University Press, 1988. First published 1852.

Morreall, John. "The Comic Vision of Life." *British Journal of Aesthetics* 54, no. 2 (2014): 125–40.

Munro, Alice. *Lives of Girls and Women.* New York: Signet, 1974. First published 1971.

Museum of Modern Art. "Publication Excerpt from *MoMA Highlights: 375 Works from the Museum of Modern Art.*" New York: Museum of Modern Art, 2019. https://www.moma.org/collection/works/78455 (accessed 2 March 2020).

Nardin, Jane. "A New Look at William Carus Wilson." *Brontë Studies* 27, no. 3 (2002): 211–18.

Neufeld, James. "A Complicated Contract: *Young Rebels of Literature and Dance.*" *Queen's Quarterly* 112, no. 1 (2005): 99–106.

Nobbs-Thiessen, Ben. "Reshaping the Chaco: Migrant Foodways, Place-making, and the Chaco War." *Journal of Latin American Studies* 50, no. 3 (2017): 579–611.

O'Brien, Tim. *The Things They Carried.* 1990; TTTC full text, 2009. https://www.boyer-townasd.rg/cms/lib/PA01916192/Centricity/Domain/777/TTTC%Full%20Text%20mariner.pdf (accessed 3 December 2019).

Omhovère, Claire. "Beyond Horizon: Miriam Toews's *A Complicated Kindness* and the Prairie Novel Tradition." *Commonwealth Essays and Studies* 33, no.1 (2010): 67–79.

———. "Pop Culture and the Construction of Ethnicity in Richard Van Camp's *The Lesser Blessed* and Miriam Toews's *A Complicated Kindness.*" *RANAM: Recherches Anglaises et Americaines* 46 (2013): 151–62.

Park, Noon. "Rebirth through Derision: Satire and the Anabaptist Discourse of Martyrdom in Miriam Toews' *A Complicated Kindness.*" *Journal of Mennonite Studies* 28 (2010): 55–68.

Parry, Albert. "Samizdat Is Russia's Underground Press." *New York Times,* 15 March 1970. *New York Times* Archives. https://www.nytimes.com/1970/03/15/archives/samizdat-is-russias-underground-press-russias-underground-press.html (accessed 3 February 2019).

Patterson, Marc C., Thomas B. Cole, Eliot Siegel, and Philip A. Mackowiak. "A Patient as Art: Andrew Wyeth's Portrayal of Christina Olson's Neurologic Disorder in *Christina's World.*" *Journal of Child Neurology* 32, no. 7 (2017): 647–49.

Peters, Avery. "Tragedy and Comedy in Mennonite Life." *Canadian Mennonite* 17, no. 7 (2013): 33–34.

Peterson, Anna L. *Seeds of the Kingdom: Utopian Communities in the Americas.* Oxford: Oxford University Press, 2005.

Posner, Michael. "Helen Weinzweig Turned Personal Pain into Beautiful Prose." *Globe and Mail*, 23 February 2010, updated 2 May 2018. https://www.theglobeandmail. com/news/national/helen-weinzweig-turned-personal-pain-into-beautiful-prose/ article/1208937 (accessed 8 January 2020).

Primeau, Ronald. *Romance of the Road: The Literature of the American Highway*. Bowling Green, OH: Bowling Green State University Press, 1996.

Radonjic, Aleksandar. "The Undiagnosed Patient in *Christina's World*." *American Journal of Medicine* 133, no. 2 (2020): 253–54.

Ratnarajah, Dorothy, and Margot J. Schofield. "Survivors' Narratives of the Impact of Parental Suicide." *Suicide and Life-Threatening Behaviour* 38, no. 5 (2008): 618–30.

Reader's Guide to Miriam Toews' *A Complicated Kindness*. One Book, One Community. Word Press: Medicine Hat, Alberta, 2006. https://1book1community.files.wordpress. com/2009/06/readersguide2006.pdf

Redekop, Magdalene. "Charms and Riddles in the Mennonite Barnyard." *English Studies in Canada* 19, no. 2 (1993): 209–27.

———. "Escape from the Bloody Theatre: The Making of Mennonite Stories." *Journal of Mennonite Studies* 11 (1993): 9–22.

———. "The Importance of Being Mennonite: Hilarious, Heart-Breaking Comedy Told by a Gifted, Creative Liar." Review of *A Complicated Kindness*, by Miriam Toews. *Literary Review of Canada*, October 2004, 19–20.

———. *Making Believe: Questions about Mennonites and Art*. Winnipeg: University of Manitoba Press, 2020.

———. Review of *Swing Low: A Life*, by Miriam Toews. *Journal of Mennonite Studies* 19 (2001): 244–46. https://jms.uwinnipeg.ca/index.php/jms/article/view/862 (accessed 8 April 2014).

Reimer, Al. "Look Homeward, Nomi: Misreading a Novel as Social History." *Mennonite Life* 60, no. 2 (2005). http://www.bethelks.edu/mennonitelife/2005June/reimer.php (accessed 21 September 2006).

Reynolds, Sheri. *The Rapture of Canaan*. New York: Berkley Books, 1996.

Rostila, Mikael, Jan Saarela, and Ichiro Kawachi. "'The Psychological Skeleton in the Closet': Mortality after a Sibling's Suicide." *Social Psychiatry/Psychiatric Epidemiology* 49 (2014): 919–27.

Rudolph, Miriam. "disPOSSESSION: Exploring Mennonite and Indigenous Land Usage in Paraguay through Art." *Journal of Mennonite Studies* 38 (2020): 23–34.

Rushton, Amy. "A Bubble in the Vein: Suicide, Community, and the Rejection of Neoliberalism in Hanya Yanagihara's *A Little Life* and Miriam Toews's *All My Puny Sorrows*." In *World Literature, Neoliberalism, and the Culture of Discontent*, edited by Sharae Deckard and Stephen Shapiro, 195–213. New Comparisons in World Literature. New York: Palgrave Macmillan, 2019.

Sanderson, Richard K. "Relational Deaths: Narratives of Suicide Survivorship." In *True Relations: Essays on Autobiography and the Postmodern*, edited by G. Thomas Couser and Joseph Fichtelberg, 33–50. Westport, CT: Greenwood Press, 1988.

Scarry, Elaine. *The Body in Pain: The Making and Unmaking of the World*. Oxford: Oxford University Press, 1985.

Schrock, Rae. "Love Begins in the Kitchen." In *Homespun: Amish and Mennonite Women in Their Own Words*, edited by Lorilee Craker, 15–19. Harrisonburg, VA: Herald Press, 2018.

Schwartz, Alexandra. "A Beloved Canadian Novelist Reckons with Her Mennonite Past." *New Yorker*, 25 March 2019. https://www.newyorker.com/magazine/2019/03/25/a-beloved-canadian-novelist-reckons-with-her-mennonite-past/ (accessed 9 September 2019).

Schweid, Richard. *The Cockroach Papers: A Compendium of History and Lore*. New York: Basic Books, 1999.

Shakespeare, Tom. "The Social Model of Disability." In *The Disability Studies Reader*, 4th ed., edited by Lennard J. Davis, 214–21. New York: Routledge, 2013.

Shakespeare, William. *Hamlet*. Rev. ed. Edited by Ann Thompson and Neil Taylor. The Arden Shakespeare. London: Bloomsbury Press, 2016.

Shear, M. Katherine. "Grief and Mourning Gone Awry: Pathway and Course of Complicated Grief." *Dialogues in Clinical Neuroscience* 14, no. 2 (2012): 119–28.

Sheehan, Lindsay, Patrick W. Corrigan, Maya A. Al-Khouja, Stanley A. Lewy, Deborah R. Major, Jessica Mead, Megghun Redmon, Charles T. Rubey, and Stephanie Weber. "Behind Closed Doors: The Stigma of Suicide Loss Survivors." *OMEGA—Journal of Death and Dying* 77, no. 4 (2018): 330–49.

Small, Zachary. "The Controversial Story behind Andrew Wyeth's Most Famous Painting." *Artsy*, 31 August 2017. https://www.artsy.net/article/artsy-editorial-controversial-story-andrew-wyeths-famous-painting (accessed 23 March 2020).

Smith, Sidonie. *Moving Lives: Twentieth-Century Women's Travel Writing*. Minneapolis: University of Minnesota Press, 2001. ProQuest Ebook Central.

Solomon, Andrew. *The Noonday Demon: An Atlas of Depression*. New York: Scribner, 2001.

Soper, Ella. "'Hello, abattoir!': Becoming through Slaughter in Miriam Toews's *A Complicated Kindness*." *Studies in Canadian Literature* 36, no. 1 (2011): 86–99.

Southwick, Steven M., George A. Bonnano, Ann S. Masten, Catherine Panter-Brick, and Rachel Yehuda. "Resilience Definitions, Theory, and Challenges: Interdisciplinary Perspectives." *European Journal of Psychotraumatology* 5, no. 1 (2014): 1–15.

Steffler, Margaret. "Breaking Patriarchy through Words, Imagination, and Faith: The Hayloft as *Spielraum* in Miriam Toews' *Women Talking*." *Canadian Literature* 243 (2020): 61–78.

———. "Fragments and Absences: Language and Loss in Miriam Toews's *A Complicated Kindness*." *Journal of Canadian Studies* 43, no. 3 (2009): 124–45.

———. "The Presence of Absence: Sister-Loss and Home-Loss in Miriam Toews's *All My Puny Sorrows*." *Mennonite Quarterly Review* 90 (2016): 51–72.

———. "Thebes Troutman as Traveling Tween: Revising the Family Story." *Girlhood Studies* 11, no. 1 (2018): 126–40.

———. "Writing through the Words of Those Lost: Memoir and Mourning in Novels by Rudy Wiebe and Miriam Toews." *Journal of Mennonite Studies* 36 (2018): 117–35.

"Steinbach, Manitoba." Wikipedia, 30 May 2021. https://en.wikipedia.org/wiki/Steinbach,_Manitoba.

Steinbeck, John. *The Grapes of Wrath*. New York: Penguin, 2006. First published 1939.

Styron, William. *Darkness Visible: A Memoir of Madness*. New York: Random House, 1990.

Szasz, Thomas. *The Myth of Mental Illness: Foundations of a Theory of Personal Conduct*. Rev. ed. New York: Harper and Row, 1974.

Tal, Kalí. *Worlds of Hurt: Reading the Literatures of Trauma*. Cambridge, UK: Cambridge University Press, 1996.

Tannen, Deborah. *You Just Don't Understand: Women and Men in Conversation*. New York: Ballantine, 1991. First published 1990.

Thacker, Robert. *Alice Munro: Writing Her Lives: A Biography*. Toronto: McClelland and Stewart, 2005.

Thomas, Dylan. "Do Not Go Gentle into That Good Night." In *The Poems of Dylan Thomas*. New York: New Directions, 1953. https://poets.org/poem/do-not-go-gentle-good-night (accessed 8 September 2021).

Thomson, Rosemarie Garland. *Extraordinary Bodies: Figuring Physical Disability in American Culture and Literature*. New York: Columbia University Press, 1997.

———. *Staring: How We Look*. Oxford: Oxford University Press, 2009.

Tiessen, Paul. "'It was like watching my own life': Moviegoers in John Rempel's *Arena* (1967–1970) and Miriam Toews's *Irma Voth* (2011)." *Mennonite Quarterly Review* 87, no. 1 (2013): 49–71.

———. "Plotting the City: Winnipeg in Selected Fiction by David Bergen, Sandra Birdsell, Miriam Toews, David Waltner-Toews, Armin Wiebe, and Rudy Wiebe." *Journal of Mennonite Studies* 28 (2010): 13–31.

———. "Re-framing the Reaction to *Peace Shall Destroy Many*: Rudy Wiebe, Delbert Wiens, and the Mennonite Brethren." *Mennonite Quarterly Review* 29, no. 1 (2016): 73–102.

———. "Revisiting Home: Reading Miriam Toews's *A Complicated Kindness* and Sandra Birdsell's *Children of the Day* through the Lens of Ontario-Mennonite Literature." *Mennonite Quarterly Review* 82, no. 1 (2008): 127–46.

Toews, Miriam. *All My Puny Sorrows*. Toronto: Vintage, 2014.

———. "*All My Puny Sorrows* Helps Author Miriam Toews Work through Some Very Real Grief." Interview with Eric Volmers. *Calgary Herald*, 20 April 2014. http://www.calgaryherald.com/story_print.html?id=9757308&sponsor (accessed 26 June 2014).

———. "'Authentic Emotional Truth': An Interview with Miriam Toews." With Melissa Steele. *Prairie Fire* 27, no. 1 (2006): 6–13.

———. With Dianne Rinehart. "Author Miriam Toews Talks about the Family Experiences that Lead [*sic*] to *All My Puny Sorrows*, Her Latest Book." *Toronto Star*, 14 April 2014. https://www.thestar.com/entertainment/books/2014/04/14/author_miriam_toews_talks_about_the_family_experiences_that_lead_to_all_my_puny_sorrows_her_latest_book.html (accessed 5 June 2014).

———. *A Boy of Good Breeding*. Toronto: Stoddart, 1998.

———. *A Boy of Good Breeding*. Rev. ed. Toronto: Vintage, 2005.

———. *A Complicated Kindness*. Toronto: Vintage, 2004.

———. "A Complicated Kindness." Interview with Rachel Kohn. *The Spirit of Things* (radio broadcast, Australian Broadcasting Company), 5 June 2005. abc.net.au/radionational/programs/spirit of things/a-complicated-kindness/8443242 (accessed 4 April 2006).

———. "A Complicated Kind of Author." Interview with Di Brandt. *Herizons* 19, no. 1 (2005): 20–24, 44–45.

———. "A Father's Faith." In *Dropped Threads: What We Aren't Told*, edited by Carol Shields and Marjorie Anderson, 191–97. Toronto: Vintage, 2001.

———. *Fight Night*. Toronto: Alfred A. Knopf, 2021.

———. *The Flying Troutmans*. Vintage Canada, 2018. First published 2008.

———. "How Miriam Toews Gave a Voice to the Rape Victims of the Horrific Bolivian Mennonite Atrocity." Interview with Joseph Brean. *National Post*, 16 August 2018. https://nationalpost.com/entertainment/books/how-miriam-toews-gave-a-voice-to-the-rape-victims-of-the-horrific-bolivian-mennonite-atrocity (accessed 10 April 2019).

———. Interview with Sabrina Reed. Online, 20 March 2020.

———. *Irma Voth*. Toronto: Vintage Canada, 2012. First published 2011.

———. "'It Gets under the Skin and Settles In': A Conversation with Miriam Toews." With Natasha G. Wiebe. *Conrad Grebel Review* 26, no. 1 (2008): 103–23.

———. "Miriam Toews Breaks Out." Interview with Dave Weich. PowellsBooks.Blog, 20 January 2005. http://www.powells.com/blog/interviews/miriam-toews-breaks-out-by-dave (accessed 18 June 2014).

———. "Miriam Toews Brings *All My Puny Sorrows* to Studio Q." Interview with Jian Ghomeshi. *Q with Jian Ghomeshi*, CBC Radio One, 22 April 2014. https://www.youtube.com/watch?v=5n4cphavKms (accessed 8 June 2020).

———. "Miriam Toews: 'I Needed to Write about These Women. I Could Have Been One of Them." Interview with Katrina Onstad. *Guardian*, 18 August 2018. https://www.theguardian.com/books/2018/aug/18/miriam-toews-interview-women-talking-mennonite (accessed 13 September 2019).

———. "Miriam Toews: 'I Worried People Would Think, What Is Wrong with This Family?'" Interview with Alice O'Keeffe. *Guardian*, 2 May 2015, modified 22 February 2018. https://www.theguardian.com/books/2015/may/02/miriam-toews-interview-all-my-puny-sorrows-mennonite (accessed 3 March 2020).

———. "Miriam Toews on Her New Novel *Fight Night* and How It Explores 'the Fight for One's Mental Health.'" Interview with Tom Power. *Q with Tom Power*, CBC Listen, 1 September 2021. https://www.cbc.ca/listen/live-radio/1-50-q/clip/15863732-miriam-toews-novel-fight-night-explores-the-fight (accessed 1 September 2021).

———. "Miriam Toews on What Forgiveness Means in the #MeToo Era." Interview with Hannah Lillith Assadi. Literary Hub, 2 May 2019. https://lithub.com/miriam-toews-on-what-forgiveness-means-in-the-metoo-era/ (accessed 26 September 2019).

———. "A National Literature." Keynote Address, Edinburgh World Writers' Conference, 25 October 2012. http://www.edinburghworldwritersconference.org/all-keynotes/toews-in-toronto-keynote-on-a-national-literature/ (accessed 1 July 2020).

———. "Novelist Miriam Toews: A Mennonite Story." Interview with Elizabeth Palmer. *Christian Century*, 8 May 2019, 33–34.

———. "'No Wonder People Are Reluctant to Talk about Mental Health': An Interview with Miriam Toews." With Anna Fitzpatrick. *Hazlitt*, 7 May 2014. https://hazlitt.net/feature/no-wonder-people-are-reluctant-talk-about-mental-health-interview-miriam-toews (accessed 5 June 2014).

———. "On Studying Psychology." *Open Letters* 2, no. 6 (2000). https://openletters.net/2000/10/miriam-toews-on-studying-psychology-2/ (accessed 26 July 2022).

———. "Peace Shall Destroy Many." *Granta* 137 (2016): 13–21.

———. "'A Place You Can't Go Home To': A Conversation with Miriam Toews." With Hildi Froese Tiessen. *Prairie Fire* 21, no. 3 (2000): 54–61.

———. "'Profound Despair Can Strike Anybody': In the Wake of Her Sister's Suicide, Miriam Toews Found Herself Writing Her Way Toward Real-Life Redemption Again." Interview with Kate Taylor. *Globe and Mail*, 12 April 2014, R3.

———. "Road Tripping with Miriam Toews." With Claire Kirch. *Publishers Weekly*, 1 September 2008, 22.

———. "The Rumpus Interview with Miriam Toews." With Meredith Turits. Rumpus, 9 January 2015. http://therumpus.net/2015/01/the-rumpus-interview-with-miriam-toews/ (accessed 12 May 2016).

———. *Summer of My Amazing Luck*. Winnipeg: Turnstone Press, 1996.

———. *Summer of My Amazing Luck*. Rev. ed. Toronto: Vintage Canada, 2006.

———. *Swing Low: A Life*. Toronto: Vintage Canada, 2005. First published 2000.

———. "Why a Nine-Year-Old Girl Narrates Miriam Toews's New Novel, *Fight Night*." With Shelagh Rogers. *The Next Chapter*, 1 October 2021. Updated on 5 October 2021. https://www.cbc.ca/radio/thenextchapter/full-episode-oct-2-2021-1.6193424/why-a-9-year-old-girl-narrates-miriam-toews-s-new-novel-fight-night-1.6193427 (accessed 6 June 2022).

———. *Women Talking*. Toronto: Alfred A. Knopf, 2018.

———. "The Women Will Write Their Own Stories: A Conversation with Miriam Toews." With Christine Fischer Guy. *Los Angeles Review of Books*, 2 April 2019. https://

lareviewofbooks.org/article/the-women-will-write-their-own-stories-a-q-and-a-with-miriam-toews-on-women-talking/ (accessed 4 September 2019).

Toron, Alison. "Funny Feminism: Humour in Canadian Women's Fiction." PhD diss., University of New Brunswick, 2011.

Tykwer, Tom, dir. *Lola rennt* [*Run Lola Run*]. Produced by Stefan Arndt. X-Filme Creative Pool, 1988.

Ungar, Michael. "Introduction to the Volume." In *The Social Ecology of Resilience: A Handbook of Theory and Practice*, edited by Michael Ungar, 1–9. New York: Springer, 2012.

———. "Social Ecologies and Their Contributions to Resilience." In *The Social Ecology of Resilience: A Handbook of Theory and Practice*, edited by Michael Ungar, 13–31. New York: Springer, 2012.

Unger, Andrew. "The Top 50 Most Common Russian Mennonite Surnames." *Daily Bonnet*, 29 September 2017. https://dailybonnet.com/top-50-common-russian-mennonite-surnames/(accessed 16 July 2020).

Urry, James. *Mennonites, Politics, and Peoplehood: Europe—Russia—Canada 1525–1980.* Winnipeg: University of Manitoba Press, 2006.

———. "Of Borders and Boundaries: Reflections on Mennonite Unity and Separation in the Modern World." *Mennonite Quarterly Review* 73, no. 3 (1999): 503–24.

Ussher, Jane. *Women's Madness: Misogyny or Mental Illness?* Amherst: University of Massachusetts Press, 1991.

van Herk, Aritha. *No Fixed Address: An Amorous Journey*. Toronto: Seal, 1987. First published 1986.

Viljoen, F.P. "Hosea 6:6 and Identity Formation in Matthew." *Acta Theologica* 34, no. 1 (2014): 214–37.

Walter, Tony. "A New Model of Grief: Bereavement and Biography." *Mortality* 1, no. 1 (1996): 7–25.

Weir, William. "John Dillinger: Dead or Alive?" Excerpt from *History's Greatest Lies. History Magazine*, August–September 2009, 37–40.

Wenger, John C. "Funk (Funck) Family." *Global Anabaptist Mennonite Encyclopedia Online*, 1956. https://gameo.org/index.php?title=Funk_(Funck)_family&oldid=146439 (accessed 15 May 2020).

Whalen, Tom. Review of *Run Lola Run*, by Tom Tykwer and Stefan Arndt. *Film Quarterly* 53, no. 3 (2000): 33–40.

Wiebe, Christoph. "'The tail end of a five-hundred-year experiment that has failed': Love, Truth, and the Power of Stories." Translated by Gerhard Reimer. *CMW Journal* 3, no. 2 (2011). https://mennonitewriting.org/journal/3/2/tail-end-five-hundred-year-experiment-has-failed/#page8 (accessed 12 September 2019).

Wiebe, Natasha G. "Miriam Toews' *A Complicated Kindness*: Restorying the Russian Mennonite Diaspora." *Journal of Mennonite Studies* 28 (2010): 33–54.

Wilder, Laura Ingalls. *Little House on the Prairie*. New York: HarperTrophy, 1971. First published 1935.

Will, Martina E. "The Mennonite Colonization of Chihuahua: Reflections of Competing Visions." *Americas* 53, no. 3 (1997): 353–78.

Williams, Alex, dir. *The Pass System*. Narrated by Tantoo Cardinal. Produced by James Cullingham. Tamarack Productions, 2015.

Winterson, Jeanette. *Art Objects: Essays on Ecstasy and Effrontery*. New York: Vintage, 1997. First published 1995.

———. *Why Be Happy When You Could Be Normal?* Toronto: Vintage, 2011.

Wyatt, Edward. "Live on 'Oprah,' a Memoirist Is Kicked Out of the Book Club." *New York Times*, 27 January 2006, A1, A6. ProQuest Historical Newspapers: The *New York Times* with Index (accessed 12 June 2020).

Wyeth, Andrew. *Christina's World*. 1948. Tempera on gessoed panel. Museum of Modern Art, New York.© Estate of Andrew Wyeth / SOCAN (2022).

Wyss, Johann. *The Swiss Family Robinson*. Edited by W.H.G. Kingston. Translated by Agnes Kinloch Kingston. Santa Rosa, CA: Classic Press, 1968. First published 1812.

Yacowar, Maurice. "*Run Lola Run: Renn* for Your Life." *Queen's Quarterly* 106, no. 4 (1999): 557–65.

Zacharias, Robert. *After Identity: Mennonite Writing in North America*. Winnipeg: University of Manitoba Press, 2015.

———. *Rewriting the Break Event: Mennonites and Migration in Canadian Literature*. Winnipeg: University of Manitoba Press, 2013.

INDEX

Mills, Claudia, 174

Mittelstadt, Martin W., 123, 139

Moodie, Susanna, 17, 74

Morreall, John, 13

mosquitoes, 72

mothers and motherhood: in
  A Complicated Kindness, 47–48, 50;
  in *The Flying Troutmans*, 97–99; in
  Summer of My Amazing Luck, 100–101.
  See also, Toews, Elvira

mourning, 178–79

Munro, Alice, 61, 102, 163

N

Narfa, 109, 140–42

Neufeld, James, 27

No Fixed Address (Van Herk), 70,
  76, 227n1

Nobbs-Thiessen, Ben, 118

nostalgic tourism, 48–52, 53

O

O'Keeffe, Alice, 84, 85

Olsen, Christina, 43, 45

Omhovère, Claire, 19, 31

On the Road (Kerouac), 71, 74–75, 227n1

Onstad, Katrina, 136

P

pain, 207–11

Palmer, Elizabeth, 4

Park, Noon, 34

parody, 88, 94–95

The Partridge Family (tv show), 50

patriarchal communities, 108, 129–30

Patterson, Marc C., 43–44

The Poisonwood Bible (Kingsolver), 60

Posner, Michael, 228n5

Power, Tom, 207, 214

Primeau, Ronald, 77, 78–79

Prozac, 58–59

Q

quest narrative, 102–3, 180, 183

R

The Rapture of Canaan (Reynolds)

Redekop, Magdalene, 25, 115, 144, 159,
  164, 206–7

Reimer, Al, 26

religious fundamentalism: and art, 215;
  in *A Boy of Good Breeding*, 8, 22; in
  A Complicated Kindness, 8, 27–28,
  30, 38, 57, 67–68; in *Fight Night*,
  204, 205; and resilience, 30, 205–6;
  and similarity to authoritarianism
  in mental health care system, 193;
  Toews's view of, 4, 29, 30, 67,
  165, 192–93

reparation: M. Toews to Mel Toews,
  170; through autofiction, 7, 158,
  207; through writing about suicide,
  177, 201, 222

resilience: and acceptance of uncertainty,
  9; in *All My Puny Sorrows*, 5–6, 196,
  201, 202, 221–22; as author's choice
  of theme for this book, 5–6; in *A Boy
  of Good Breeding*, 54, 67, 68, 69, 221;
  and caring for the mentally ill, 92; in
  A Complicated Kindness, 66–67, 68–69,
  133, 221; connection to home of,
  16; connection to pairs of sisters in
  Toews's novels, 197; dark side of,
  132–33, 134–35; and depression, 59,
  60, 156, 172; in *Fight Night*, 201, 204,
  205–6, 212–17, 219; in *The Flying
  Troutmans*, 71, 73, 98–99, 104, 221;
  and fundamentalism, 30, 205–6;
  in *Irma Voth*, 10, 105, 145–46, 153,
  155–56, 221; as learned/inherited,
  219; as loving ourselves, 221; and
  luck, 97–98; M. Toews's explorations
  of, 221–22; M. Toews's view of, 107;
  of Mennonites, 7, 107; of Miriam
  Toews's parents, 172; from pain, 211;
  as persistent theme of Toews work, 2,
  6–7; as seen in tv and movies, 53; and
  sexual abuse, 137; social supports for,
  6, 66, 84, 85–86, 219; as submission,
  219–20; and suicide survivorship,

WEBER, Max. *The Religion of India: The Sociology of Hinduism and Buddhism* (Hans H. Gerth and Don Martindale trans). Glencoe, IL: Free Press, 1958.

WILLIAMS, Raymond. *Marxism and Literature*. New York: Oxford University Press, 1977.

WORDSWORTH, William. *Wordsworth's Poetry and Prose* (Nicholas Halmi ed.). New York: W. W. Norton, 2014.

YOUNG, Robert J. C. *White Mythologies*. London: Routledge 2010.

ŽIŽEK, Slavoj. *The Sublime Object of Ideology* (Jon Barnes trans.). London: Verso, 1989.

——. "Revolutions That as Yet Have No Model: Derrida's 'Limited Inc.'" *Diacritics* 10 (December 1980): 29–49.

——. "Scattered Speculations on the Subaltern and the Popular." *Postcolonial Studies* 8(4) (2005): 475–86.

——. "Sex and History in Wordsworth's *The Prelude* (1805) IX–XIII." in *In Other Worlds: Essays in Cultural Politics*. New York: Routledge, 1998, pp. 46–76.

——. "Teaching for the Times." in Anne McClintock, Aamir Mufti, and Ella Shohat (eds), *Dangerous Liaisons: Gender, Nation, and Postcolonial Perspectives*. Minneapolis: University of Minnesota Press, 1997, 468–90.

——. "Three Feminist Readings: McCullers, Drabble, Habermas." *Union Seminary Quarterly Review* 1-2 (Fall–Winter 1979–80): 15–34.

——. "Three Women's Texts and a Critique of Imperialism." *Critical Inquiry* 12(1) (Autumn 1985): 243–61.

——. "Tracing the Skin of Day." in *Undated: Nightskin*. Dubai: 1x1 Art Gallery, 2009.

——. "Unmaking and Making in *To the Lighthouse*." in *In Other Worlds: Essays in Cultural Politics*. New York, Routledge, 1998, pp. 41–62.

——. "Who Killed Patrice Lumumba?" Keynote address at the conference "Translating Postcolonial into French," Columbia University, New York, March 26, 2010.

TAYLOR, Charles. *Multiculturalism and the Politics of Recognition*. Princeton, NJ: Princeton University Press, 1994.

THOMAS, Peter. *The Gramscian Moment: Philosophy, Hegemony and Marxism*. Leiden: Brill, 2009.

TYLER, Mary. *My Years in an Indian Prison*. Harmondsworth: Penguin, 1978.

VALÉRY, Paul. *Charms and Other Pieces* (Peter Dale trans.). London: Anvil Press Poetry, 2007.

VARADARAJAN, Siddharth (ed.). *Gujarat: The Making of a Tragedy*. New Delhi: Penguin India, 2002.

VATTIMO, Gianni. *Nietzsche: An Introduction* (Nicholas Martin trans.). London: Athlone, 2002.

VERGÈS, Françoise. "Creole Skin, Black Mask: Fanon and Disavowal." *Critical Inquiry* 23(3) (Spring 1997): 578–95.